Captain McNeill
and His Wife the Nishga Chief

Captain William Henry McNeill

Captain McNeill
and His Wife the Nishga Chief

1803 – 1850

From Boston Fur Trader
to Hudson's Bay Company Trader

Robin Percival Smith

ISBN 0-88839-472-1

Cataloging in Publication Data
Percival Smith, Robin, 1929–
Captain McNeill and his wife the Nishga chief, 1803–1850

Includes index.
ISBN 0-88839-472-1

1. McNeill, William Henry, 1803–1875. 2. McNeill, Matilda,
1810?–1850. 3. Hudson's Bay Company—Biography. 4. Haida
Indians—Biography. I. Title.
FC3822.1.M26S64 2001   971.1'02'0922   C00-911421-1
F1088.S64 2001

Printed in Canada—PRINTCRAFTERS

Cover: Fort Rupert, 1866 sketch, courtesy of the Hudson's Bay Company Archives
Frontispiece: Captain William H. McNeill, courtesy of the Vancouver Maritime Museum

We acknowledge the financial support of the Government of Canada through the
Book Publishing Industry Development Program for our publishing activities.

Published simultaneously in Canada and the United States by

HANCOCK HOUSE PUBLISHERS LTD.
19313 Zero Avenue, Surrey, B.C. V3S 9R9

HANCOCK HOUSE PUBLISHERS
1431 Harrison Avenue, Blaine, WA 98230-5005

(604) 538-1114   Fax (604) 538-2262
(800) 938-1114   Fax (800) 983-2262
Web Site: www.hancockhouse.com   *email:* sales@hancockhouse.com

Contents

Illustrations

Maps

The Author

Robin Percival Smith was born in 1929, within the sound of London's famed Bow Bells. He was educated in England, at Oakley Hall School at Cirencester, St. Johns School at Leatherhead, Gonville and Caius College (1950), Cambridge and the Westminster Hospital Medical School.

He emigrated to Canada in the Royal Canadian Air Force and was posted to Vancouver in 1958. He practised family medicine in the city of Richmond from 1961 to 1971, then accepted a position as Staff Physician with the Student Health Service at the University of British Columbia. He became interested in women's health, researching and writing a number of articles on screening for various conditions. His work on intrauterine contraception and post coital contraception led to his involvement with the Canadian Committee for Fertility Research and the World Health Organization. In 1981 he was appointed Director of the Student Health Service. He retired from medical practice in 1989 to devote unlimited time to his passion for sailing on the west coast of Canada aboard his sailing vessel, *Tremethick II*.

To Emma

From *Voyage*

Old men come, old men go,
Children huff and young men puff,
Old men glitter when they know
Emma flutters in their luff.

Driven forward against all odds,
Wind, wave and spewm, strains
The bulwarks of the sea Gods
When Emma's hand sheets the reins.

Preface

I first visited Queen Charlotte Strait in 1985 but did not go far enough north to visit the small town of Port McNeill on the east coast of Vancouver Island until 1990. I asked the way to the Port McNeill Library, an institution of a size that was not hard to find but easy to miss.

"Who was McNeill?" I asked the duty librarian.

She did not have an immediate answer. I asked her if she knew that Captain McNeill had been master of the SS *Beaver*, the first steamship on the northwest coast? "Oh yes, now I remember!" she exclaimed.

I had learned about Captain McNeill from Stephen Hillson's, *Exploring Puget Sound and British Columbia*. He quoted a story told by McNeill's grandson, which I later obtained from the British Columbia Archives. This story implies that the Hudson's Bay Company was unable to get rid of McNeill and his brigantine *Llama* from the coast, even by armed intervention, and was forced to employ him as a result. This apocryphal story is not supported by the logs of the *Llama* or the Hudson's Bay Company's vessel, *Cadboro*. The true story, however, is even more interesting and romantic. My quest for more information on Captain McNeill did not take off until I read, *A Guide to B.C. Indian Myth and Legend*, by Ralph Maud. In this book he quotes the story of Captain McNeill's Kaigani Haida wife who had been married to Chief Sakau'an (Sharp Teeth), a Nishga from the Salmon Eaters clan of Gitiks village on the Nass River, before she left him to join in marriage with Captain McNeill. I was surprised that there was no biography of McNeill, outside of those in the *Dictionary of Canadian Biography* and in the *Hudson's Bay Record Society*, volume 7. Neither of these have information of his life before he joined the Company at the age of twenty-nine years. He was the only American citizen on the Pacific coast to become a chief trader and a chief factor of the honorable Hudson's Bay Company during his lifetime.

In writing *Captain McNeill and His Wife the Nishga Chief*, I have used historical accounts taken from the logs of his voyages, journals that he kept aboard ships, letters he wrote to Josiah Marshall in Boston, to John McLoughlin, Sr. at Fort Vancouver (Washington) and to Sir George Simpson after McNeill became a Chief Trader in 1839. I have drawn heavily on the information about Fort Vancouver in the *Hudson's Bay Record Society*, volumes 3, 4, and 7 and the *Fort Victoria Letters*, volume 32. Other sources have included private letters to James Hargrave, Edward Ermatinger and Sir George Simpson from other chief traders and chief factors. John Work traveled with McNeill in 1835 and kept a diary of his experience trading furs while aboard the *Llama*. Sir George Simpson also comments on McNeill in his *Voyage around the World in 1841-42*. It was from this source that I found the origin of 'Ma-ta-hell'.

I have kept the use of "would have," "might have," or "perhaps," to a minimum and written in a positive narrative style to make the story flow. However, this is not fiction. William McNeill was born in Boston, did go to sea at eleven years of age and was on the brigantine *Paragon* in 1818. His life as a boy at sea is compiled from various diaries and accounts of his times. I have written in the present tense for Augustus Wright, Bernard Barry, Charley Beardmore and Hladerh in an attempt to give the reader an experience of living at that time.

Every factual experience that is told is supported in the written record and only my interpretation is fictional. For example, Augustus Wright was a boy on the *Convoy* and *Tally Ho*; he did join in the crew's refusal to go to their duty; he did see seaman Low suffer loss of vision and Isaac Marsh suffer from venereal disease, and he was punished for stealing rum. Charley Beardmore was a young Indian trader at Fort Simpson who was posted to Fort Rupert under McNeill from the start of the fort's construction. He really did carry a shillelagh with him at all times. His account of the building of the fort is based on factual information in the Fort Rupert journal, Beardmore's letters to Aaron Chapman (a director of the Company in London) and Andrew Muir's diary. He kept the fort journal when Blenkinsop and his family were on sick leave and by an Indian wife he had a daughter who was known as Princess and the baby was christened by Governor Blanshard.

When William McNeill was born in Boston in 1803 he entered a community whose prosperity derived from the maritime trade. Some of the greatest wealth accrued to the merchants who specialized in the sea otter fur trade obtained from the Pacific northwest coast of America. His choice of a career at sea when only eleven years of age was expected, not exceptional for a boy at that time and he was not exceptional. To rise to the rank of master of a vessel required skill in mathematics and an understanding of the cosmos for navigation. That gift alone marks William McNeill with above-average intelligence. He wrote in a simple style without any indication of a literary bent or quotation from the classics. His writing is individual and his mode of spelling, for example, "occation" or "hawled," is consistent. His use of capitals for Sea and Sails occur throughout the logs as does his use of Steering Sails over Studding Sails. All these quirks of style identify the writing as his own.

William was a red-head, tall and heavy set. His temper was on a short fuse and, when threatened, he was aggressive in his action, impetuous, blusterous, a little given to exaggeration and not fond of waiting to see how things might turn out. He was reared by a mother who was strict and imbued with religious conviction, "a sincere Christian," he said to Sir George Simpson in writing of the news of her death. He was probably a first mate at fifteen years of age on the brigantine *Paragon* and a master mariner at twenty-one. By the time he joined the Hudson's Bay Company, he was a competent and experienced master mariner and fur trader.

Matilda

Matilda McNeill was born into the Kaigani Haida, a culture of artistic splendor to vie with any ancestral house of Europe. It was a culture, however, without written records or history, making precise dates difficult to reconcile with the Gregorian calendar. Her year of birth can only be estimated from two events. Her first child, Helen, died on March 27, 1869, at a recorded age of forty years and six months. Helen would have been born in October, 1828, and conceived early in that year. Matilda bore McNeill's twin girls in November, 1850, and died after their successful delivery. Assuming her span of fertility from seventeen to forty years of age, Matilda would have been born around 1810. For Matilda to inherit the Wolf-Bearmother Chiefship in common with her brother Neeskinwaetk, at the village of Gitradeen (Angydae) on the Nass River, implies that her mother was a Nishga chief's daughter in a political marriage. It is not unreasonable to extrapolate such an arrangement as a means for securing trade between two families to ensure a supply of shrowton (eulachon oil) in return for sea otter pelts. Matilda's parentage is not known for certain. However, her brother Neeskinwaetk was a friend of Chief Tsebassa, and joint Chief of the Wolf-Bearmother clan at Gitradeen. Her Kaigani Haida sister did visit Fort Simpson and told John Work the story of Captain John Bancroft's murder on the brigantine *Llama*.

The details of Matilda's birth, childhood, training, first menstruation, marriage to Sakau'an and death experience come from the anthropological research by Boas, Deans, Dawson, Swanton and others at the latter part of the nineteenth century and also from Edward Curtis, Marius Barbeau and others at the beginning of the twentieth century. This material was collected three generations after Matilda's birth by which time the great northwest Indian culture had been decimated by small pox, venereal diseases and measles epidemics.

The Haida of Queen Charlotte's Islands (now known as the Queen Charlotte Islands) had a population of 20,000 at the time McNeill first arrived, but by some estimates, this was quickly reduced to as little as 500 souls on the coast. For this reason I have placed greater reliance on the observations of Joseph Ingraham, Jacinto Camaano, Stephen Reynoulds, William Sturgis, and Johnathan Green, all of whom were in the Pacific northwest before and up to the time of Matilda's youth. I used W. F. Tolmie's description of his first visit to Fort Vancouver as the source for Matilda's first trip to that fort. In this account of her life, I present a reconstruction that no doubt contains some of the romantic musings of the author! Women were little mentioned by all these male characters and a good deal of Matilda's reconstructed life is gleaned from the remarkable book, *During My Time: Florence Edenshaw Davidson, A Haida Woman* by Margaret B. Blackman.

Hladerh, a Nishga carver from the village of Gitiks, was a friend of Chief Sakau'an and helped him raise the tallest totem pole on the

Nass River about 1860. They were both enemies of Chief Sispagut of the Killer Whale clan. Sakau'an is reputed to have been pursued by supernatural beings who conferred on him his power over fire. This information comes from Boas' report to the British Association in 1895 and from an account given to Marius Barbeau by Chief Mountain whose uncle, Chief Sakau'an, was responsible for Mountain's education.

McNeill

McNeill was twenty-nine years old at the time of his "marriage." His impetuous, stubborn nature, added to his strict disciplinarian views, made life hazardous for those of unruly behavior under his command. From his logs and letters, he appears also to have been given to exaggeration. In the incident at Fort Rupert, Andrew Muir gives an almost Falstaffian caricature of him as he enters the great hall, cutlass in hand and pistols in his belt, shouting his displeasure at the miners in general and Andrew Muir in particular. Captain McNeill dealt with mutineers by flogging them and putting them in irons on a diet of ship's biscuit and water before shipping them back to Oahu or delivering them into the hands of the Russians at Sitka. But this was normal practice for sea captains of his time. He ordered a dozen or two dozen lashes for disobedience or desertion. His record of punishments to his crew on board the *Llama* in 1831–32 was excessive, even for the times, with Robinson put in irons for theft and later flogged twice within a week for fighting. In transferring the mutineers, Dean and Rouch, at Sitka, he could not resist paying them off with a dozen lashes before sending them ashore even though Rouch had already been given two dozen before he was put in irons. But in fairness to McNeill, he was ruling by the example of his youth, since he was brought up under similar punitive coercion at school in Boston and as a boy on board ship.

McNeill was a man who would keep "a bee in his bonnet" and would "carp on so" about certain issues that affected him or upset him. He constantly threatened to resign, but never did. McNeill had a penchant for getting on the wrong side of people including Captain Wilde, Marshall, later with Chief Trader John Work and all the inebriated mates and captains of the Company's vessels. Even Sir George Simpson, in the end, did not trust him.

None of these blemishes should take away from McNeill's accomplishment at sea, his contribution to the Hudson's Bay Company or his dedication to his wife and family. He served loyally as a ship's captain and was sober and attentive to his duties. He was also a kind man with a genuine love of children. He is said to have brought the first fireworks to Victoria for the amusement of the children. He was an enthusiast, ever ready to embrace a new assignment and pursue it with great energy and dedication. He was fastidious in maintaining both ships and forts under his command and took pride in their appearance. He was trusted by the Indians as a fur trader and he treated them as equals with respect. He made friends with some of the chiefs, as all the Boston traders did, to improve trade. He was not a sentimentalist and fully appreciated that the Indians would take advantage of him, even attack his ship, if he let down his guard. He was against the missionaries' interference with the religious life of the tribes and expressed his belief that the missionaries were corrupt and did less to further the civilization of the Indians than did the officers of the Company. The Indians rewarded him by placing him atop a totem pole, now in the museum at Campbell River. He had a pedantic sense of humor as evidenced by the eleven conundrums at the back of the log of the *Convoy* and the poem at the front of the log of the *Llama*. He rose to be a chief trader and later a chief factor in spite of being an American citizen. While his name is not as well known as James Douglas or John McLoughlin and he did not occupy the front seat of history, his biography in the *Hudson's Bay Record Society*, volume 7, is nonetheless almost as long as that of James Douglas.

In later life, he offered to give land for the building of a new lieutenant governor's house in Victoria in spite of the difficulty he had encountered in buying it in the first place, because the Company said he was not a British subject, a fact that in the past had not stopped them appointing him a captain on a British vessel against their own laws. In the end he was bitter and signed the petition to President Grant asking for the annexation of British Columbia to the United States.

Acknowledgments

For their help in obtaining information on many aspects of McNeill's life, I wish to thank the staff of the British Columbia Archives; the staff of the Hudson's Bay Company Archives in the Manitoba Provincial Archives; Brent Sverdloff at the Baker Library of Harvard University, for searching the Bryant and Sturgis correspondence for information on the brigantine *Llama*; the staff of the Houghton Library, Harvard University, for providing me with a copy of the microfilm of the Marshall and Wilde correspondence and accounts; and the staff of the University of British Columbia, Koerner Library, Special Collections and Map Division for their help in obtaining information relevant to McNeill's life and times.

Thanks too, to Corisande, my wife, for her tolerance during the research and writing of this book that took me away from home to write in the calm and peace of Otter Bay on North Pender Island. I also appreciate the support from my sisters, June Simington and Anne Armitstead, as well as Peter Armitstead, all of whom willingly read for me and gave their advice and criticism.

Thanks to the "gang" at Otter Bay: Chuck, Kay, Tom, Roger, Jessica, Allan and Jeanne, who listened to my readings from the manuscript. To Knud and Bente Nielsen I say "Cheers!" for all the times we have discussed this book over elevenses.

Special thanks to my son Christopher for his care and attention to the maps.

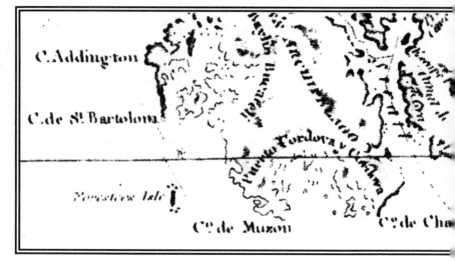

Southeast Alaska from Captain George Vancouver's map, 1793.

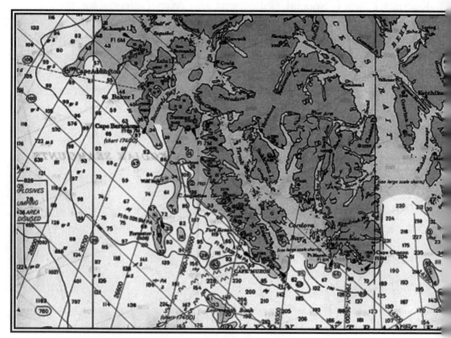

Southeast Alaska from United States marine chart 16016, 1993.

CHAPTER 1

Early Days

Working Lunars is a tricky business, for any error in the observation brings a thirty fold error in the result.
—S.E. Morison, *Maritime History of Massachusetts*

Rumors of a naval engagement right under their eyes, abounded in Boston and reached a climax on May 31, 1813. Murmurs turned to shouts when the powder was put aboard their frigate, USS *Chesapeake*. Next morning, citizens of the town watched from the wharfs for signs that *Chesapeake* was about to slip her anchor and move into Boston Bay to challenge the blockading HMS *Shannon*. In early afternoon a favorable wind sent a large proportion of the town's population of 25,000 souls up onto Beacon Hill to watch their champion hammer the hated enemy. Bostonians still seethed with contempt against those arrogant colonialists responsible for the Boston massacre. Among them nine-year-old William Henry McNeill, no friend of the British, ran and shouted his excitement with his school mates, braving the punishment of absence from their master's classroom. The boys were confident after the news of the capture in rapid succession of HMS *Alert* by their USS *Essex*, HMS *Guerriere* by their USS *Constitution* and HMS *Macedonian* by their USS *United States*.

Young boys, who had been caught up in admiration of the heroes of naval engagements, gave no thought to long term consequences. Just the past winter of 1813, they had whooped their greetings at the arrival of USS *Constitution* both for her defeat and burning of HMS *Java* and her courageous passage into port through the fog of Boston Bay to evade the British blockading squadron. They watched the prisoners of war herded into captivity to await their

17

exchange and, as the crew came ashore, sat with sparkling eyes of hero-worship to listen to their tales of naval prowess. The hard Boston winter had done little to dampen the enthusiasm of these boys as rumors spread that USS *President* and USS *Congress* were waiting for a foggy ebb tide to sneak out of harbor unseen and sail the Atlantic Ocean to harass the British merchant vessels en route to Halifax or the Caribbean.

William, on high ground overlooking the harbor, saw the tips of topmasts moving slowly down to the Nantasket Roads; his ears straining for the sound of gunfire. After two anxious hours of nothing but silence, and he was free to rejoice at the success of their two men-o'-war evading the British blockade.

But that was yesterday. Now the crowd moved up the hill to watch, with the confidence of conquerors, for yet another defeat to the British navy. A carnival atmosphere pervaded, opportunist hawkers worked the crowd; there were telescopes for hire, provender for sale, books opened for bets and pockets for the boys to pick. A hush went through the crowd when *Chesapeake*'s sails appeared and a cheer went up when she rounded Boston Light; the small pilot cutter following in the warship's wake and a flotilla of small boats straggling out far behind as the *Chesapeake* picked up speed. HMS *Shannon* laying on and off in Boston Bay, saw her quarry and turned out to sea.

She headed for the gap between Cape Ann and Cape Cod. Two hours of anticipation passed before the two frigates came within range at 5:50 P.M.; the crowd quiet and still. A thousand or more hearts beat in unison, all eyes on the ships, strained as the distance lengthened. Telescopes were trained to bring the action closer. Then, suddenly, the flash and smoke, followed, after a short delay, by the rumble of guns.

The pilot cutter, closest to the action, looked on in horror as both vessels closed for action and sailed to within forty yards before the flash, smoke and thunderous power of two simultaneous broadsides shattered wood, slaughtering both gun crews. From that first broadside, *Shannon* sent a fatal blow that killed *Chesapeake*'s sailing master and mortally wounded Captain Lawrence. In the roar and confusion of battle, a captain's plea, "Don't give up the ship!" went unheard and unheeded. In fifteen minutes of shattered dreams of victory, *Chesapeake*'s colors were struck; the crowd, stunned and silent, drifted away in disappointment and despair. The pilot cutter hurried back to Boston Harbor to spread the news of defeat.

Not all of Boston was unhappy with the defeat of *Chesapeake*. The merchants suffered from loss of trade and, with the town besieged by the blockade, openly expressed the view that such defeats might shorten this federalist war, a war that stopped reliable trade for most consumer goods and left Boston men pining for their wine and other comforts while their wives were starved of tea and good Canton silks for fashion. But there was another side to the war. It enabled this newly emerging nation to produce for itself and never again be reliant on foreign sources for cotton, duffel (thick woolen fabric), canvas, furniture and other household goods.

William saw this battle, felt the pain of defeat and years later told his grandchildren about it.

The defeat was made worse by the inexplicable joy of the mercantile population. Did he slink home with tears dripping from nine-year-old eyes? Did his mother greet him with tenderness or stiff-backed disapproval at such a childish display of emotion? Life was harsh for a new immigrant family, and she, a determined and respected woman, drove her children to achieve, first in school and then in work. Their little leisure was devoted to the biblical passages that disparaged idleness and sparing of the rod. William, a harbor-watcher since the start of memory, had crewed in boats to fish or supply the ships at anchor and earn a few cents to add to the family income. Could he have imagined then that his destiny lay on the Pacific northwest coast of America?

Matilda

Matilda was born into a longhouse some ninety feet long and thirty-six feet wide. The longhouse post and beam construction allowed for decorative images to be carved on all the posts and the encompassed floor space was terraced down to the main floor where the fire was laid under the smoke-hole in the roof. The occupants were her chief father's own family on the upper terraces, as well as his commoner kin on the lower terraces and slaves on the lowest floor. Their lives were controlled by a set of customs and beliefs to match those of puritan Boston. With those beliefs came a set of ceremonies to be followed with the same meticulous care of a Christian Mass.

Matilda's birth was attended by two midwives and a shaman. Her father would attend only if a male child was expected. The shaman was present to ensure that no taboos were committed that might hinder the transfer of the reincarnate spirit from the Commander of the Land to the newborn infant for which he would be the mediator. When Matilda's birth was imminent, the junior midwife placed Matilda's mother with her head to the sea so that the newborn would not observe the sea before the land, for such a sight was a bad omen against the child's life. Senior midwife took the goatskin out of the clothes chest and placed it over the outstretched arms of the shaman so that he could ask the Commander of the Land for the blessing of his presence before the skin was placed beneath the mother's hips. Both midwives looked down on a serene face; a mother was not allowed any sign of anxiety or pain from her long labor to show on her face lest the Commander of the Land would decide to return this important spirit for some more stalwart mother's child. Perhaps this spirit was a seventh reincarnation and the destiny of its life on earth must be followed absolutely if this spirit was to achieve everlasting life and enter into the paradise of the Commander of the Land.

During the progress of the pregnancy the shaman had read the destiny of this child for the mother, predicted a female child and Matilda's mother dismissed her husband, confident that he was not needed to sever the cord of a male infant. As the baby's head crowned, the midwives raised the mother's shoulders so that she could reach down to control the infant's head.

As like as not, after a long hard labor the baby would be face up to the world and bring delight to the three of them for such was an omen of a good obedient life. The senior midwife assisted the mother with the cutting of the cord of her infant daughter.

The shaman took the infant Matilda, stood in front of the Commander of the Land to receive the Spirit into his lungs and breathe it into the infant and then, taking some water in a short tube of kelp, cleansed her mouth. The junior midwife held the child to the mother's breast to suckle and so stimulate the discharge of the afterbirth. The senior midwife proudly accepted the afterbirth to bury it in the forest at the back of the house—an act that bestowed great honor.

Ceremonies immediately began for introducing this new infant to the community, first to her chief father and close kin. Then the house was opened to the other chiefs and their entourages, before the child was swaddled in the skin of a young goat. The chief threw shrowton oil extracted from the "little fish" (eulachon), into the fire to raise a great flame and smoke to drive away the evil spirits from the infant's presence.

At about six weeks Matilda's mortality was recognized with a naming ceremony in which a nick-name is given based on some observed habit or appearance. As in all cultures, there existed that same humor that allows a tall child to be called Shorty. In Haida society a large infant might be named Sguii, a flea!

Matilda, up to the age of six, was given the freedom of the village. She roamed with a group of her friends, entered houses to demand and was granted food or drink. When the children asked for a story from some elder, he, seating them at his feet, retold one of the great myths that subtly informed the children of their tribal beliefs and laid a framework for their future morality.

Although there was no "little red schoolhouse," youngsters were soon thrown into a tough education that, in a boy's case, could not be entrusted to the soft sentimentality of a parent. The boys were taken by their hunter uncles for training and the girls by their mothers.

Matilda, no doubt a strong-willed daughter of a strong-willed chief father, found the reins held by her mother restrictive, traces to be kicked against. Already she knew that she was above the others in her house. She looked down on them with a little boastful indulgence from time to time. Had not her chief father the rings of six potlatches on his hat, symbols of their power?

Matilda learned the manners and responsibilities of her royal power; she was no longer able to run free but now to walk with regal hauteur and stand for hours without complaint as long speeches of welcome droned on. When her chief father was absent from the house leading the hunt, she stood outside the longhouse beside her mother, oblivious to pelting rain or hail, until his return; no whimpering or whining, just that serenity of manner her own mother displayed during her birth. The Kaigani Haida were a stoic people!

William

At ten years of age, William came up against the reality of the commercial world, lowered his emotional patriotism and hoisted the mercantile reality as he wasted away precious months of potential experience and pay at sea. Not until he was eleven years old did he get away to sea for the first time. What pull or circumstance brought him to acceptance by Josiah Marshall can only be imagined; the church as probable as any place for patronage in Boston. Of his early life at sea, there are no records to guide us except his log kept on board the brigantine *Paragon*, owned by Marshall and Wilde, with Captain Dixey Wilde her master. One thing is sure, he went from boy to man on his first voyage. There was no adolescence in nineteenth century Boston. At fifteen years of age, the log does not record his position, but the rank of first mate was not unusual at that age. The ship's log was usually the responsibility of the first mate and it was kept in William's handwriting.

William, aged eleven years, did not "go to sea with his gloves on!" unlike Richard Cleveland, who learned his seamanship from the comfort of his merchant father's ship. If the small boats of the harbor had, as yet, denied McNeill the rolling gait of a sailor, he came on board with the rope-seasoned hands of a small boat's crew. His unmentionables were tight around his waist and hung loose to his feet, and his black hat, low-crowned with a ribbon hanging down the left side, still lacked the varnish of a Jack tar's.

What of his sea chest? Check shirts, neckerchiefs, socks, boots, hussif (sewing kit) and long combinations, perhaps a string vest knitted by Sarah, his young sister. He also had a Bible given to him by his devout mother and for certain, a copy of Nathaniel Bowditch's treatise on navigation. At this time in Boston it was said of a boy wishing to go to sea that he should sleep with a copy of Bowditch under his pillow. To interpret this advice literally would have been most uncomfortable. This heavy tome, almost as large as the Holy Bible, contained cosmology, calculus and geometry that demanded considerable knowledge and skill in mathematics for its application in navigating a ship by dead reckoning.

On arrival at the gangway, greeted by a first mate with gruff manners, he was shown to steerage to live among the coils of cordage, spare sails, ship's stores and junk as yet not identified by him. A berth, if he was lucky, pallet and blankets, but built too short to accommodate his growing bones, the space beneath designed to just, only just, house his sea chest. Not that he saw too much of this

The forecastle of an American vessel.

small space for soon those gruff orders rang in his ears, "On deck boys, tumble up, look sharp now, do you hear the news!"

In this microsociety at sea, the hierarchy of captain, first and second mates, clerk or supercargo (manager of sales) ruled his life. In some larger vessels, there were third and fourth mates, older boys despised by the seamen in the forecastle as sailor's waiters, but they at least occupied the cabin area and quarterdeck.

Boys, like William, were ambitious to join this cabin set and be served from a better menu by the steward. William, as he tumbled up with the crew mustered for their captain's address, nodded his head as the captain suggested that "with God's blessing may we have a safe passage," and again as he called for "hard work and pull together as a team." Perhaps William's mind drifted in a pleasant day dream of his own future address to his crew, but he was cruelly awakened by the loud roar next his ear, "McNeill!" the first mate's accusing finger, "play soger again, you'll be for the top, lay forward now!" He had dreamed of hearing and speaking such language but without the first mate's insult that he was a mere soldier.

Although the orders were a confusion to his young ears, William took pawl in hand, strained to "anchor up" and heard the snap of wind in sail and creak of block and tackle as the yards braced. He might have snatched a sight of Boston Light as they moved under topsails into Nantasket Roads and said to himself, "From which I take my departure."

First impressions: messing in the forecastle, boys were barely tolerated by the seamen and suspected of being forecastle rats; a place where silent observation was a wise station. A new language, forecastle slang, slowly became understandable over the days of travel. The mate too, a hardnose, already called him a soger and threatened him with the topmast. What next? The mate might suggest salt-eel for their supper and already he'd referred to them as squeakers or younkers. A younker discovered soon enough the meaning of salt-eel—the ropes end!

Boys with names like Thompson, Kelly or Barker went to sea at ten years old. There were three or four such boys on each brigantine that left Boston. Brewer and McNeill were classmates and went to sea as comrades, a safe haven for each other's confidences. Some boys went on to be master mariners, others became seamen and a great many found they were not suited for the sea. One of the older boys was a bully perhaps, or fond of playing practical jokes. Bully or no, he would be their interpreter of the salty language of randy seamen who, as they approached the next harbor, indulged in the comedy of double speak on their prospects of, or delight in, drink and human copulation.

On the first day at sea, William heard the eight bells of the middle watch strike as he came out of sleep, then the bellow of the first mate's voice, "Tumble up, boys!" He jumped to the orders, "Rig the pump," glanced at the carpenter come up to start his repairs and the sailmaker to rigging and sails but had little time to envy those "idlers" who did not keep watch. Did he skive off out of the mate's sight? He would not have dared to slack and have the mate haze him daily until, discouraged, he deserted or at best, never went to sea again. As his "bible," a square of grinding stone, smoothed the flooded deck, he could daydream in the monotony. As he flogged the deck dry, he took a few moments to take pride in the symmetry of the boards and in those seconds of admiration, the mate's bellow, "Standby, lad, slush the mast!"Still half an hour to breakfast. Did he turn aside his bowl of unloved burgoo (porridge)? Ugh! A boy learned to eat anything that would fill his empty legs!

The swell of the open sea was different to any sensation in the harbor. Was he frightened and seasick or lucky? Just frightened!

How many days did he spend on a yardarm before his confidence stilled the terror of falling into a sail? Did he check a scream and have the nonchalance to laugh it off as the quickest way to the deck?

By tacit agreement, one man ruled the forecastle, either Stitches the sailmaker, Bungs the cooper, Chips the carpenter or some burly Jack tar. One among the crew drew the boys' respect to act as role model, a quiet example of courage, a man to guide a boy's elbow in the direction of right over wrong, goodness over evil and truth over superstition or hard work over idleness, no bluster of a coward and no boasting of a nastyface! The boys were silent observers no doubt, like rats, hoping to feed unseen, unnoticed and unclobbered! No matter if the cook was as black as the ace of spades, "curry favor with Cook," the advice of their mentor, "if you want dry socks from his camboose" (a galley built on deck). What did William make of his first treat of hot "scouse," the bucket of ship's stew, taken from the cook's camboose to the forecastle for consumption by the crew.? How quickly did he become a devotee of hot tea with molasses? That was the drink that greeted them at night when called up on watch; "water bewitched," the sailors called it. In his first storm at sea, was he washed the length of the deck, his canteen emptied of its precious brew and replaced with salt water? Did the start of tears bring an image of his mother's disapproval? He could hear her say "straighten your shoulders, Laddie!" and then join the laughter of his shipmates. "A man's no sailor if he can't take a joke," they told him as they slapped his back. At the same time each tipped a little of his precious brew into William's canteen; not to share was tantamount to thievery.

As they moved east and south, the borderless sea smoothed and the breeze moved them with a regular rhythm. The boys were assigned to Stitches, Bungs or Chips to learn those trades so essential to the ship's progress that they were detailed in the log every day. The boatswain or senior able seaman trained them in knots, belays, splices and blocks or, rigging a gant line, taught them to tar the shrouds. When William rose up into the sky he looked down on the quarterdeck. His solitary Captain Wilde — judge, jury, king and schoolmaster, paced the deck deep in private conversation with himself. A thought might run through William's mind to visit the kindly gentleman who had greeted him in the offices of Josiah Marshall with a warm handshake.

When did he discover that a formal visit to his captain put him on the way to his first tryst with the "gunner's daughter" (the gun to which a boy was lashed for flogging)? Unusual punishment for a boy? No, it was only different from his schoolmaster's cane in the severity of pain from the rope's end on his breech. How did he take his gruel? In silence, t'was a point of honor!

At noon, as the sun rose to its full height, the boys were invited to the quarterdeck with their sextants to take a fix on the height of the sun and from the measured angle determine the ship's latitude. On those mornings in which the sun and moon were visible in the sky together, the angle measured between them was used to determine longitude, a calculation that took four hours to complete. For those boys like William, destined to be masters of vessels, it was a keen challenge to come up with the correct answer, not from fear of punishment but from apprehension of a failed ambition.

William McNeill became an assiduous navigator embracing dead reckoning adjusted by these cosmic observations. In spite of the advent of chronometers, William was never able to trust them and continued to take lunar observations whenever an opportunity presented itself.

One evening as his ship moved south in the fits and starts of the doldrums towards the "Line," (for William, his first crossing) he heard a cry from the topmast.

"Sail ho," from the lookout.

"Where away?" asks the first mate.

"Off the starboard bow!" the lookout shouts back.

"What she look like?"

"Low black schooner, sir!" the reply.

The crew hustled William along with the other boys into the forecastle, blindfolded his eyes and tied his hands behind his back.

"Silence!" was the command issued to this small band of innocents.

From above, William was puzzled by the sounds from deck, scraping and splashing and a solemn greeting to their visitor from the black schooner.

"Ship ahoy," a voice from off the bow, "are any of my children aboard?"

"A few," he heard a sailor reply.

Crossing the line.

Old Neptune had arrived to the music of an iron hoop scraped across the lip of an empty barrel—eerie and threatening.

"Let me see some of my children!"

Roughly handled up from the forecastle, William's bound wrists burning under the tight bonds as they sat him on a bench, he winced with pain as they held his head firmly by his queue. A filthy mixture of soap, slush and tar was lathered on his face and shaved off with the iron hoop.

Questions came at him from unseen lips and demanded obedience to the Society of Old Neptune.

27

"Will you pledge yourself never to kiss the maid when you can kiss the mistress, unless indeed, you should like the maid best?"

Questions that might tickle the lewd fancy of the audience were added to pledges of loyalty to this fraternity of seamen. Questions to strengthen the bonds between officers and crew that included a test of seamanship knowledge. Then Old Neptune requested a pledge of solidarity in the forecastle community, brothers pledged to give each other protection with social support that allowed them to go where they wished in the world without fear of molestation. Questions which William faithfully answered with, "all due respect."

"Rinse him," Old Neptune's voice demanded.

In front of a sail full of water, blind William was pushed back into the brine, struggling to release his wrists but prevented by the bonds that bit into his skin. As time and again he came up for a gulp of air, he spluttered and gasped. The ceremony continued until he was considered cleansed. This was his baptism of admittance to the society of sailors and as he stood dripping on the deck, with hands free, he shook the hand of Old Neptune, a new initiate into this elite community of sailors.

Between 1814 and 1818, McNeill learned his seamanship, each voyage bringing him closer to the cabin via the loneliness of that in-between phase of being bunked in steerage as second or third mate. A time when he was despised as "a sailor's waiter" by the crew and not yet admitted as an officer by his captain. Serving as general dogsbody on board provided training that could make him as strong and good, or better, than any seaman aboard.

In January, 1819, the brigantine *Paragon*, under Captain Dixey Wilde, outfitted for fur trading on the Pacific northwest coast of America, left Boston Harbor. The log of the *Paragon* is in McNeill's handwriting and it was usually the first mate's responsibility to keep this record unless the captain decided he wished to make the entries. William McNeill, just turned fifteen years old, was young for such a responsibility. As first mate, William McNeill was responsible for the orders to sail the ship. From first light, attending to the washing down of the decks, sending men up or down the topmasts or yards, ordering changes in the sails, setting the studding sails, taking in reefs or in bad weather balancing the ship's sails to better ride out the storm; although these orders were given under the watchful eye of his captain. A captain who wanted a fast passage trucked no excuses when too few sails were set, yet blamed the mate when, overpressed, the sails gave out with the thunderous sound of a fired cannon.

On the voyage of the *Paragon*, a leak somewhere in the bows made them put into Rio de Janiero, unscheduled, to make repairs. The American vice-consul dined on board with the captain. McNeill dutifully listened to their conversation. Was it here that Captain Wilde got wind of the intended Russian ukase (edict) that would forbid American brigantines from participating in the fur trade in Russian territory backed up with two men-o'-war with seventy-four guns.

In Rio de Janiero, McNeill as first mate experienced disciplinary decisions for the first time. One seaman returned from liberty, perhaps disappointed by the lack of female company and in his cups, spouted language that left doubt about the heredity of the mate! The cooper too, went absent without leave for twenty-four hours. No action was recorded in the log but a dressing-down and a fine for both was doubtless meted out by the captain!

The log of the *Paragon* detailed the uncertainty of rounding Cape Horn. Forty days of drenching cold, beating against huge rough seas thrown up by the roaring forties and interspersed with agonizing calms that let the easterly current set them back again. Even the quality of his writing seemed to echo the fatigue. They sighted Diego Ramirez, an island south of Cape Horn, passed it, drifted back, passed it again with one saving grace, they were sure of their longitude!

Was it fatigue, early effects of scurvy or frustration that led to disorder among the crew?

Many logs recorded near-mutiny in the south Pacific after rounding "the Horn." Not long after passing Cape Horn, the steward was punished with a dozen lashes for disobedience. McNeill at fifteen, may have carried out his captain's order, with rattling line, the log records. Did the crew oppose such punishment? Richard Dana, who witnessed the flogging of two of his mess mates in 1834, recorded in 1850 such disgust that "even the word brought up feelings that he could hardly control." In spite of his feelings though, he writes: "Yet not to have the power of holding it up 'in terrorem', and indeed of protecting myself, and all under my charge, by it, if some extreme case should arise, would be a situation I should not wish to be placed myself, or to take responsibility of placing in another."

Melville was absolutely certain that flogging a seaman was a heinous crime against humanity. In *White Jacket* he devotes three chapters to the evil, unlawfulness and lack of necessity of continuing this practice in the U.S. Navy. He argues, "is it lawful to scourge a man that is a Roman? asks the intrepid apostle, well knowing, as a Roman Citizen, that it was not. And now, eighteen hundred years after, is it lawful for you, my country men, to scourge a man that is an American?"

Many seamen did not oppose corporal punishment for a thief or for any disobedience or act that put the ship and their lives in danger. Before arriving at the Sandwich Islands many a seaman would have approved when the cook, found guilty of "dirty cooking," was seized and given a dozen with "the cat." But why rattling line for the steward and the cat for the cook? Was the cook, a Negro, to be treated like a dog? Many of the cooks on board Boston ships were Negroes; on the *New Hazard* between 1811 and 1813, the Negro cook was flogged with the cat four times and the Negro steward three times.

A wise captain resorted to such punishment only when the crew condoned it. This was a lesson that McNeill found difficult to grasp when his hot-headed temper ran away with his reason. McNeill, like many of his contemporaries, dealt with disobedience with the authority of a raging bull! In the logs of his ships and the journals of his forts his knee-jerk reaction to strife led him to a course of action that sober reflection probably caused him to regret.

Once round Cape Horn, the *Paragon* crew prepared their ship, rolled out their guns and boarding netting for trade in the Marquesa Islands. There they collected sandalwood for the Canton market prior to proceeding on to the Sandwich Islands.

While furs were the main trading article at Canton at the beginning of the nineteenth century, the American brigantines were always on the lookout for other items of trade. Sandalwood abounded in the hills of the Sandwich Islands and the local inhabitants could trade it for goods brought out from Boston. The unit of measurement was in piculs, a Chinese measure equal to one hundred catties or about sixty kilograms. Depending upon its scarcity or abundance in the Canton market it fetched from $6 to $10 a picul

Flogging a seaman.

and 5,000 piculs would trade for considerable quantities of tea, chinaware and silks. By 1819, sandalwood was becoming expensive at the Sandwich Islands and the ships found secondary sources of supply.

The log of the *Paragon* finished on arrival at the Sandwich Islands in June, 1819. The supplies for the northwest coast trade were off-loaded at Oahu and used to resupply their own brigantines already on the coast. The log continued in May, 1820, on the voyage from Canton towards Boston. The *Paragon* left Canton in convoy with two other brigantines to run the gauntlet of the pirates operating in that part of the China Sea. The log ends with the *Paragon* in the Pacific Ocean in July, 1820. It is known from the correspondence between the agents in Oahu and Josiah Marshall in Boston, that the *Paragon* returned to the Sandwich Islands before returning to Boston.

That William McNeill remained in the Sandwich Islands is known from the log of the *Llama*, in which he tells the reader that this is his fifth time round Cape Horn. He was paid wages from the Marshall and Wilde's brigantine *Parthian* that sailed between Canton and the Sandwich Islands during this time. He arrived back in Boston in 1824 on the *Paragon*, left the same year in the *Convoy* and returned to Boston in 1828 in the brigantine *Golden Farmer*. In a letter to Sir George Simpson in 1848, he proclaimed that he made four voyages to China. There is certainly no other period in his life when it was possible for him to have made those voyages to Canton.

Captain Eliah Grimes brought the brigantine *Inore* from Boston to the Sandwich Islands arriving in early July, 1821. The voyage around Cape Horn had nearly destroyed his vessel as he writes in his letter to Marshall: "...the weather off Cape Horn was very severe so much so I lost both boats, camboose, house, spars. bulwarks, rose the Starboard plankshere about 3/4 of an inch, washed two men off deck, fortunately both got on board again."

He took the schooner *Eagle* from Sandwich Islands to the California coast and arrived back in time to greet the brigantine *Owhyee*, under Captain Henry, on its arrival in December, 1821.

Mr. Jones, Marshall's agent at Oahu, writes in his letter to Boston: "Capt Grimes is pleased with the Brig but complains much of the scanty way in which she was fitted out; he has been obliged to purchase here at an advanced price, cutlasses, pistols, boarding pikes, blunderbusses and other articles of defence, not an article for cabin stores, no sugar and nothing to drink but NE Rum" (New England rum).

There was a shortage of crewmen and provisions at the Islands at this time due to a large number of whaling ships in Oahu Harbor. He continues in his letter: "A Mr Welty, long acquainted with the coast, and formerly an officer with Capt Grimes in the St Martin, will go Chief officer of the Owhyee, Mr McNeil has shipped as second officer, for crew they will be obliged to take whoever they can obtain and those at advanced wages, a great mistake has been made in sending the vessel out so poorly manned, others on the coast will have much the advantage of Capt Grimes."

Captain Grimes, however, was quite optimistic and pleased to have acquired Mr. Welty because he was well acquainted and knew many places that he did not and having a good vessel and cargo, wished to take every advantage and not go in company, although he had powerful competition to contend with.

William McNeill was with experienced company and no doubt eager to learn, not only the handling of the brigantine in and out of tricky anchorages but also the manner of trading with the Kaigani Haida, Haida, Tlingit, Bella Bella, Tsimshian and Nahwitti Indians of the coast. An ambitious Boston boy like William McNeill, brought up with stories of great wealth derived from the fur trade on the northwest coast and having seen the opulent mansions of the merchants of Franklin Square, would take a demotion from first mate in order to gain experience of the northwest coast in preparation for obtaining a captaincy of a brig destined for the fur trade. A captain was paid wages of $20 per month plus 5 percent of the value of the furs he traded at the end of each voyage, a sum far in excess of his wages as first mate. The *Owhyee* sailed from Oahu on February 4, 1822, and William's training for the northwest coast fur trade commenced.

Matilda

At the age of six years, Matilda was taken under the wing of her mother for her education. Not a different education from others in her group of children, and yet as a chief's daughter, a subtle difference of expectation set her apart from the children of commoners or slaves. She saw the world out of a face varnished with train oil and colored with red ocher, from the upper gallery of their house and her kinship came with the obligations of wealth and station—ambition, self-respect, cleverness, hard work and obedience. At public feasts, seated in full view of the village, she ate sparsely, denied herself favorite delicacies and maintained a politeness of manner. She learned to admire her father's headdress with its rings that told of the number of potlatches given by him.

Her father inherited his chieftainship and name from his maternal uncle, but his ongoing chiefly status was due to those hard-earned rings. Matilda's very status as a noblewoman was dependent on those rings. After the feast she was expected to sing one of her inherited songs, perform one of her own dances or participate in a performance of a secret society and keep the secrets of its magic.

As she aged, this expectation was ever more rigid, and lack of conformity corrected with no room for laxity. The shaman played an important part in her spiritual life as a priest did in the lives of European nobles. A recalcitrant Matilda suffered the pain of the shaman's magical power if she strayed from the path of righteousness, that path of her foretold destiny.

The skills of survival that all women must learn started as winter supplies dwindled. Her mother taught Matilda to trap small animals to keep the wolf from the door (this type of pun was at the heart of Haida humor). In early spring she helped collect and prepare the herring spawn that attached itself to the cedar fronds placed in the high tidal water. Soon after, an expedition would leave their winter village in their large trading canoes. They paddled across Dixon Entrance to enter Portland Inlet where the canoes were joined by the herds of seals and sea lions, killer whales and right whales. Ahead, the water was white from myriad gulls whose rackett calls harmonized with the woodwinds of whales and sackbuts of sea lions. Beyond the gulls, the pure white of the Nass Basin awaited the breakup of the winter ice. Every species was on the same quest, to fish for the eulachon, "the little fish," as the Natives called them. As the men set their nets under the ice, the women prepared the vats for maceration of the female fish and the racks for drying the males. These little fish were so full of oil that when dried they were lit as candles. Fires burned to heat the rocks to throw into the vats to release the yellow oil—butter for a nation.

Early summer brought Matilda back to her village to gather the salmonberries, soapberries, huckleberries, strawberries, Oregon grapes and crab apples to be laid down for winter as well as eaten fresh. All the time her mother taught her a taxonomy of plants with their food and medicinal value, identified animals from their droppings, detailed the uses of bark and roots and discussed the trapping of the small mammals of the forest. Did Matilda test her new knowledge with devil's club and get purged? Did she believe that she must not cross the path of a land otter or talk to these creatures who could take away her senses and turn her into a useless Gogiid (imbecile or idiot)? When Matilda was older her mother taught her to paddle a canoe, took her across the sea and, looking at the heavens, told her of One-in-the-sky who received the spirits of dead hunters and recounted the story of one of her relatives, a great whale hunter perhaps, whose spirit was received by One-in-the-sea and reincarnated into a great killer whale. When they had beached and set up camp on some island, the bright fire burning, did her mother tell her the myth of Natsalanee, that tells of the origin of the killer whales from yellow cedar.

In the time between the berries and the coming of the salmon, Matilda accompanied her mother to Kigarney Point with their sea otter furs and tails to haggle with the Boston traders. Seated on deck, their furs spread out for inspection, under their wide-brimmed hats that hid their tell-tale eyes, they waited for the bargaining to begin. From a Haida point of view, some of the toughest bargainers with their furs were the women. Many a Native husband remained mute until a sign from his wife allowed him to close the deal. Matilda observed and then practiced the art of haggling for that little extra from the white-face tribesmen. She learned to almost reach agreement, then call on a neighboring Haida with some humorous comment that would send both into a paroxysm of laughter. Is there anything more disconcerting to us than a joke that we are unable to mutually enjoy? She would have learned to sense the moment when the Boston trader's guard was down and with cunning, add a little sauce to the pot; another fathom of cloth or gill of rum and make for a hasty closure of the deal.

Was this when Matilda first saw the man who was her fate, the second mate of the *Owhyee*, her Matahell?

In the fall, at their salmon river, Matilda learned to dry and smoke the fish for the winter. After the salmon had run their course up river, she went into the forest again, this time to receive the gift of the cedar tree, its bark that formed the basis of their cloth. She woul prod for the spruce roots, raw material used to manufacture the different twines used in their basketry. All along the months of spring, summer and fall, her mother taught her the prayers of gratitude to the roe, little fish, berries, salmon, cedar bark or spruce root that were said on each occasion of harvest, thanking the bearer of these gifts of nature.

These prayers to the spirits of trees and animals became as familiar to her as "give us this day our daily bread," that William recited to his one and only God in his nighttime prayers. In the winter, the ceremonials were no longer just entertainment, but a body of history to be learned and passed on to the next generation with the same accuracy of a printed book. Each year she had listened to her chief father retell the story of their origin:

> The One-in-heaven was angry with the constant battles between our ancestors. During the great conflict between the warring tribes, one village was under attack at the time a young girl was isolated with her grandmother in anticipation of her becoming a lady. After the battle they found that they were the only survivors from their village.

Grandmother was sad and in her mourning cried out to the One-in-heaven, "Who will marry my daughter?"

"I will marry your daughter," this first suitor, a squirrel in the form of a small man, answered.

"How will you protect us when under attack?" Grandmother asked scornfully.

The small man ran to the base of a tree, shinnied up the trunk to the first main branch and ground his teeth at them. Then he ran out on the branch and dropped cones on their heads. Grandmother was not impressed even though some cones hit her head.

Each time she cried out, a different animal responded to her call. She rejected them all until a grizzly bear answered. His big claws scratched at the air, his mouth snarled and he almost convinced her of his suit. But grandmother remembered how the brave hunters of her village tracked down and killed the bears, ate their meat and slept on their soft fur.

"Go!" she told him, "you're not fit to protect us." Then she cried out once more through the thick fog of the morning, beseeching the One-in-heaven to hear her call. So thick the morning fog that she could hardly see her daughter standing next to her.

A new voice, silvery and musical, "I will marry your daughter," a voice that seemed to surround her, a different tone, humble, as he offered his hand.

The young man appeared out of the fog, shining with surface energy that made the mist around snow white. She was not impressed by his slight body; beautiful, yes, but not strong.

"How are you going to protect us when we are attacked?"

The young man took a short rod from under his cloak and pointed it to the east. As his hand moved the tip of the rod towards the west, the earth tilted to such a degree that grandmother and daughter were hanging onto a tree to stop them rolling off the earth.

"Stop! stop!" Grandmother yelled, "let me think this over."

As Grandmother stood thinking and while pondering on his lack of strength, the earth started to tilt again. Grandmother and daughter knelt at his feet and she begged him to be her son-in-law. He put out his hand to them so that they would rise.

"I will take you on a long journey," he told the daughter, "through space and up into the heavens on one condition." He took her under his right arm and held her off the ground, "Do not open your eyes, even if you do feel frightened by strange noises."

Grandmother begged to go with them and he took her likewise under his left arm. They left the ground and flew upwards into the sky. At the first feeling of sudden elevation Grandmother wanted to see where they were, but she resisted. When she heard the frightening moaning all around her, she had to open her eyes. Immediately they all fell to earth like stones.

The young man was angry with Grandmother, pulled a branch from out of an old spruce tree nearby and stuffed her into the knot hole. After he had replaced the branch he told her, "You stay there until the end of time and the people will hear you!"

Matilda's chief father cast his eyes around the assembled villagers and with dramatic gestures, "That is why you can hear her when the east wind blows in the tree that moans out, 'Ska twa,' which means, who will marry my daughter!"

Her chief father continued his oration after a shiver of fear echoed through the assembly.

"You can open your eyes now," her young man informed the daughter.

They were in front of a strange and beautiful house, obviously a spirit house.

"Come, meet my family," and they entered to stand before his father, Simoiget, the first chief.

"Take your young lady," he commanded his son, "and bathe her." He pointed to the bath in the corner of the room.

The servants took off her clothes and placed her under water. Her skin peeled off to make her appear like the servants. They were all different, all like lit glass of different colors, as she followed them to her own private quarters. They showed her the mat to sleep on. Her husband was ordered to sleep on the balcony at the far end of the house, two floors above her. As he stood on the balcony he was consumed by light to become a sun and she never saw him again.

She was with child even though she had not known a man. Simoiget took the child from her, washed him, stood on the infants feet and pulled on his arms to stretch him to his own height. Yet again she was with child and once more Simoiget stretched the boy to his size.

On the third occasion she bore a daughter for Simoiget to stretch and he was able to name the three, Liggeyoan, Akagee and Goestella. Now he was ready to prepare their return to earth on his special mission.

At this point in the story, Matilda always found her mind full of images that deflected her attention from the rest of the myth.

37

Matilda's mother was from the Nass River, the village of Gitradeen. Matilda inherited, with her brother Neeskinwaetk, the chiefship of the Wolf-Bearmother clan of that village. She learned the Nishga version of many of the myths and visited the village with her mother to attend winter ceremonials at Gitradeen to be able to fulfill a double duty to her offspring.

One aspect of Matilda's education was absolutely contrary to a puritan Boston woman. On the open terraces of her house, which provided little privacy for its members, copulation was a normal and observable pleasure for the Kaigani Haida. Before puberty, it was the prerogative of her grandmother (or if no longer alive, an older aunt) to instruct her in sexual pleasure, encourage her to tryst with a young hunter and learn the art of love. However, once her first menses started, Matilda learned that she would be under a strict code of abstinence until betrothed and married. Pregnancy before marriage in some tribes warranted the death sentence at worst, or forced marriage at best.

Matilda was endowed with a hereditary name at about the age of ten years. At the time of her naming she was assigned a slave to serve her by her chief father. Not long after, Bearmother, Wolf and Raven were tattooed on her back and chest. It was not immodest for Kaigani Haida women to bare the upper body and proudly display their crests. At a similar time, the shaman made a small incision under the lower lip to insert a small labret (ornament fashioned from whale bone and abalone shell). Whether Matilda continued to enlarge her lower lip to the point that it produced their prized sibilant speech is not recorded. If William was like other Boston men he would not have liked a lower lip that could be stretched to cover the eyes, and probably discouraged it.

William

In July, 1822, Captain Grimes wrote a long letter to Marshall from Tamgass Harbour (also spelt Tumgass and Tomgass) detailing his success aboard their own brigantine *Owhyee*, or lack of it in some quarters. He arrived late in the season and found many boats in opposition to him. Sea otter furs were hard to come by and the price too high for profit. He suspected that the Indians were holding out for high prices, for it was common for the American ships to offload their supplies late in the season in a last effort to obtain skins before sailing for the Sandwich Islands. In this letter he writes to Marshall:

> On a consultation of all the masters on the coast that is Capts Clark, Cross, Harris, Stetson we have thought it for the interest of our owners to purchase the remains of Capt Martin's cargo as he was determined to give 9 or 10 Fathoms for a skin with all the presents, in that case we should not have been able to have got a skin, we know for a fact that the natives have kept them back for that purpose what we bought is the best of his cargo for which we have paid 16 Prime skins, 16 cubs, 30 Beaver and 30 Land otter each.

The ruse paid off and he reported a month later that he had bought seventy-four prime skins and forwarded them to Canton.

Young Mr. McNeill watched this wily Captain with his experienced first mate and learned the art of bargaining, the language of Chinook jargon, which were the most productive villages to visit, the most obliging manners to endear himself to the Indian chiefs, how to deceive the opposition to be the sole trader at the various anchorages and last, but not least, how to outrun the Russian frigate, *Apollo*!

When a great chief of the Kaigani or Tsimshian visited the *Owhyee*, William learned to entertain and honor them with a feast of the ship's finest fare. The chiefs and their families were allowed to spend the night on board. Sometimes a chief, wary of remaining for such entertainment requested a hostage be sent ashore to sleep in his house. So, at Chucknahoo, did William go to Chief Cogwealth's house in exchange for his son, as a mark of mutual trust?

When William visited the house one fall evening he was greeted by the sight of the chief, naked, toasting his light brown body in the heat of the central fire. A bustling household gathered around him, not just the seven or eight souls expected, but people occupied in various activities that abruptly ceased; and now forty pairs of eyes looked at him with astonishment. Courtesy was demanded by the chief and a slave brought a chest for him to sit on by the fire and shooed away the dogs sniffing and snarling at his feet. His eyes followed the smoke out of the roof and adapted to the dusky light. The central floor was surrounded by three terraces; small cubicles gave space to individuals or couples but little privacy. Goods were piled in cedar boxes, dried fish hung from racks on the roof, blankets were stowed away in piles. William was fascinated by a woman taking a hot stone from the fire to place in a cooking vessel to poach the tubers. Food was offered from carved wooden bowls, dry salmon with shrowton, roast halibut and licorice plants, sweet and succulent. He realized shipboard hospitality must seem equally strange to his counterpart.

Both hostages were destined to sleep the night in unfamiliar beds and surroundings. A length of blue cloth and a pillow of furs was laid out on the upper terrace in honor of his station, but when the chief's lady offered William a girl for comfort, he declined; not without a blush at the lack of privacy! Was it because he was too young or because he was attracted to the chief's daughter? Her eyes lowered and raised again as she flirted her curiosity at him. Even the vermillion paint beautified her face and offset the oiled black hair falling down her back. He frowned at her lack of modesty in showing off her tattoos, Raven and Wolf, over her nubile developing breasts; his frown was not for the tattoos!

Did William, at some later date visit and tryst with her? Did his shyness yield to her caressing hands? Did he see her as an uncaged bird of paradise to transport back to the Islands?

McNeill

Captain Grimes was critical of Marshall for not sending goods that would sell. He was specific about the cloth or duffel he required and then went on to recommend:

> Kendrick muskets are no more value than the French in fact they are not so saleable the Speak muskets is of more value, one or two bales of India chintz will do well to purchase Land furs & tails. Send buck shot instead of lead except what is wanted for balls I have tried in the most compact way and find there is from 25 to 30 per cent loss in running lead into shot, the great proportion wants to be of the largest kind as it is used altogether for hunting Otter, more than one half the lead is already gone I shall not have enough to last half next season, I should say it would take 20 or 21 cwt for the year and two thirds or more of it buck shot.

The sea otter pelts were sorted into red, black, adult or pups, and the sea otter tails were traded and listed separately. Unlike the

Russians on the coast, the American ships did not go hunting for the sea otter themselves. However, they were conversant with the needs of the Haida, Tlingit or Kaigani Haida hunters.

McNeill observed the sea otter hunters at work and learned their needs. He noticed that some of the hunters were missing parts of their fingers. He most likely read Captain John Meares' account of the sea otter, written in 1788 at the time that Meares built an establishment at Nootka:

> This animal, like the river otter, is of an amphibious nature, but their peculiar element is the sea. They are sometimes seen many leagues from land, sleeping on their backs on the surface of the water, with their young reclining on their breasts. As the cubs are incapable of swimming till they are several months old, the mother must have some curious method of carrying them out to sea, and returning them to their hiding place on shore, or in the cavities of rocks that project into the sea. Indeed, they are known to sleep with their young on their breast, and swim with them on their back, but if they should be unfortunately overtaken by the hunters, the dam and her brood always die together; she will not leave her young ones in the moment of danger, and therefore shares their fate.
>
> From the formation of their lungs, they are able to remain under water no longer than two minutes, when they are forced to rise to the surface for respiration. It is this circumstance which gives their pursuers such advantage over them, though the wonderful swiftness with which they swim very often baffles the utmost attention and skill of the hunter. Nature has furnished the sea otter with powerful weapons of offence and destruction. Its fore-paws are like those of the river otter, but of much larger size and greater strength: its mouth contains most formidable rows of teeth superior to any other marine animal except the shark.

Captain Grimes described the difficult season which resulted from much sickness among the crew. There were two deaths, one from consumption and the other from fever, an illness that kept from three to seven crew off duty daily and required a long list of medications:

> They complain of violent colds pains in the breast and head which I think is owing in a great measure to Brig being so fully salted she is damp from one end to the other, ...Also medicines such as Antimonial wine, Burgundy Pitch, Dover powders, half of it doses 15 gr each other, flaxseed half in powder, Paragoric,

Essence of peppermint, Spirits of Nitre dulcified, Syrup of Squils, Spirits of Hartshorn, Tincture of Myrrh, Balsam popacia, Laudanum, gum kino in powder, Rhodaldock, Elixir vitriol, Turlington Balsam, Camphor—I have reason to believe if those medicines had been on board, the complaints might have been removed as they were occasioned by colds.

The medicine chest in Dr. Helmcken's house in Victoria attests to the space needed to carry this variety of medicaments on board ship. Today we may smile at the infusions, elixirs, tinctures, spirits, balsams and gums used by people at the beginning of the nineteenth century, but they set great store by these medicines. The Fort Simpson journal under John Work blames their absence for deaths during the 1830s and when the great fever hit Fort Vancouver, Dr. McLoughlin notes in a private letter that he ran out of some of his essential medicines that led to unnecessary deaths. There were no surgeons or apothecaries on Boston ships and the responsibility fell to the captain to be physician and nurse to the sick. Naturally, they all disparaged any use of the Indian shaman's remedies!

Captain Grimes reported that he had been quite unwell himself with rheumatism and that crew members had made threats against his life: "I shall also send a mutinous fellow by the name of John Rees who was out one of the Liberty's crew who shipped from Boston which Capt Wilde knows the particulars. I have had a serious proof of his conduct also two other who resorted to pistols, knives, axes & clubs. I intend getting two of them to the Islands if I can."

William McNeill learned to outrun the frigate *Apollo* on those sorties into Russian-claimed territory that took the *Owhyee* up Chatham Strait to Ennacanoe, Hood's Bay and Chuckanuck to where the Klukwan and Chilkat Indians sold their furs. Then further south into Sumner Strait to visit Henegea and Coyou, explore Clarence Strait to anchor at Chucknahoo and Tamgass before a visit to the Nass River Indians at Kincolith. At Kigarney, they anchored across from the Indian village of Hogin (Howkan) where the *Owhyee* spent time protected from the fall gales before running south to California and then returning to the Sandwich Islands.

In the fall of 1822, did McNeill visit the village of Chasina at Chucknahoo? Did he attend the feast of Bearmother when Matilda took the role of Peesunt (sometimes spelt Rhpeesunt)?

Matilda

During the winter ceremonials each year, various myths and histories were re-enacted on the stage of the village ceremonial house. Matilda took part in these performances and was familiar with both the Haida and Nishga versions of the myths. Perhaps Chief Cogwealth invited young William to attend one of her performances that told the story of Bearmother.

A strange hush goes through the ceremony house, not immediate silence, but a repeat of the sighing sound on the beach at William's first visit as hostage against the kidnapping of Chief Cogwealth's son. The sound rushes through the room like a breeze sweeps through the trees of the forest with everyone's attention drawn to an elder approaching the chief to accept the talking stick. Male performers move onto the stage, each and every one of them naked to receive the costumes of their characters. Three young nubile girls enter, the center one taller, broader, stronger and statelier. Shifts are placed over their heads before they don their chilkat cloaks and berry baskets. Two boys come forward to receive chasubles of bearskin with carved bear's heads attached that act as the hoods. The dimming light of late fall gives an eerie reality to the actors.

The actors spread out over the stage as the elder stands to one side to begin the narrative which guides the actors' action.

The storyteller opened his narrative:

"Shit," Peesunt announced, as she slipped on the bear droppings, fell heavily onto her back and broke one of the backstraps from her forehead that held her berry basket. Her two companions stopped their songs and laughed back at her lying on the path.

Laughter of approval greets this unusual opening to the Bearmother myth. The master storytellers are appreciated for their ingenuity of humorous puns in presentation.

"With the bears so close, you should not swear," one of her companions told Peesunt as she helped put the berries back into her basket. Her other companion helped repair the strap.

"Pooh to the orphan who did this!" Peesunt replied angrily.

"Shush!" both companions charged, "and don't forget to sing as you walk or the bears will think you mock them!" and they all set off again along the path.

The audience applauds their approval. The storyteller has included all the essential elements of their traditional story with unusual economy and skill.

William is enthralled by Peesunt's performance, her subtle movements that mime the narrative.

His eyes are rivetted on her; his mind reflects on her image outlined in his mind before she received her shift. Her mature figure, a shimmering image standing on the stage, proud and of a beauty that imparts an unnerving shift of blood between his thighs.

The younger children giggle with pleasure. What child could fail to find merriment in the bathroom humor of slipping on bear poo! William senses from their bright eyes their keen anticipation of the rest of the story to come.

> As Peesunt lifted her basket onto her forehead again, the straps broke. She called out to her companions for help but this time they ignored her.
>
> "Bastards," she cried out in anger instead of singing, as the bears expected of her. As she tried to mend the strap, dusk was putting out the lights of day.
>
> "Sister, are you in trouble?" Peesunt looked up into the face of a young hunter dressed in bearskin. "Nobody to look after you?" he asked as his brother helped him replace the berries in her basket.
>
> "Come with us, we will help you carry your berries!" The two younger hunters told her with cunning.

The old storyteller's eyes glint as his head nods at the audience until all the heads nod back with him—nervous giggles from the women and leering grins of seduction from the men before laughter. Then he holds up the talking stick for silence.

A further group of actors come on stage to accept their costumes. The group includes one tiny child, no more than three years old, who is helped into a mouse suit so real that even William joins in the applause.

"Tseets," William learns from the old lady next to him, "the grandmother!" She chuckles as William sees her own resemblance to the mouse.

One huge naked man stands before the great carving of Bearmother as helpers seem to stuff him into a bearsuit with a carved bear's head that covers his own and makes him compete with the ferocity of the statue behind him. He sits back into the lap of the Bearmother as if on a giant throne and his large stomach ripples with triumphant laughter, reminding William of the Chinese God of laughter in Canton. A very small hissing sound, started by the children, builds to a crescendo of disapproval at the villain.

The storyteller craves silence.

The brothers led Peesunt up the mountainside to a large house. They entered through an entrance decorated with two Ravens. One carried the moon in her beak and the other the sun in his beak. The house was crowded with people attending a feast. The sight of the Chief, huge, strong, fierce with his grizzled hair took Peesunt's breath away and she felt faint. She knelt in front of him as bidden and looked up at his cruel face. She felt a little tug on her robe, looked down to see Tseets, the little grey mouse with long hair to camouflage her presence.

"Granddaughter," she whispered, "the bears have you in their den. You will now become one of them, have their children or," the mouse disappeared into the Chief Grizzly Bear's fur just as one of the brothers stood in front of his chief.

"Chief Grizzly-Bear, Uncle, I bring you Peesunt." He lifted her up and thrust her forward before the chief. She stood bowed before him shaking with fear. To Peesunt, it felt a whole day and night before he gave her leave to unbow her head.

"Has she agreed?" he asked his nephew.

"Agreed?" Peesunt inquired.

"To be wife to my nephew, heir to this house, and bear his children?" he asked.

There is general but groaning laughter around the room. William does not understand the simplicity of the storyteller's pun.

Peesunt asked boldly, "and if I refuse?" her question asked with a boldness that she soon regretted. Four of the bear cubs took a limb each and held her over the fire.

The story teller stops and the action on stage takes over the story as they roast Peesunt over the flames. The audience moans with pity as small pieces of Peesunt's cloak catch fire and fall into the flames. It appears as if her whole body will soon be ablaze as one of the cubs lets go her arm and it falls into the flames.

Peesunt lets out a heart-rending scream, "I will marry your nephew!" sobs out and once more she screams with the burning pain. The cubs throw her at the feet of Chief Grizzly Bear in a bundle, her whole body smolders as she shakes in fear before him. He raises his huge foot-paws over her and clenches the claws with the pleasure of his dominance.

There is deafening applause all around the room, William feels the goose bumps on his bare arms begin to settle after the tension of the drama subsides. The story teller holds up his stick for silence from the audience and the drums begin to beat softly.

> Peesunt bore her husband twins, a male and female, half human and half bear. Meanwhile in her village, her own brothers continued their search for their sister. One winter's day she saw them in the vale below the Bear's village. She pressed some snow into a large ball and let it roll down the scree to attract her brothers attention. Her brothers climbed the mountain and slew her husband, Chief Grizzly Bear's nephew. As he lay dying he taught them two ritual songs to be given in his memory over his body.
>
> Peesunt did not let her brothers kill her half human children but in their place they killed all the members of the house in front of the cruel Chief Grizzly Bear before they turned on him.

The thin falsetto voice of the shaman floats across the audience as Chief Grizzly Bear lies dying at the foot of the Bearmother statue. As the second ritual song starts the attendants place the body of the chief in a small cedar sarcophagus, so that his knees touch his chin. The shaman stands singing beside the body and as the song ends the detached claws of the bear float up out of the coffin, form themselves into a necklace that encircles the shaman's neck. As the last beat of the drum sounds, the claws clench into his neck and blood runs down his chest.

There is a gasp, then applause for their great shaman, followed by calls for all the actors to join them to reassure them that no one has actually died. The elder storyteller comes to centre stage, holds up the stick and the room is silent. He turns to find their new visitor and speaks to him directly.

"Simoiget McNeill, this is the legend of the birth of the Grizzly Bear phratry within the Raven Clan. All members of this phratry have come down to us from those two bear children. Who knows if the hunter has killed a distant kin of their own? Reverence the bear whose meat you will eat at the feast and remember, the songs must be sung before we can partake of his meat."

William

Two seasons on the coast was enough to try the patience of most of the crew of the *Owhyee* and in Captain Grimes' letter to Marshall in December, 1823, he asks for a clear policy in the employment articles when young men are enlisted, citing the practices of both Boardman & Pope and Bryant & Sturgis as examples. Similar grievances came up time and again in the letters and dispatches of the Boston merchants' correspondence and there was always a shortage of first rate seamen and junior officers.

Captain Grimes writes to Marshall: "…my officers also wish to go home — McNeil would have stopp'd another season I think had not Capt Wilde written for him to come home, he is a smart young man and I am sorry to part with him at this time and think it would have been as well for him to have remained in the Brig and not to have gone home at this particular time."

William McNeill sailed from the Sandwich Islands in the brigantine *Paragon* and arrived in Boston on 26 August 1824. He had been away nearly six years and was ready to become a master mariner at the age of twenty-one years, at which time he could apply for a master's position. Clearly, Captain Wilde had picked him out for the northwest coast trade, groomed him with Captain Grimes and planned to give him command as soon as he arrived back in Boston.

His stay in Boston lasted only seven weeks before he was at sea again.

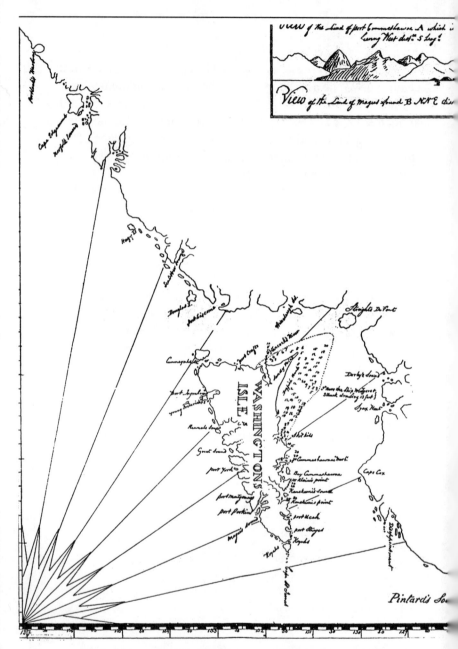

Map of Queen Charlotte Islands drawn by Captain Joseph Ingraham
of the brigantine *Hope* in 1790.

CHAPTER 2

The Voyage of the Brigantine *Convoy*

The passage around Cape Horn from Eastward I positively assert is the most dangerous, most difficult and attended with more hardships, than that of the same distance in any other part of the world!

—Captain Porter, U.S. Frigate, *Essex*

William McNeill, twenty-one years old, arrived back in Boston on board the *Paragon* in August, 1824. He obtained his Master Mariner certificate and knew from Captain Dixey Wilde that the firm had plans for him to take a ship out to the Sandwich Islands and proceed to the northwest coast.

Imagine young Captain McNeill admiring the two-masted, two-hundred-ton hermaphrodite brigantine *Convoy*, after Josiah Marshall and Captain Dixey Wilde had informed him that he was to be her next master.

McNeill had already achieved the first of his two dreams; to go to the rich fur trade of the Pacific northwest. Now the second was in sight; he was to be captain of his own vessel. Tomorrow he would bring his own ship to the wharf for outfitting. There was no time to dream, the longboat was waiting at the jetty to take him out to his vessel that was riding on her best bower (an anchor with chain). Mr. Little, his first mate, greeted him aboard with perhaps a smile for grinning Joseph Carter, second mate, who had been a mere boy five years before, on the *Paragon*. No time for sentiment, there was work to do.

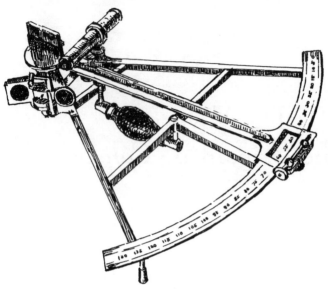

Ramsden sextant. Jesse Ramsden F.R.S., an optician and astronomical instrument maker in London in the second half of the eighteenth century, made several instruments carried aboard the HMS *Discovery* and HMS *Chatham*.

That morning, his old captain, mentor and employer, Dixey Wilde, had spread the charts of the north and south Atlantic oceans on his desk.

"Take her well to the east, 27 west of Greenwich before turning south, avoid the horse latitudes and make the most of the clockwise currents. Pick up the northeast trades off Africa and head for the Cape de Verde Islands, try to keep east of 27 west before crossing the line, and then ride the southeast trades to take you down the coast of Brazil."

"Into Rio, Sir?" McNeill, not beyond teasing his old captain.

"May God protect you from those saucy bastards!" Dixey Wilde exclaimed, in memory of their unscheduled visit in the *Paragon* in 1919.

"Into the soundings off the south coast," Dixey Wilde continued, placing his finger off the south coast of Brazil, "and take the breezes out of Rio de la Plata to head west of the Falklands." Such was the advice of the experienced captains to the new masters. William became restless with Captain Wilde's exposition of the obvious. He was eager to refresh his knowledge about the course northeast from the Sandwich Islands and details of Indian villages for trade and harbors safe from the vicious southeasterly storms that would pass and as quickly turn to northwest gales.

In the front of the log of the *Convoy*, all harbors and straits are detailed with latitudes, appearances of their entrance, hazards to avoid, both outside and inside those anchorages. Names like Kigarney, Tatterskey, Tamgass, Clement Cittie, Tongas, Nass, Chucknahoo, Tucketsarn, Henegea, Ennacanoe, Chuckanuck, Skidegate, Cumshewa, Masset, Sebashes and Nahwitti, visited under Captain Grimes, peppered the logs of *Convoy* in 1825 and *Tally Ho* in 1826.

Also at the front of *Convoy*'s log, was a complete list of the inventory stowed aboard. That list included bales of cotton, duffel, and calicoes, pipes of brandy, hogsheads of rum, cases of musquits (muskets), knives and other hardware goods, all for the trading of fur. Items needed to sustain them for the five-month voyage included casks of bread, flour, rice, molasses, oil, salt beef and pork. Each item was assigned a value with the total outfit worth over $15,000 American. By Sunday, October 24, 1824, the *Convoy* was ready to sail.

Imagine the youthful McNeill sitting in his cabin and lowering his writing flap to enter the events of the day into the log. Was he overwhelmed by detail? As you read these four days of the "Civil Account," surely you will agree that he would have wished for anything other than this:

Boston Harbour Sunday October 24th 1824
Fine breezes and pleasant, scaled our large Guns. continued pleasant this day.

Monday October 25th
Pleasant and fine breezes from the Westward employed in preparing for Sea filled up our empty water casks Making in all on board Nineteen Hundred & Forty Gallons.

Tuesday October 26th
Commences moderate & pleasant at 1 P.M. a fresh Gale from the S.E. with rain found the Brig dragged her anchor, let go the best Bower which brot' her up. Sent down Royals and top gallant Yards. In attempting to get further into the stream, we drifted to the North of Battery Wharf, until close of day we lay aground when she floated.

Wednesday October 27th
At 2 AM more moderate hove up and made Sails run off into the Stream and came to anchor in 6 1/2 Fathoms water. Sent up Top

Gallant & Royal Yards. At 8 AM Pilot came on board at 9 Got
underweigh at 11 Past Boston Light with a pleasant breeze from
the Westward. Discharged the Pilot
Here ends civil account.

Thursday October 28th Nautical Account
Commences pleasant weather and a moderate breeze all sail set.
At meridian Boston light bore W by N from which I take my
departure. May God bless us with a safe and speedy passage.
Ends moderate, Winds W.N.W.
Latitude 41°.54' N
Variation 6° West
Longitude 67.58 W

The *Convoy* took the course prescribed by experienced Boston
mariners and crossed into the tropics east of 30° west, longitude.
Soon after entering the tropics they picked up the northeast trade
winds. The *Convoy*, "proved stiff and going very well free," and by
the time the brisk trade winds pressed her sails the log records,
"crew employed on the rigging which was in a very bad state when
we left Boston." Such remarks are frequent in the logs of McNeill's
voyages, a little like politicians new in office blaming the previous
set for the state of the account books.

A leak reported coming in from the bows into the forecastle
gave rise to some anxiety and on November 8 the log records: "A
heavy sea on with the wind S.E. and close braced to it, the Brig very
wet and the leak increasing a little. We find it very difficult to work
the pumps on account of the coals working thro' into the wells
room. We often bring up two quarts at a time with the box. If the
leak increases, I think we will be of the necessity of putting into one
of the Cape de Verde Islands to stop it, as we cannot do it at Sea."

Over the days, however, the pumps were cleared of coals and
the leak not mentioned in the log, particularly when they got to
6° north latitude. For nine days of indifferent and variable winds
they struggled in the doldrums to reach the equator and crossed it at
a longitude of 28°50' west. Here they almost immediately picked up
the southeast trade winds. During the fine sailing days in the south
Atlantic they put their house in order. Each day the log records the
activities of the crew and then specifically those jobs done by the
carpenter, sailmaker and armorer. Even in late December there was
no change in the routine and in keeping with puritan Boston tradi-

tion, Christmas Day was bereft of all pagan celebrations. There were no jolly rope makers on board to outwit this Puritan taboo by celebrating the Feast of St. Catherine of Alexandria, Patron Saint of their profession, on 25th December every year! New Years Day was a calendar event without the word "Hogmanay" entering the log. Early in the new year McNeill writes: "...the Brig Sails and rigging, are now in good order for doubling Cape Horn."

On the mornings of January 10 and 14, 1825, the log of the *Convoy* reports:

> Calm thro' the night at 5 AM a light breeze from the N.E. with thick foggy weather Set all Studding Sails. People employed watch and watch at sundry jobs. Ends with thick foggy weather. To the Sd & Wd of C. Horn 75 days out.
>
> Squally at times wind S by W with showers of rain and hail, out all reefs and Set the Fore top Gallant Sail. At 3 P.M. wore Ship to the Westward. At 4 P.M. wore Ship to the Eastward. At 8 P.M. Tacked Ship to the Westward. At 10 Tacked Ship to the Eastward. Saw the land Cape Horn bearing by Compass W by N distant 20 Miles. Latter part hard Squalls take in and make Sail as occation required. Since we made Cape Horn we find ourselves 4 Degrees to the eastward of our Reckoning having had no Lunar Observation since leaving Rio de la Plate.

Four degrees eastward of his reckoning would have put McNeill approximately fifteen miles east of his expected position due to the strong west to east current that sweeps around Cape Horn. It does not mean that he was four degrees of longitude east of his position.

These entries into the log while off Cape Horn give testament to the routine difficulties encountered by Boston mariners. They contended with fluky winds from all directions or head winds to beat against. The swell set up by an endless fetch in the roaring forties gave a small ship constant discomfort, but most of all, an uncertainty of their position in a navigational method that relied on dead reckoning corrected by daily latitude observations and occasional lunar observations. The sighting of Cape Horn was undoubtedly a tremendous relief to Captain McNeill and his crew. The other navigational aid recorded in the log was the sighting of Diego Ramirez, a small island south and west of Cape Horn that gave them a correction for their longitude. But it was five days before they were to sight this island. Not until January 20, 1825, was McNeill able to consider that he had rounded "The Horn"—ten days of frustrating progress that averaged only twelve nautical miles per day.

What of his crew in this constant cold and wet? They rode a bucking bronco, one hour in screaming wind and hail bouncing on a yardarm. They pulled in sail with benumbed hands reefing or furling them. The next minute they sat becalmed in a current that set them back from where they came. Weather that often did not allow the camboose fire to be alight, no hot meal, no "water bewitched." Even if hot food was available it was like walking a tight rope back to the forecastle without falling, not just because of the motion in a heavy sea, but the constant swooshing of the sea along the foredeck could wrest the feet from under a seaman. There was no fresh food for days to ease their bleeding gums. All of this contributed to a sullen mental state that accompanied increasingly sore bones, heralding the onset of scurvy. No wonder there was a clouding of judgment that would lead a crew to disobedience, even mutiny. To add yet another irritation, since crossing into the tropics in November, the crew was rationed to three quarts of water per man per day, and this was reduced to two quarts in mid-January. Yet the log shows little sign of discontent on board, with no mention of punishment or disobedience.

On February 1, 1825, Juan Fernandes was sighted thirty miles away bearing west by south, an island akin to a desert oasis on the sea. Fresh peaches, nectarines and other fruits grew wild over the hills of the bay. The need for water forced McNeill to stop his voyage:

> In the Harbor of Juan Fernandes filling water, Stowing the hold and other necessary Jobs. Still continued rainy with gusts of wind from the mountains at times. The boy White deserted while employed in filling water. We had nearly completed our watering late in the afternoon, when it being light and baffling winds concluded to remain until morning and fill the remainder of our casks and endeavour to catch the deserter. While in pursuit of him the Sailmaker, Carpenter and Thomas Alexander deserted from the boats crew. Took a man on board to work his passage to the Islands.

The next morning another party went ashore to bring back the deserters. They searched for the four deserters for two hours before it became obvious that they would not find them. At 4:00 P.M., with a light breeze from the southeast, McNeill decided to set sail and leave the deserters at Juan Fernandes. In the time-honored tradition, the deserters' effects were sold by auction to the crew for the benefit of the owners, for $57.10.

The loss by desertion of the carpenter and sailmaker created difficulties on the leg from Juan Fernandes to Oahu. McNeill appointed an able seaman to be sailmaker. Most able seamen assisted the sailmakers on board and had a reasonable ability but not so with the carpenter. During the passage from Boston to Juan Fernandes Island, McNeill had a crew of two officers and one clerk in the cabin, six seamen, three boys and five idlers in the forecastle—a total of fourteen that was cut to ten by the desertions at Juan Fernandes. Mr. Warren, a working passenger taken on board at Juan Fernandes, was co-opted as carpenter and, with McNeill, did the necessary jobs on board; their appointment was referred to with a certain cynical humor in the log: "Fine pleasant weather thro' the day with moderate trades. Crossed the Tropic. Crew employed on the rigging. Carpenters! on the Bulwarks Sailmaker repairing the Mainsail &c'."

The *Convoy* made a forty-day passage between Juan Fernandes and Oahu with the log recording 200 miles or more per day. His course took him northwest to 20° latitude north and for three days he ran due west until he sighted the Sandwich Islands. During this section of the voyage, Charles Jeffs was chastised for disobedience. When three dozen jackknives went missing, they were found in steward Thomas Morante's sea chest and he was seized and given two dozen with rattling line. Both punished men deserted ship in Oahu. The cause for their desertion was as likely from the cold shoulder treatment by their shipmates as from their whippings.

Once anchored and attached to shore in the harbor of Oahu, the log was handed over to the second mate, Joseph Carter. McNeill went ashore to recount his problems to Captain Grimes, the agent for Marshall and Wilde in Oahu in the absence of Mr. Jones. After arranging for the transfer of some cargo to the Marshall warehouse McNeill wrote a long letter to Josiah Marshall, followed by a shorter one five days later:

Horrura, Whoahoo March 21st 1825.

Dear Sir

I arrived out in One Hundred and Thirty six days from Land to Land and found Capt Grimes in charge of the business, the Owhyee is now on the coast and has been from here about 12 mos. We shall land some casks of Rum & other articles, what they will be and what quantities will be determined by Capt Grimes before we sail the coast, the bleached Cotton is in very much demand and is 'going off rapidly' the calicoes are not taken up quite so quick they will probably do better for the California market, Mr Elwell has gone down on the Spanish main in the Schooner Washington with what goods we had here for the California coast. Capt Grimes has been very unwell since the Parthian left so much so that his life was dispaired off for several days, there was fortunately a Russian Man of War in the Harbour at the time, the Doctor of which/under providence/ was the means of saving his life. He is now as well as usual and has mentioned that he should probably go on the coast with us, we were under necessity of stopping at Juan Fernandez for water, having been on allowance of two quarts per day for six weeks and but one cask remaining, we filled all our water casks & got underway with four hands short, who deserted they were William White (boy) Willcut /carpenter/ Clough (sailmaker) & Alexander (seaman).

In doubling Cape Horn we ran inside of Falkland Islands and were in sight of land on the West side up to the Straits of Magellan the Brig proved to be an excellent sea boat and sails remarkably fast altho' we was so deep that the sea was continually coming in over the bows & rolling aft to the break of the quarter deck, we have altered and new fitted everything on board of her since we left Boston (in fact she has been completely new rigged) and made a suit of new Sails the principle part of the work has been done on the quarter deck in consequence of her being so wet forward where it was impossible to do anything except in calm weather. We shall not be ready for the coast under 8 or 10 days as the vessel wants caulking and we have our boarding nettings to make, but I expect we shall be off before the Griffin arrives, the Tamaahanaah Capt Meek is going to Lima to be sold in a few days. we arrived here 6 days after the vessel that brought news of the King and Queen's death, the bodies have not yet arrived. It is more than probable that there will be a war among the natives upon arrival of the King & Queen's remains

— Billy Pitt has secured the principle part of the army that were in the hands of the natives. King Jamonu is dead and his son George has had a battle with Pitt in which he was defeated and is now in prison at large at this Island. The ship Volunteer sent down 600 skins the first season Capt Ebbets remaining here for the purpose of closing his business, the market is entirely drained of goods there is scarcely an article of trade on the Island, Rum is in great demand & commands an extra price.

I have shipped a few hands here to supply the place of those who deserted at Juan Fernandez I shall ship 4 or 5 Kanackers for the coast & I shall do my utmost to obtain a share of Furs, no exertion shall be wanting on my part to obtain a large a share as any vessel on the coast. Mr Dana has chartered the Waverly & gone on a sealing voyage, he has been absent twelve months & has not yet returned. There has no occurences taken place of material importance I believe than those I have mentioned in my letter the ship that takes this is now in the offing underway.

> I remain with respect
> Your & T
> Wm H. McNeill

Honorura, Woahoo Mar 26 1825

Dear Sir

I wrote you by the Ship Thomas Capt Coffin on 21st Inst. Since then the Griffin has touched here and sailed again for the coast on 25th Inst. We shall not be detained here longer than Wednesday at the furthest and am in hopes to be on the coast soon after the Griffin, there is a possibility of your receiving this letter as soon if not sooner than that by the Thomas, as Capt Meek takes but a few goods to dispose of in his vessel and proceeds immediately home natives. King Jamonu is dead and his son George has had a battle with Pitt in which he was defeated and is now in prison at large at this Island. The ship Volunteer sent down 600 skins the first season Capt Ebbets remaining here for the purpose of closing his business, the market is entirely drained of goods there is scarcely an article of trade on the Island, Rum is in great demand & commands an extra price. I have shipped a few hands here to supply the place of those who deserted at Juan Fernandez I shall ship 4 or 5 Kanackers for the coast & I shall do my utmost to obtain a share of Furs, no exertion shall be wanting on my part to obtain a large a share as any vessel on the coast. Mr Dana has chartered the Waverly & gone on a sealing voyage, he has been absent twelve months & has not yet returned. There has no occurences taken place of material importance I believe than those I have mentioned in my letter the ship that takes this is now in the offing underway.

> I remain with respect
> Your & T
> Wm H. McNeill

While in Oahu, the *Convoy* employed up to four carpenters daily for two weeks to bring the bulwarks and hatches up to snuff. New seamen reported on board with Native Kanakas and the carpenters were busily constructing a new bulwark and accommodation for the Natives who were housed separately in steerage. A new steward was appointed to the cabin and a third mate, Mr. Hall, came on board. Meanwhile, Joseph Carter and up to eight hands daily worked on shore making boarding nettings to hang from the yardarms to the bulwarks and cocoon the ship against surprise attack. These were furled along the bulwarks ready to raise by block and tackle attached to the yardarms. The fact that the *Convoy* was delayed so long made Captain Grimes scold Josiah Marshall: "It is to be regretted the Convoy has been detained on account of her boarding nets — the cost of them in Boston would have been but triffling to them here — and detention — I strongly recommend all such things put on board and made on the passage out and the vessel made ready especially when they sail so late — the brig ought to have been copper'd higher up as the coast is full of worms should she remain on long will be much injured, if the Brig Owhyee is to remain in that trade she must have copper sent out the first opportunity, that was sent out for her has been sold by Capt Wilde to the French, the goods I have kept are,…etc."

The *Convoy*'s armorer was reported to be busy cleaning their big guns ready for defense and two swivels and a blunderbuss were brought on board and mounted at strategic points for defense of the ship. Muskets were cleaned and oiled, as were the fowling pieces used on shore to hunt for fresh provisions. Muskets were assigned to the crew members and stored in the arms chest. They were also used by the wood cutters and water parties on shore for defending themselves against attack by the natives. When the brigantine *Tamaahmaah* sailed, *Convoy* gave her a five-gun salute which was returned.

The brigantine *Griffin* arrived 150 days out from Boston, a fact that would normally have pleased McNeill who always noted in his log whenever he outsailed another vessel, but now the opposition had got ahead of him. The *Convoy* left eight days later for the Queen Charlotte Islands in haste to catch up with the opposition.

Queen Charlotte Sound from
Captain George Vancouver's map, 1793.

Queen Charlotte Sound from Canadian
Hydrographic Service chart
L/C-3000, 1994.

CHAPTER 3

The *Convoy* on the Coast

Next to a beautiful woman and a lovely infant, a prime Sea Otter skin two feet by five, with its short glossy black fur, was the finest natural object in the world.

—William Sturgis, Boston, 1844

The brigantine *Convoy* set sail from Oahu on April 2, 1825, and apart from three short periods of heavy sea when they shipped a good deal of water, they made a fast passage and sighted Point Buck on the Queen Charlotte Islands on April 17. There the *Convoy* was delayed two days west of Dall Island:

> ...standing off and on during the night. At 4 AM made Sail and run for Kigarney. At 8 AM a canoe come off from the shore and was informed that the Owhyee had left the coast. Continue turning to windward for Bowles Harbor. At 4 P.M. came to in 14 Fathoms water rocky Bottom. Commenced breaking out the hold to put it (in) order for Trading, which will be attended with considerable difficulty, as we are so full as not to be able to carry our cable below deck, and not room enough in the hold, to put a spare barrel. but shall make the best possible arrangements and hope we shall obtain our share of skins. I shall lie here no longer than I can possibly help as I am in hopes that the Owhyee is still on the coast, and shall endeavour to find her as speedily as possible. Closes calm and pleasant.

The ship was so congested that McNeill had five bales of goods in his cabin. Even so, business continued: "...this day commenced Trading and bought 4 Prime 20 Beavers, 10 Land Otters 12 Tails 10 Co Cotsacks (fur robes) and Some Small furs. I intend to stop here one day longer to obtain all the furs the natives have at this place and finish our Stowage."

꿈

Augustus (Gus) Wright, a strong, lean and healthy ship's boy of thirteen in 1824, looks out over the starboard bulwarks. The north island of the Queen Charlotte Islands is visible fifteen miles to the northwest. It is two days since he hauled the hemp cable on deck and bent the best chain anchor to the starboard bow. All through the voyage out, Gus has hidden his fears induced by the long swell, shinning up the mast or standing out on a limb in a rough sea, hiding behind a wall of cheerful bravado. Captain McNeill responds to his cheerful spirit, if not his mathematics. Gus knows his station and will remain a seaman and never be a navigator.

For two days Gus has stood his watch in light airs and a calm sea, waiting for a wind to take them round Point Kigarney. During his trick at the helm he hears Mr. Little discuss their position with Captain McNeill. To the south lies Forrester's Island, with Wolf Rock to the northwest and their destination a distant point of land to the east-southeast ten leagues away.

Next morning when he tumbles up for the morning watch, there is at last, a breeze from the northwest to run them down to Kigarney to anchor in front of the village. Colorful canoes are launched from the beach in front of the austere buildings that meld with the forest behind them. They are manned by male and female occupants and head toward the brigantine. The nearer they come, the firmer Gus grips his loaded blunderbuss, his finger ready on the trigger.

A massive forty-foot canoe glides toward the *Convoy*, her freeboard almost as high as the ship's. Bitter bile of fear rises into Gus' throat when he recognizes the apprehensive eyes and expressions of the slave paddlers. At her stern, high above the slave paddlers, is a fat figure, sitting in state. "That's Smoke-it Douglas," one of the older seaman declares and the others nod. "A great Haida Chief from Kyusta," Gus hears them say, "famed for his marauding warriors that lay waste from Cape Flattery to Cape Scott, feared for his cruel disregard for his slaves." Today he has come to Kigarney, not with furs, he trades them at his village, but with potatoes cultivated for trade. "Why Douglas?" Gus asks Joe, the Kanaka interpreter. Joe tells him that this great chief of Kyusta, a village on the northwest tip of the north island, befriended Captain Douglas, one of King George's men, and in esteem of one another they exchanged their names during a feast in the captain's honor.

The stature of these Haida Natives is tall, stately and Herculean, unlike those tribes further south. Here their skin is almost white, their hair black and their women as tall and strong as their men. Chief Douglas is adorned in a magnificent Chilkat cloak with his crests woven into the cloth, a sea otter fur undergarment with a copper clasp across the front and on his head, a cedar bark cloth hat whose center of seven rings make him tower above all his commoners and slaves. Those seven rings denote the largesse of his seven potlatches.

But Gus' eyes are diverted by an equally grand woman, her shift clinging around her calves as she walks toward him. Almost as tall as the chief and certainly more graceful, with broad shoulders draped in a magnificent bearskin cloak. Her long black hair, held by a slide, reaches her waist and her head is surmounted by a broad rimmed cedar bark hat. Her strange sibilant speech puzzles him and he notices a mother-of-pearl plaque beneath her mouth. This puzzles him until she bends forward, then the huge lower lip flap falls vertical to reveal the abalone labret that creates what is to them, this beautifully distended appendage. She gives imperious orders to a young girl, "her daughter," Gus thinks. She removes her cloak to reveal a state of nature from the waist up.

Beautiful clear, sun brown, nubile skin that make his cheeks burn with embarrassment at his rising desire. He cannot keep his eyes off the raven tattooed over her right breast or the beaver over the left; she turns, a leaping killer whale across her back. As his eyes take in her oiled vermilion face, a gleaming white sea otter tooth attached to a tiny abalone labret in her lower lip attracts his attention; she is looking him eye to eye, lowers her eyes and returns them in a flirting ritual to make him weak at the knees. The grand Native lady withers him with a glance that tells him, "Not a chance, Augustus!"

Captain McNeill greets Smoke-it Douglas on board. That is how Simoiget sounds to Boston ears, a pronunciation that makes Joe, the Kanaka interpreter, grin.

Furs are laid out on deck, inspected and sorted so that the haggling can begin. Gus watches, watchful, his blunderbuss primed.

The captain measures six, then seven fathoms of cloth across his broad chest. The Indian faces of rejection make him add a bucket or a mirror, which elicits scornful laughter. An hour or more goes by before a gill of rum catches their attention and Gus' eyes thirst for a taste, longs for its mind-numbing effect. He has become partial to his grog ration with its ability to bolster his confidence and allay his fear.

Captain McNeill, pleased with the results of his trade, distrusts the holding capacity of the rocky bottomed bay and Gus strains on a capstan pawl to raise the ship's anchor. The sails fill to transport the *Convoy* two miles north into a snug harbour and bury the best bower into its welcoming mud.

"Taddy's Cove," the armourer calls it.

"Tatterskey," Joe corrects him.

Captain McNeill pays a visit to the brigantine *Griffin*, under Captain Peirce, owned by Bryant and Sturgis of Boston. On watch, Gus hears Mr. Little tell Mr. Carter that he has gone to seek news of the *Owhyee*, and when he returns, Gus learns of their plan for a visit to Skidegate.

It is common knowledge on the *Convoy* that they are on the lookout for the brigantine *Owhyee*, under Captain Kelly, of Marshall & Wilde. Life on board is cramped by the stores for the *Owhyee*. So little space is left that they are not able to stow their anchors, chain and cables below decks.

Dusk settles over the two ships, a fine mist on the water in light baffling airs, portends a morning fog as the *Convoy* enters Dixon Entrance. The *Griffin* appears to take a more northerly course as if for Tamgass and the *Convoy* lags behind, not wanting to give its destination away.

Up on deck on the morning watch, Gus marvels at the glowing orange ball of sunrise that imparts color to the dripping yards and shrouds. The mist soon thickens to a soupy fog. The *Convoy*, in her Sunday best, moves gracefully in the swirling northwest airs. The mate assigns Gus to assist the leadsman standing on his platform at the bow. The leadsman's weight whirls in the air before flying forward off the bow, the line pays out from its coil and slithers over the bulwark like a scared snake. "No bottom," they rejoice silently as Gus recoils the line. As the fog thickens, the swish of the rope, the plop of the weight that now falls into the sea ahead and out of sight, is all they hear. Toward the end of the morning watch, the fog starts to swirl along the waist in a freshening breeze, the westerly swell lifts the stern and foam breaks along the bends.

"Fog'll clear soon, younker," the leadsman assures him.

Gus hears the sound of breakers off the larboard (port) bow and his anxiety stirs. He cannot see his captain smile in the knowledge that their course is fair.

The *Convoy* emerges from the fog bank suddenly, to reveal Point Rose off the starboard bow, a rock to larboard and white breakers beyond formed by the tidal flow over the ledge against the westerly swell. Another plop excites a cry of "five-o!" from the leadsman. The *Convoy* is over the ledge and passes Point Rose two cables off the starboard beam. And there she is ahead, the *Griffin*, as if their trusty pathfinder, but not welcome!

Gus knows that they hope to trade at Skidegate as he eavesdrops on the captain's discussion with the mate on the need for defense and vigilance at Skidegate. He learns that the chief at Skidegate is more powerful and cruel than Douglas and Captain McNeill says he buries his slaves alive in the pits of his house posts or totem poles. This information only serves to increase his dismay in this rock-strewn sea and deserted land of mountainous forest.

The brigantine *Owhyee*, their partner on the coast, is not at Skidegate and Captain McNeill anchors outside the inner harbor, leaving it to the competition, the *Griffin* and *Volunteer*.

A steady northwest breeze during the evening watch sends Gus up to set the studding sails. With his matey, John Holland, on the yardarm, he unfurls the light sails. Below on the quarterdeck, they see Captain McNeill's glare at Mr. Little for not setting the studding sails an hour earlier. John says, "The mate'll haze us now!" and they both shinny down the rigging to the deck, looking eager and trying not to put a foot wrong. When Gus tumbles up for the morning watch, there are islands off the starboard beam. "Scott's Islands," he hears the captain tell Mr. Carter while he takes his trick at the helm. There is a narrow passage ahead, where there are white breakers on the surface of the sea and it seems to take the *Convoy* forever to reach them. The tide turns, the sea smooths and the *Convoy*, assisted by the flood tide, moves into the passage for Nahwitti Sound. The passage widens, there is a village on the larboard beam. The cannon speaks, but the village appears deserted. The *Convoy* turns to starboard into Shushartie Bay. Yet again, the *Owhyee* has evaded them.

Gus mans an oar on the longboat to carry an anchor out to deeper water. The *Convoy* has fouled aground on a rock. The kedge (a light anchor used to warp a vessel forward using a capstan or windlass), drops twenty-five fathoms, the coil of cordage whirls out and snaps on the surface of the sea. A violin plays the capstan step to aid the crew to pull together and heave the *Convoy* away from shore. The tall trees of the forest bend and creak in the westerly wind, yet there is little more than a ripple on the water of this protected bay. Since there was no answer from the Natives of this place to the fired cannon, Gus joins the wood cutters and watering crew ashore where he bathes and washes his clothes in the luxury of a fresh water stream. Next day the Indians arrive from Scott's Islands. Although they had heard the cannon, they could not leave because of gales and rough seas. Among them is another big canoe, commanded by Chief Nancy who exchanges a greeting of friendship with Captain McNeill, allowing the crew to relax its vigilance. They haggle over two dozen skins and a pile of small sea shells which, Hiqua Joe the Kanaka tells him, is valued as money by the northern tribes.

The *Convoy* stood out of Shushartie Bay at 9:00 A.M. driven by a light easterly wind that was insufficient to overcome the flood tide. Not until 5:00 P.M. did they make progress with the ebb tide over the Nahwitti bar to leave the Islands of Galiano and Valdes (renamed Nigei and Hope Islands respectively) to the east. McNeill worked the ship to windward and across to Cape Caution. He set his course for the east side of the Queen Charlotte Islands. By sunrise next morning the log expresses his surprise:

> At 6 AM Saw the land, some of the Nass Islands bearing N.W. distant 6 Miles. We must have had a very strong current as I shaped my course from Newittie for Charlottes Islands and never was more astonished in my life than when I found myself on the Nass shores. At 11 PM stood inside of the Islands to the Southward of Banks Island for Sebashes as we could not fetch outside of the land. Strong Gales and thick weather. At 2 PM sent the boat to sound for a harbour at 5 the boat returned filled away

and stood under the lee of our Island and came to in 7 Fathoms Soft Bottom. Surrounded by rocks on all sides which I was not aware of until we let go the Anchor. At Midnight hard Squalls of wind which set her adrift, let go the Bower which brought her up.

Next day, strong Gales from the S.E. with thick and rainy weather got the hawse on Shore hove up both anchors, winched her Set Jib and Mainsail run her up the harbour and came to in 25 Fathoms water with the chain. at 7 breeze increasing struck adrift let go the Bower and brot up stern close on the rocks. At Meridian got the Spare Anchors on the bows bent a new hawse to it and a coil of Manilla Rope carried out to 120 Fathoms Strait ahead and hove up both Anchors in doing it we broke one of the flews from the Chain Anchor. Warped off to the third Anchor in attempting to get underway from it we broke ground and were obliged to come to again in 25 Fathoms. At 6 PM carried out the Anchor again hove of to it and let go the Bower in 25 Fathoms Soft Bottom took the spare Anchor formerly her Bower for a chain. Our Kedge is so light that we do not use it at all.

On the following morning, the storm abated, the rain poured down and McNeill made a prudent decision: "At 10 AM when a breeze Set in from S.S.W. with thick rainy weather and being unacquainted amongst these Islands & rocks judged it prudent not to get underway at present. the wind being ahead and the crew beat out having had but little rest during the last 40 hours remained at anchor the rest of the day."

Every anchor, chain, cable, hawse and cordage had to be man-handled, rowed out and dropped over the side without capsizing or damaging the longboat. The cold wind and rain of this gale would have chilled the small crew of fifteen men to the bone and at no other time in the log does McNeill record paying homage to his crew by giving them a rest.

At the end of this ordeal they still had to seek out and find the *Owhyee*. The *Convoy* weighed anchor and went to the west side of Banks Island in search of Scedunsk Harbor. Two days later, McNeill boarded the *Owhyee* in Hecate Strait and both ships went to the harbor to exchange trading goods to *Owhyee*, defense goods and a kedge anchor to *Convoy*.

Once the *Convoy* and *Owhyee* had transferred cargo they parted company. They did not wish to compete for the same furs and yet they did not want to allow the other three boats, *Griffin*,

Volunteer and *Rob Roy* to have free range along the coast. Off the harbor, *Owhyee* went south toward Nahwitti and *Convoy* north toward Skidegate and then along the east side of the Queen Charlotte Islands.

The *Convoy* announced its presence with a cannon but no Natives came off land in canoes. McNeill decided to head north and anchored in Tatterskey (a Kigarney harbor) in company with *Volunteer* and *Griffin*. Captains Cross and Barker visited the *Convoy* and in the log, McNeill complains of the too high a price these two captains were paying for the furs. Nonetheless, he reports that he was able to trade for the black sea otter furs because he had superior musquits and duffel.

McNeill left Tatterskey in company with *Volunteer* and recorded his pleasure at outsailing the opposition. He was hoping to be first into Chatham Strait to visit Ennacanoe (Rowan Bay), Hood's Bay and Chuckanuck (Swanson Harbour) all three anchorages occupied by the Tlingit sea otter hunters. The northwest wind that allowed him to sail out of Kigarney now headed him on the outside of Dall Island. Together with *Volunteer* he made slow progress up to Cape Addington and for three days was at a standstill. As the winds increased and persisted he turned east to enter Davidson Inlet and anchor in the Port of Henegea (Edna Bay) seven days after leaving Tatterskey. McNeill had shaken off the opposition and did a brisk trade with the Henegea Indians of Tuxekan alone at anchor for four days. Henegea Indians were described in his notes on harbors as: "...a well disposed tribe as any on the coast and great hunters but sell most of their furs to the Kaigani tribe and others."

This anchorage was also good for wood cutting, watering and: "...one of the best for herring, salmon and other fish."

The *Convoy* left Henegea with a favorable wind from the southeast in the early morning and by early afternoon was abeam of Point Ellis. North of this point McNeill was in Russian-claimed territory. Here he saw a vessel coming out of the harbor of Ennacanoe and, even though the Russian edict was said to have been lifted, his anxiety turned to relief as he identified it as the *Volunteer*. Initially he outsailed *Volunteer* in an effort to get to Hood's Bay first. The winds became light and baffling and McNeill lost the advantage, so the two brigantines anchored together in the bay. Discretion, the better part of valor, made McNeill agree to share all furs with the

Volunteer and prevent the Indians from extracting too high a price from competition. After three days at Hood's Bay both ships sailed to Chuckanuck, an anchorage (Swanson Harbor) at the junction of Icy Strait, Lynn Canal and Chatham Strait, for two more days of joint trading.

McNeill left Chuckanuck to return to his previous anchorage at Hood's Bay and reported seeing the *Volunteer* standing down the Strait. Once again he had the trade to himself without opposition. However, when he sailed down to Henegea, McNeill found *Volunteer* in port. He did some repairs and waited for the *Volunteer* to leave before taking up trade with the Henegea Indians who had promised him some twenty skins. Indeed, for the next two days he bought twenty-six black sea otter skins for seven fathoms of cloth each, a bargain price of about nine dollars in cloth for a skin worth $41 in Canton. When he arrived back at Kigarney he recorded obtaining a further twenty prime skins.

McNeill intended to leave Kigarney for Tamgass Harbor, but unfavorable winds made him seek shelter in Cossacks Harbor at Sebashes. He remained in Cossacks Harbor for eight days to do repairs, met with *Owhyee* and exchanged more trade goods. He also obtained the use of *Owhyee*'s carpenter to do some essential repairs to the hatches. McNeill, with the *Owhyee* in company, went toward Skidegate, the *Owhyee* turned south for Cumshewa and the *Convoy* anchored three miles off the shore at Skidegate to trade with canoes. When he got underway in the morning he reports in the log:

> At 9 AM got underweigh and stood to the Northward with a light wind from E.S.E. a number of canoes came off out of which I bought 22 Black Sea Otter Skins & 40 Prime Tails, the best and largest I have seen on the coast. As we were running along the shore off Cape Ball our keel just touched some rocks lying off there, but immediately got off we were going three knots at the time. from this time the wind gradually increased in all Studding Sails and other light sails down Royal Yards and housed the Mast the Mainsail came over and carried away the straps of the sheet blocks.

Passing Kigarney Point in fresh gales from the southeast at 2:00 A.M. they fired a cannon, but it was blowing too fresh for canoes to come off. The *Convoy* bore away for Henegea. In the afternoon McNeill congratulated his crew, as the ship had run from

Skidegate to Henegea since seven o'clock the previous evening, in about twenty-two hours. Finding no Henegea Indians in the village, McNeill sent his Kanaka interpreter, Joe, to find them and inform them of his presence. In the meantime, he sent two other Kanakas to dive under the vessel to inspect for any damage done when they grounded off Cape Ball. They reported no damage but a considerable quantity of grass attached to the keel and bottom. The next day, July 4th, the crew celebrated the anniversary of American Independence with a double allowance of grog for each member of the crew. The *Convoy* spent one day preparing the boarding nettings for defense and then sailed north for Hood's Bay and traded without opposition. For three weeks they were unopposed from Chatham Strait to Tamgass Harbor. At Ennacanoe, north of Point Ellis, McNeill cleared the grass off the bottom and payed the bends (cleaned the hull at the waterline) on both starboard and larboard sides. From Ennacanoe, the *Convoy* sailed for Henegea again and here McNeill confided his concern with sailing on the coast without a carpenter:

> We have a great number of Jobs for a Carpenter to do and for want of one we are under the necessity of doing the best we can ourselves which is but poorly. We have not had a Carpenter since we left Juan Fernandez and I think there is no place in the world were one is wanted more than on this coast. For Instance, if a vessel runs ashore and gets injured badly which is often the case here you could not repair the damage immediately but for want of a Carpenter would have to lay by a month or more, besides their work adds to the appearance of the vessels, for the expense that is incurred for stock is no more than the labour to go on shore to obtain it, but however we have done so far without one and am in hopes to arrive at the Islands without finding one absolutely necessary.

Augustus Wright is less anxious in the presence of these Native Indians. Trading has been brisk and Captain McNeill is in a buoyant mood. Even the weather has been kindly disposed and as he keeps watch he recognizes the landmarks as they pass on the way to Tamgass Harbor. The work has been tiring with two men off duty, sick.

From Tamgass Harbor, the *Convoy* runs up Clarence Strait for Chucknahoo in a pleasant southeast wind. Gus looks down from the helm at poor Thomas Low, off duty and on deck, who gazes out of his one good eye. He looks thin and ailing, the bad eye swollen and crusted.

Captain McNeill asks Mr. Little if he can suggest some medicine that might counteract the damage by small pox and the venereal. Gus wipes his own eye and ponders the ravages of the venereal. Isaac Marsh, too, has been off sick more than once since leaving Oahu with the same disease that in his case, makes him double over with cramps and complain, "I can't piss!"

Gus remembers hearing voices of encouragement from the main cabin by the captain in response to Isaac's moan of distress. In the forecastle they had all laughed at him when he went pale at the description of the long silver tube the captain passed down Isaac's wanker to let out the piss. The crescendo of distress from Marsh had been so harsh as to make him wonder if he will ever dare a visit to the bordello. Yet, there was Isaac, burned with flapdragon (gonorrhoea) in more than one port before, at liberty in Oahu, heading for merry legs in the nunnery; and two days later pissing cream! "Better keep a girl in your cabin you can trust, like the captain," he thought. But his matey, John Holland, says a wife on board'll bring bad luck and turn the brig into a hen frigate!

The crew has been kept busy these fine sailing days, chasing furs from Chucknahoo to Masset and across to Kigarney. Now Captain Peirce on *Griffin* has ruined trade with high prices and too much rum. Musket fire from the village brings the captain and mate on deck to inspect the defenses. Canoes from shore tell of five men killed and some wounded, North Island "Smoke-it" being one of them.

"Load the guns and blunderbuss, Mr. Little," Captain McNeill orders, and as Gus stands watch, the firing continues all night ashore.

"Lemnar's son and Douglas' party," he hears the Captain tell Mr. Carter.

Rumors and facts fly around the forecastle with the Indians blaming the rum traded from *Griffin* for their trouble and now threatening the *Convoy* for trading it! The crew prays for a wind to take them out of this hostile shambles and next morning Gus, in the boat's crew, pulls on his oar with a passion to get away from this

71

place. On the way to Henegea, Gus overhauls his musquit. He's glad to be going north among the more friendly tribes along Chatham Straight.

ᶜ∿⠙

Captain McNeill was aware that the Natives, particularly the Haida, would look for redress from any Boston vessel whether the perceived wrong of selling rum was perpetrated by that individual vessel or not. The *Griffin* had left and he expected the Natives to attack the *Convoy* in its place. He did not return to Kigarney until the next season aboard the brigantine *Tally Ho*.

On July 26, McNeill wrote to the Sandwich Islands that the *Convoy* and *Owhyee* had 800 prime skins and 3,000 land furs between them. They had paid high prices for them and were already out of woolen goods. The *Convoy* continued to trade in the north for the rest of August and came to anchor at Henegea at the end of the month. McNeill bought eleven more prime skins and announced: "I intend to remain here one day longer in hopes of obtaining pay for a fowling Gun I let a chief have sometime since."

This is the only time the log recorded a trade that was not paid for at the time the bargain was struck. It would be a year before McNeill received payment.

The *Convoy* traded in the north for the rest of August 1825 and at the end of the month was once again anchored at Henegea. As with the *Owhyee* in 1823, the *Convoy* contended with much sickness and in early September the log records: "Five Hands off duty and the Cook unwell, making our crew the weakest ever on the coast having but seven White men in the Forecastle altogether and Four of them sick."

Due to southeast gales the *Convoy* did not get out of Henegea for a week and then made a fast passage to Tamgass Harbor. Here the *Convoy* made ready for the voyage to the Sandwich Islands. In harbor, the *Owhyee* gave assistance with the loan of their carpenter to do essential work and it took nearly three weeks to prepare the *Convoy* for the crossing of the Pacific. Here too, McNeill ran into trouble with his crew: "…Quit work to get dinner @ 3 PM at 4 the People forward were ordered up to their duty, when Thomas D. Low, Francis Thompson, Augustus Wright, John Coster, John Holland, James Hutchins & Antonio Dean refused, also Isaac Marsh although sick and off duty joined the others and made use of mutinous language. The Forecastle was then closed upon them and half a pint of water and half a biscuit a day for each man was ordered for their allowance."

This incident did not stop the *Convoy* from starting on its passage to the Sandwich Islands, leaving the white crew in the forecastle. Care, however, was always given to the sick. Isaac Marsh, in spite of mutinous activity, was taken from the forecastle, put into the steerage, allowed the liberty of the deck and given suitable medicine for his venereal disease.

Augustus lies in his forecastle bunk. Life in the closed forecastle becomes claustrophobic; pangs of hunger and thirst rack him and the stench of human confinement blunts his sense of smell. As the *Convoy* sails toward the north Pacific, a constant bucking adds to the discomfort of these grim days. On the third day after the one biscuit and the allocation of water is consumed, the effect of the long days and weary nights causes a discontent that splits the resolve of the "mutineers." Gus joins Holland and Dean and they become restless with anxiety at the feel of the long swell of the ocean increase. Then the wind rises. Any sailor knows what's coming. They remain sullen for two days as Holland, their spokesman, argues for a return to duty, but still the hold-outs refuse to listen.

However, even when the brigantine is kept under reduced sail and the movement and hunger prevent them from having a restful sleep, the hold-outs do not demur. As the storm force winds rage, their survival instinct tells them that they are needed on deck and may flounder in the huge seas if they don't respond to the captain's offer. Then a quarter of a biscuit handed down the hatch with just a gill of water breaks the resolve of the hold-outs. They accept the captain's terms and return to duty to greet the comfort from the fresh air of the storm.

Yet another gale hits the *Convoy* a thousand miles from their destination. The wind drops but the swell persists and passes under the ship to tumble them from larboard to starboard on their beam ends as the waves wash through the foredeck of this long-legged ship. Mr. Little orders Wright, Holland and Dean to ascend the rigging to send down the topgallant mast. Not an hour later and they're ascending again to send the mast up and they grumble to each other of this inexperienced first mate who is constantly changing sails and rigging, scathing him with the name, Staysail Jack! The *Convoy* rolls again and again in the high seas before the terrible snapping sound warns of danger and the small topmast breaks free. Gus hangs on to the rope and swings toward the shroud to gasp and grasp.

"Man overboard!" he hears, before he realizes his friend Holland has dropped into the sea.

Gus hurries down, oblivious to his rope-torn palms, to join the boat's crew. Mr. Carter prevents him and tears of frustration burn his eyes at the loss of a true friend. The *Convoy* heaves to, pitches and falls on the tumbling sea. His body does not feel the motion as his eyes search among the rolling breakers.

"A head!" he hears, shouted from the lookout even as the blocks squeal and the small boat drops into the sea.

A body is hauled out of the sea into the small boat, a cry of "alive-oh!" sends a cheer through the ship's crew and Gus' tears no longer burn, but flow in gratitude.

∽

In late October, 1825, the *Owhyee* arrived back at Oahu. Captain Wilde complained to Marshall that: "...he had no idea that we should have been able to have left one vessel on the Coast this winter, and should, if they had not given such high prices."

This harsh criticism seems unfair to both McNeill and Captain Kelly after all the letters of request for a better quality of outfit for sale on the coast. As it was, Marshall received $19,676.34, and Captain Wilde $6,558.78 from the income of the voyage of the *Convoy* alone, to cover the cost of the inventory and crew expenses. McNeill received a commission of $905.97 on the 340 black skins and a proportion of land furs to add to his salary of $20 per month that amounted to $291.33 by 10 April 1826.

On arrival at Oahu, the *Convoy* underwent a refit for the coast of California that entailed removing the trade room in steerage and converting it into stowage space. In the log, while anchored at Oahu at the end of November, Mr. Little writes: "At 2 PM Mr. Carter after much abusive language left the Brig in a very abrupt manner without requesting liberty. This being the second time since our last arrival it was deemed necessary to note it in the Log Book."

The reason for his two outbursts may possibly have been from jealousy. Mr. Little, first mate, was promoted to captain in charge of the schooner *Washington* and in his letter to Josiah Marshall he displays a bitterness that was not expected from the account of the voyage in the log of the *Convoy*. He also displays a familiarity with Marshall's son when signing off the letter and this may have made Mr. Carter suspect favoritism.

Josiah Marshall Oahu 20 December 1825

Dear Sir.

I am happy in informing you of the safe arrival here of the Convoy after a successful cruise on the coast, considering the number of vessels with which we had to contend, governing myself by your admonition I have submitted to almost every indignity that malice jealousy and ignorance could invent determined to remain by the Brig untill the close of the voyage, which is now terminated, at the request of Capt Wilde and with the consent of Capt McNeil I have left the Convoy and taken command of the Washington bound for the coast and gulph of California, hoping that by diligance and perseverance the voyage may be to the advancement of your interests and so conducted as to meet with your approbation and ensure future employment.

> My regards to your son & family
> Your obed servt
> William C. Little

In McNeill's account of the voyage in this letter to Marshall, he writes in a style of uneasy waffling about his position.

Josiah Marshall Honorura, Whoahoo 1825

Dear Sir.

We arrived at this place from the NWCoast on the 3rd November last — On our arrival on the coast we laboured under many disadvantages in consequence of not finding Capt Kelly immediately and a report from the Indians of his having left the coast.

We however made the best arrangements for trading that we possibly could in our crowded situation as it respected our cargo. We fortunately however soon fell in with the Owhyee to whom we delivered cargo to the amount of 3,800 Dolls and then proceeded to the different ports on the coast in the prosecution of our voyage. There being in all four vessels on this season, we had to use every exertion in our power for the purpose of obtaining an equal share of skins with the other vessels and were fortunate enough in collecting as many as any one on the coast, during the time we were on, being about 340 black skins and 1,200 land furs. We should no doubt have obtained a larger number if our Blankets and Duffel had not been expended some time before we sailed. I think the Brig is much better calculated for the California trade than for the NWCoast, she being much too small and her accomodations for trading rather inferior. There are at the present time two or three vessels on the coast of California, whose cargoes will in all probability be disposed of in the course of two or three months. I think if the Brig had been ordered to Canton for a cargo suitable for the Spanish Main, she would no doubt have made a good if not a great voyage.

The partitions and other temporary accomodations that were put up in the cabin for the NW trade have all been taken down since we have arrived with the intention of proceeding with the vessel for coast of California and if she now returns to the NWCoast the expense replacing them will be again incurr'd.

My orders from Capt Wilde at present are to remain here till the last of April and if no vessel arrives on or before that time to take what cargo remains here and proceed for the coast or direct for Norfolk Sound as I shall think best, the idea of cruising the whole extent of the NWCoast, during the summer without one solitary blanket or one fathom of Duffel on board (the most essential article of trade) is one which if persisted in I am confidant will not prove profitable. Therefore if no vessel should arrive previous to the time stated I shall proceed to Norfolk Sound without delay, as I cannot but think, altho Capt Wilde and Capt Meek have both been there, and have done nothing of consequence, it will be preferrable to visit that place first and then be govern'd in my future plans as circumstance will permit. Capt Ebbett, proceeds for China in the Brig Pamaah, much for the purpose of procuring a cargo for the Spanish Main and I think will do extremely well, while I am fearful I shall make a broken voyage.

The Brig Harbinger arrived here a few days since from Boston and brought me letters, which is perhaps not a surprising circumstance to those engaged in commercial pursuit to this part of the world, she had 206 days passage being unable to double Cape Horn on account of the severity of the weather and was obliged to put away and come by the way of the Cape of Good Hope. As I shall forward this by the Parthian any information I have omitted will no doubt be communicated to you by Capt Wilde.

I remain
Yours & T
WmHyMcNeil

When the Convoy arrived at the Sandwich Islands, McNeill took two actions that upset Captain Dixey Wilde. He demanded his commission to be paid him and later refused to give up command of the *Convoy*. Part of doing business at the Sandwich Islands was never to pay out cash if exchange of goods could be arranged. As Wilde complained to Marshall: "…his (McNeill's) obstinacy deranged my plans very much as you will see by the arrangements I had made the Convoy should have gone to the Main." In a later letter he complained to Marshall: "I do not think Capt McNeil well calculated for the voyage & have requested him to exchange with Capt Grimes & take the Owhyee and I remain here until a cargo arrives for the coast & Capt Grimes take charge of the Convoy (which he willing to do) and go to the Gulph as he is well calculated to trade with the Spaniards, but Capt McNeil absolutely refuses to make the exchange or give up his vessel, he is very obstinate."

McNeill's intransigence may be related to the girl he brought from the coast. In the ledgers of account at Marshall & Wilde in Boston, an entry appeared on 10 June 1828 in Captain McNeill's account. The exact wording in the ledger entry reads:

Own Brig Owhyee....for bringing girl to Sandwich Islands...$180.00
Own Brig Convoy.... carrying ditto to coast & back.......$320.00

McNeill may have needed cash to house her in Oahu during the time he waited to return her to the coast. The identity of the girl is not mentioned.

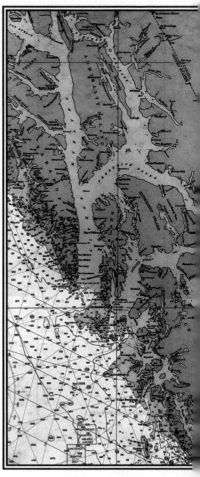

Chatham Strait from
Captain George Vancouver's map, 1793.

Chatham Strait from
United States marine chart 16016, 199?

CHAPTER 4

The *Tally Ho* on the Coast

A wise marchant neuer adventures all his goodes in one ship.
—Sir Thomas Moore

In late 1825, after his period of leave, Mr. J. C. Jones left Boston on the brigantine *Tally Ho*, to replace Captain Grimes as agent for Marshall and Wilde. The *Tally Ho* met with another vessel returning to Boston and they exchanged letters.

Feb 1st 1826

Brig Tally Ho at Sea
Lat 41.40 South
Josiah Marshall Esq Long 55 West

Dear Sir
I have only a moment to say that we have progress'd thus far on our voyage all well. The Tally Ho is the best vessel that ever floated on the ocean, all on board is as it should be. To a letter I have written by this conveyance to Josiah I refer you In great haste

Your Obed Servt
JC Jones Jr.

The correspondence between the agents in the Sandwich Islands and Captain Wilde with Marshall in Boston reveal a management style that was muddled and imprecise. Wilde was a pragmatist who tended to take the route of quick gain without regard to consequences. Captain Grimes told Marshall that he was upset when Wilde sold the copper to the French when their own ships, going to or coming from the teredo-worm-infested shores of the northwest, would need it themselves.

Captain Grimes and Mr. Jones, like the captains of vessels, were paid on commissions based on what they sold. Captain Wilde was a part owner, usually with a quarter interest, and concerned with immediate results. He came and went between the Islands, Canton and Boston at his own will. The letters he wrote to Marshall were often at odds with their employee's reports.

The letters sent by Captain Grimes and Mr. Jones tended to pass blame from themselves onto lesser lights in the organization. In the administration of business the appalling time that each letter took to travel and an answer to return made long-range planning impossible.

McNeill fell foul of Captain Wilde for demanding his commission be paid and aggravated him by refusing to give up the *Convoy*. Some failures were therefore ascribed to him that should have landed on another's doorstep. Josiah Marshall's promise of a new ship to be sent out in 1826 was conveyed to Captain Grimes by Captain McNeill when he arrived in the *Convoy*. The holds on this new vessel, *Tally Ho*, were packed with supplies for both the *Convoy*, and *Tally Ho* herself, to trade on the northwest coast.

Final plans for 1826 were not made until Captain Wilde got back to the Islands from Canton and in his letter he reported to Marshall of McNeill's obstinacy. When Captain Wilde left the Sandwich Islands, his understanding with Captain Grimes was that McNeill would wait until the end of April for the new vessel to arrive. If no vessel came, McNeill was to take the *Convoy* to the California coast.

Matilda

Matilda was now approaching the age of puberty. In nineteenth-century Europe, the age of first menstruation was much older than today. If the same trend occurred in the Kaigani Haida, Matilda would likely have reached puberty at age fifteen. Matilda's first menses was celebrated with a period of isolation in a small room at the back of the longhouse. Totally bereft of all comfort and clothing, she sat naked on her rough cedar seat, unable to lie down, fed only enough water to wet her lips. Her fast was to last for seven days at least, her mind was to be focussed on her life ahead as a consort wife to an Eagle Chief, for Matilda was a Raven. Her shaman visited her daily to monitor her progress, waiting for her to report a divine experience.

Did Matilda see Bearmother come to her hut, hug her and assure her of ancestral protection?

There are a number of reasons why Matilda might experience a vision. As Aldous Huxley points out in *Heaven and Hell* fasting, sleep deprivation and constant discomfort and pain have all been practiced by the divine to aid them in their quest for spiritual experience. The shamans of the Pacific Northwest used these techniques as well as plant extracts such as devil's club, to give them prophetic visions. The myths of Bearmother and Wolf were not "childish things" to be put aside in adulthood, but a true belief that members of her tribe were part Bear and she was surrounded by huge Bear icons just as impressive as western religious statuary. She was familiar with the Nishga version of the "Myth of Wolf and Ghost People."

For the first few days Matilda was sorely tempted to accept the kelp tube with water pushed between the boards by her friends to quench her thirst, and even tempted to drink the urine she had collected, but duty made her resist. Seeing their gifts declined, her friends no longer tempted her after the third night. Her body became numb to her trouble and her thoughts of self-pity at her discomfort receded to leave her in a blank state of trance.

By the fifth day she no longer noticed her hunger or thirst and that night she heard the drums of the ghost people and took her urine to sprinkle it around the perimeter of her room to protect herself from them. The whimpering of a wolf in agony awoke her in the night. Two points of light heralded the wolf's pacing in her room. She spoke to him to calm him before she reached into the wolf's mouth to remove a deer bone. The wolf's tongue licked her face and promised her that she would never starve. On the sixth night the chattering of the ravens outside was a soporific to send her into a deep trance.

Matilda sensed a presence in her room, then a sniffing sound made her eyes open. Two eyes looked into her own from a height above her and as she adapted to the dark she saw the shape of the furry beast. She cringed and moved into the corner. The two eyes following her every move made her tremble. A gentle voice spoke to her across the space between them, "daughter, come," in a tone that compelled obedience. Matilda stood and allowed Bearmother to encircle her in her arms. The warmth of the thick fur, the beat of the heart from the huge chest relaxed and comforted her before she accepted obedience to the destiny that Bearmother outlined in a quiet but firm revelation. On the last night of her fast, the wind blew and the rain beat down on the roof of the room. In the distance, Skwa-twa moaned from the old spruce tree to lull her to sleep. A young man appeared in her dream and transported her for an audience with the Commander-of-the-Land, Simoiget, the first chief. Just as she was to enter his room she awoke with a conviction of premonition in the dream.

For a further seven days after her fast, she was allowed only dry salmon, halibut or preserved berries, with no eulachon oil to help them down. Matilda's shaman and mother instructed her in her hymeneal responsibilities. The shaman coached her in her expected obedience to wed her father's choice of Eagle Chief without wheedling or whining. Each day the shaman tested her knowledge and assessed her will to obey her destiny. Then satisfied, he released Matilda to her mother.

Matilda's mother informed her of her responsibilities as a wife and mother. Matilda would no longer be allowed to tryst with the young men and must remain chaste until after her betrothal and marriage. After receiving Matilda's vow of obedience, her mother sent her naked to the river, to drop the round stones of fecundity along the route that would ensure her sons to protect her and daughters to pass on their hereditary property. Matilda was ordered to wash and cleanse her body with water. On her return, her mother placed a chemise of womanhood over Matilda's head that told her community that she was now cleansed for betrothal.

Matilda was fifteen at the time of her first menses and it took her chief father up to another two years to gather enough property for a great potlatch feast. Invitations went out to the Haida of Queen Charlotte Islands, the Nishga on the Nass, the Tlingit chiefs of Saxman and many others inviting them all to attend the celebration of his daughter's eligibility. In the meantime, Matilda was cosseted and fed, for who would want to wed a skinny weakling? Rumor and questions were rampant in the village, who was the Eagle chief? Which relative of her mother from the Nass? No, a Haida chief of Cumshewa surely; a speculation to last for as long as two years!

McNeill

The brig *Tally Ho* arrived just in time to stop McNeill taking the *Convoy* to the California coast. On the 5th of May, 1826, Mr. Jones, having returned to take over the agency from Captain Grimes, writes to Marshall: "I arrived here after a pleasant passage of one hundred & thirty days, The Tally Ho has proved to be a remarkable good vessel. I can find no single fault with her."

Mr. Jones then took control of arrangements for the *Convoy* and *Tally Ho* to go to the northwest coast. He transferred Captain Dominis with his crew to the *Convoy* and appointed Captain McNeill master of the *Tally Ho* with his crew from the *Convoy* and an invoice of $10,776.25. He reports in his letter to Marshall that: "...they have both sailed & I have no doubt will do well."

He instructed both captains to trade for the rest of the season on the coast and before the return voyage to meet and transfer all trading goods to the *Tally Ho*. The *Convoy* was to return with the furs to the Sandwich Islands and the *Tally Ho* was to go to Norfolk Sound and try to sell any remaining trade goods to the Russians. He also instructed McNeill to offer the *Tally Ho* to the Russian governor for sale and bring a tentative offer back with him for approval.

By the end of May the *Tally Ho* reached the Queen Charlotte Islands, bypassed Kigarney and went straight to Tongass Harbour on the east side of Cape Fox between Tongass Island and the mainland. McNeill reports in the log:

> Employ'd breaking out the hold & restowing it for convenience of Trade got a boatload of ballast off the Brig being very crank I intend to take 10 or 12 ton found two bales Blankets much eaten by mice who had eaten nearly through the head of a cask of molasses. I should smoke the vessel but being so late in the season cannot stop to do it.
>
> The natives inform me that Capts Barker & Peirce have gone round Point Rose & Allan to the Northward where I shall proceed as soon as we can get out and endeavour to get our share of skins but do not calculate to get more than 250 at the farthest Furs being scarce & we three months late for a whole season.
>
> No news as yet from Convoy I am anxious to fall in to supply her with cotton and red cloth she having none on board.

McNeill complained of being badly off for ground tackle, and expressed the opinion that: "...a vessel never ought to come on this coast without five Cables & Anchors at least."

He also found the Natives asking very high prices for furs. They declined an offer of five blankets and a musket off Tatterskey and as he entered Clarence Strait another canoe declined his offer of eight blankets. On June 10th, he writes in the log: "Natives inform that the Nass Indians have gone to Pearl Harbour being unfortunate at every Port I am almost discouraged but will cruise & try to deserve my share of Furs if I cannot fall in with them."

The Tally Ho spent most of the first part of June at or near Nass and eventually had a favorable southwest wind that allowed the vessel to sail up to Chucknahoo and on June 19th came to anchor there. Here McNeill completed a trade from the previous year as the log records: "...received two Skins from Cogwealth which he owed me last season on Convoys act."

The Indian village of Chasina was at Chucknahoo and was a common place for the Boston fur traders to visit. For McNeill to allow a chief to pay him at a later date required a considerable degree of trust and only occurred on this one occasion. This is the only clue found that might identify the family origin of the woman destined to become Matilda McNeill.

The continuing southeast winds and bad weather kept him at Chucknahoo until on the June 8 the *Tally Ho* ran down Clarence Strait, braced and stood over for Tongass with several canoes alongside. After trading with them he filled away for Nacoon and anchored, in company with the *Volunteer*. A seaman from the *Volunteer* accidentally killed a Native who was examining the blunderbuss. Capt. Barker and Captain McNeill paid off the relatives of the Indian with "20 Boxes of Shrow Ton & Ten Blankets," from each vessel, which was accepted as adequate compensation by the Indians.

This manner of appeasing the death of a Native, whether in an act of aggression or by accident, was in keeping with Haida custom. The American captains had learned this the hard way over the past forty years with the loss of several vessels. In this case observation of proper compensation prevented any reprisals against either of the ships even though the price was steep—twenty of the sixty boxes of the expensive shrowton purchased at Nass for trading at Skidegate. McNeill does not say how much he paid for the shrowton at Nass, although he gave forty boxes of it for nine sea otter skins at Skedans.

On July 6, *Tally Ho* left Tatterskey for Nacoon, stayed less than a day before crossing to Sebashes. Here they were informed that all these Indians were at Skedans. This is not surprising since the story of origin of these two tribes have a common link and the chiefs of Sebashes and Skedans considered themselves brothers.

Augustus stands watch on the thirteenth day in Skedans Harbor. The weather is warm with intermittent light rain. The crescent beach, white with sea shells and the stately houses with their colorful house posts and totem poles form a beautiful backdrop for the activities in the village. Gus is reminded of a village fete involving visits from neighboring communities, "the Fair" in full swing on a warm summer afternoon. A time when, still young, he had been free to cavort like the children on this beach.

Gus helps pack two barrels of furs, stows them in the hold and even now the supercargo has not detected the keg of rum that has been plundered with spile holes. Two years at sea, fifteen years of age, he is now a man among men, subject to all their vagaries!

In Oahu, on liberty ashore with John Holland and other members of the crew, Gus would not enter the bordello. The sight of Thomas Low's eye and sounds of Isaac Marsh in the main cabin was still fresh in his mind, he said to John, "I'll not play at hey-gammer-cock," spoken in ready forecastle slang with a grin, "an' risk flap-dragon!"

The monotony of refitting the rigging and sails day after day in harbor was drowned by one evening of excess before John hoisted Gus into the longboat and his drunken state was noted by Mr. Carter as they dragged him on deck. Common enough behavior for an old Jack tar but Augustus Wright was still a boy in the ship's manifest!

Gus stood before Captain McNeill in the cabin next morning, the little men inside hammering his head. The captain's red hair and swarthy face colored a little as Gus justified his degradation as "just another party." Captain McNeill warned him that satanic booze will take control of him and destroy him at worst or disgrace him at best. Gus brushed aside his concern with, "what else would you expect from this Boston captain of temperance!"

"Boredom!" Gus mumbles to himself on the clean-up Saturday at Skedans. The weekdays crawl by with rigging repairs, stowage of water casks, packing up furs. The captain hurries to get away from the ship to attend the festivities on shore. Rum! Now's a good time to escape detection, Gus thinks, as he descends into the hold. Once more he gets away with it. Supercargo has not discovered the spile holes!

There is little duty for Gus on Sunday except for a short trip to the yardarms to loose the sails for drying. Odd jobs of mending clothes, just one seaman on watch inside the cocoon of the boarding nettings. Gus sneers at the thought of joining the captain and his Bible-bangers on deck, then his addictive thirst impels him to visit the small keg in the hold again. The keg beckons him, all arguments against his desire refuted. Sunday worship, a good time to steal away below without detection. Alas, he falls into the supercargo's trap, and is caught without defense.

The first mate sighs resignation that Gus did not heed the captain's advice as he parades him once again in front of Captain McNeill. Gus sees the fury in Captain McNeill's narrowed eyes and flushed face. He can expect no mercy and gives no excuses for his behavior, even though theft on board ship is a major offense.

Gus seeks an opportunity to run, dive into the sea and swim ashore. Putting himself at the mercy of a Haida chief, even enslavement, seems preferable to his known fate, but he is imprisoned by the impenetrable boarding nettings and anyway Captain McNeill is invited ashore again to attend the feast that evening. Gus knows the Haida always sell the deserters back to the ship's captain.

Gus is dumb and numb as he is led the short distance to the main shrouds. A ghostly detachment takes hold of him as he removes his shirt, steps forward and allows them to bind his wrists to the shrouds. He looks up at his wrists, turns to see the nine tails hang free and desperation makes him struggle to free his wrists only to tighten the grip of his bonds. His mouth dries as terrible fear grips him with the images of others he has seen so seized and broken by the pain. Even in July the breeze cools his bare back to send a trembling shiver down his spine. The crew watches in silence, some witnesses with eyes of detestation at a thief aboard, others, like John, show pity at his plight and plead with Captain McNeill for clemency.

The mate talks quietly into Gus' left ear. Gus opens his mouth and accepts the wad of leather between his chattering teeth. Captain McNeill announces his crime and sentence—one dozen! Gus dare not look back at the executioner and closes his eyes to will the time to pass unnoticed; he startles at the whistle before a thump against his back expels all air from his lungs. Pain far worse than he imagined makes him gasp for air. A cry of surprise to vent his anguish is cut off by the second lash that drives the air out once more. "Oh, God!" implored silently at first and then yelped like an injured puppy. By the twelfth lash, all sense and sensation out of mind, he hangs by his wrists, broken and almost unaware of hands cutting him down as he sinks out of pain into unconsciousness.

Gus sits against a bulkhead trying to find a small patch of unbruised back to rest on, the irons hold his feet to a bar in front of him and the wrist irons allow just enough movement to raise the water cup to his lips or tap the barge-men out of the biscuit before chewing its strawlike texture that might quell his rumbling hunger. By the seventh day of his confinement, Gus' back has healed, but his imprisonment embitters him against such authority, such wounding punishment, such degradation in front of his peers. The imprisonment makes him crave rum as never before, to let him forget and sink into a deep sleep.

McNeill, pressed to obtain as many skins as possible, traded off Cumshewa, Skidegate and Nacoon. He exchanged goods with *Convoy* at sea and anchored in Tongass. There, he salted salmon and since the *Tally Ho* was very crank (unstable under sail), he arranged for ballast to be put on the keelson. These repairs occupied seven days before he made a further cruise to Tuxekan, Tatterskey, Tongass and Skidegate. He had collected about 150 prime skins and other furs in proportion before setting sail for Norfolk Sound.

McNeill invited the governor at Sitka aboard the *Tally Ho* and gave him a five-gun salute on arrival and departure. His intention was to impress the governor before negotiating a good deal. He secured a price of 8,500 fur seal skins in a tentative deal for approval in Oahu.

He remained at Sitka for five more days to cut spars and a new main mast before returning to the Sandwich Islands.

On 4 November 1826, Dixey Wilde writes to Marshall: "The Convoy has arrived from the NW coast, the Tally Ho left the Coast at the same time for Norfolk Sound. Capt Dominis put all his remaining cargo on board of her except some blue cloths, axes and liquor. They have collected but very few furs, they arrived too late on the coast. If Capt McNeill does not sell any part of the cargo at N. Sound we shall have a good chance this season on the coast for one or perhaps two vessels."

Between the two vessels they had collected about 1,100 furs, of which about 300 were sea otter pelts. At Canton prices this was not a profitable voyage and both captains were disappointed with their commissions, which in McNeill's case amounted to $674.84, including the commission on the sale of the *Tally Ho*.

On November 6, Mr. Jones writes to Marshall: "I have only a moment to inform you of the arrival of the Tally Ho from Norfolk Sound, she is now towing into the harbour. McNeil has made a mistake in disposing of all his blankets to the Russians consequently spoiling his cargo for another season on the coast."

This pattern of "blame McNeill" set in after his obstinacy with Captain Wilde. William McNeill was not able to counter the accusations since he knew nothing of them and these highly prejudicial letters to Marshall contributed to the closing out of McNeill's account with these merchants in 1828.

McNeill was in Oahu for two months before he got underway on 20 January 1827. He sighted Cape Omaney on the 8 February and then ran up against a series of storms that swept through north of Queen Charlotte Islands, a common winter occurrence. He did not sight Cape Edgcombe until seven days later, a distance of sixty miles. Even then it took him four more days to get into Sitka Harbor.

On February 22, the governor, saluted with seven guns this time, came on board to examine the *Tally Ho* once more to open the bargaining for the sale of the vessel. It was not until 13 March 1827 that the log records: "The Captain of Port came on board the Brig, fired a salute of 7 guns, hawled down American colors and gave up the Tally Ho to the Russians."

For some days previous to this handover, the crew transferred cargo and belongings to the American brigantine *Active*. The next day the log of *Tally Ho* closes with: "Russians with priest came on board performed some religious ceremonies & had dinner.

Remainder of the crew, with myself went on board Brig Active, Capt Cotting, bound on the coast where he is to deliver cargo on board the Owhyee. This ends the voyage on board the Tally Ho."

On March 27 1827, the *Active* transferred the cargo to the *Owhyee*, with McNeill, Carter and Davies and the remaining crew at the port of Henegea. The *Owhyee* continued to trade at all the familiar posts until May 8 when they set sail for the Strait of Juan de Fuca. After trading at Port Discovery, the *Owhyee* went to an anchorage on the north side of the Strait. The *Owhyee* log reported that they entered the harbor against a four-knot current (Race Rocks): "...hardly advancing against the land."

They finally anchored in sixteen fathoms of water. Of the harbors on the north side, only Esquimalt and Becher Bay have such depth.

The *Owhyee* sailed south from the harbor, passed Cape Flattery on 29 May and entered the Columbia River on 12 June. The *Owhyee* anchored in Baker's Bay and tested the market for purchase of beaver pelts from the Chinook tribe. While at anchor in Baker's Bay, the *Owhyee* was visited by Chief Factor James McMillan of the Hudson's Bay Company, who interviewed the mate and was told that their purpose was to obtain wood and water. McMillan was not fooled and he later discovered that the *Owhyee* was giving twice as much for furs as the Company. After leaving the Columbia River, *Owhyee* sailed to Bodega Harbour and San Francisco before crossing the Pacific to the Sandwich Islands. They sighted Mowee on 22 July 1827.

Rec'd April 12 1828 fr Capt McNeil
Josiah Marshall Oahu Nov 1 1827

Dear Sir.

Captain McNeil takes passage in the Golden Farmer for Nantucket. I have given him an order on you for commissions on Sale of Tally Ho & cargo, which when you have realised the funds please pay. His wages twenty dollars per month are payed up to this date. till his return he will be entitled to 20 Dollars per month as per agreement.

There is nothing to pay for his passage. The papers of the Tally Ho are deposited in the office of the Consulate and I have forwarded you a certificate to signify the same

Your Obt Srt
(Signed) John C. Jones Jnr

CHAPTER 5

Golden Farmer, Burton and Llama Voyages

W hen McNeill took passage on the brigantine *Golden Farmer* and left Oahu on November 11, 1827, it is not clear if he was captain of this vessel, although he was paid as if employed. He kept a journal during the voyage as if it were a log and from the first day out, the east by south winds dashed his hopes of making the Society Islands. After six days at sea he wrote that he had given up all hopes of fetching the Societies, his intention before leaving Oahu.

The *Golden Farmer* needed wood, so after two weeks at sea she was running for Christmas Island. However, a lunar observation showed that the ship was to the westward (1°26') of Christmas Island and was set on a course for Fannings Island (Kiritimati).

The chronometer measured the time difference between Greenwich and the position of the vessel at the time of taking the noon day fix for latitude. Its accuracy depended upon a pocket watch that did not vary with temperature and humidity. Captain Vancouver had three chronometers on board. Captain Vancouver measured the time east of Greenwich while the Boston captains measured it west of Greenwich. The first time McNeill recorded the use of a chronometer was in the log of the Convoy on the voyage from the Sandwich Islands to the northwest coast. However, he makes no reference to it on the voyage back to the Islands, perhaps because he was unable to correct it in Tamgass Harbor.

In the *Golden Farmer*, McNeill started out by recording the chronometer longitude alone. On arrival at Fannings Island, he reports in his journal: "...the chronometer was 15 miles to the westward owing to not having her proper rate when we left Oahu." Two days after leaving Fannings Island he stated categorically: "...from this date I shall calculate Longitude from the Chrono."

Through the long voyage to Nantucket he navigated by dead reckoning and corrected his longitude by chronometer with occasional lunar sightings to back up the chronometer. A good navigator did not rely on a single method for determining his position. At Fannings Island he sent a party ashore to collect 500 cocoa nuts and five boatloads of wood. He writes in his journal of this visit to the island: "Saw the Land F Island bearing W.S.W. 3 miles dist it being very low cannot be seen more than 15 miles from masthead in the day time. during the night making short trips to windward. At 8 a.m. went on shore where we found a party of Men Collecting Beach La Mar there were 11 Sandwich Islanders & one white man who said they had 3000 dollars worth & that a great quantity had spoiled."

Beach la mer is a sea cucumber with a soft wormlike body, varying in size from inches to two feet. The inner parts are removed and the rest boiled before drying them in the sun. Known as trepang in the Canton market, it was a delicacy used to thicken soup in Chinese cuisine.

Ten days out of Fannings Island, McNeill reported the sighting of land:

First part a light breeze at East heading South Easterly all sail set by the wind. At 2 a.m. Saw the Island of Whytootake (Aitutaki) bearing S. by W. 12 miles dist at 8 a.m. I was boarded by two Canoes from the Island two Native Missionary Teachers came off they had certificates from the Missionarys at Raiatea dated July 1st 1823. They invited us to go on Shore which we accepted, At 9 a.m. went on shore with Articles to trade.
Lat of this Island 18°56' S. Longt 159°40'W

Tuesday Dec 11th 1827

Boat on shore waiting for what we should perchase. At 3 P.M. returned on board with 32 Hogs bannanas Potatoes & Yams for which we paid Knives Scissors Shirts Fish Hooks &c. At 4 P.M. made Sail to the Southward by the wind, the Island bearing North by East 12 miles dist. This Island is of a moderate height & very fruitful there where Taro. Potatoes. cocoa Nuts. Yams. Bananas. Bread Fruit. & other Tropical Fruits. We found the Natives friendly & honest they were about the size of the Sandwich Islanders but not well formed the Females where more modest being entirely covered with white Tappos which the South Island Females but partly do The Males wore their Maro's the same but the greatest part of them where covered from the body half way down the leg. Every house has a yard made by driving Posts endways into the ground uniformly & regular walks very clean between the Houses which where built with mud sides & white washed similar to the houses on California the Tops covered with the Cocoa Nut Leaf which made a very handsome appearance from Sea. They have a Large Church 200 feet long capable of holding 2000 Souls of which there is 3000 on the Island. Before the Missionarys went there they used to eat Human Flesh but I believe have discontinued it all together. They informed us that there had but 10 Vessels visited the Island during their remembrance one of which was 5 days before our arrival.(a Whaler)

Next day, at 1 P.M. Saw the Island of Orarute (Rarotonga) bearing by Compass S. by E. Judged it to be 40 miles dist it is layed down on the chart in Lat 21°17' S. Longt 159°40' W. At 2 a.m. passed 10 miles to the west of it at 11 a.m. it bore N.N.E. 35 miles dist. It is moderately high land & can be seen a great way off in clear weather.

"Hogs" is probably a contraction of Hogsheads and not 32 pigs or sheep, although they did keep pigs aboard and one was slaughtered later in the voyage for fresh meat. From an early date in the journal, McNeill records that the ship leaked and in a boisterous sea required 300 strokes of the pump each hour. In the bad seas approaching Cape Horn this rate went up to as high as 1,000 strokes per hour. He also complains of the bad state of the ship's standing rigging as well as the bottom of the vessel: "The bottom is getting foul, Copper ragged & coming off. Leather full of Barnacles & Grass & coming off."

On January 1st 1928 he records:

Thick misty weather a moderate from W.N.W. Steering Sails on the Starboard side. I think by the bottom being so foul hinders our progress one & a half miles per hour. Another New Years day which makes me Three Years three months & four days from Boston.

Thro the night thick weather & rain at times wind variable from W.N.W. to S.S.W. Saw a Diver of the Penguin species also saw rockweed. Course to Diego Ramirez S, 76.E 2340 miles Distance.

Ends thick weather & a moderate breeze from S.W.

Lat Obs 47°33' S Longt by Chro 130°30' West 52 days out.

The journal does not record the sighting of land on the passage round Cape Horn, not even the Island of Diego Ramirez. Seventy days out from the Sandwich Islands the ship started northward into the south Atlantic, passing west of the Falkland Islands. The *Golden Farmer* was off Rio de la Plata seventy-five days out. There was optimism in the journal that they would make a fast passage to Nantucket, but as so often happened on a long voyage, the weather turned against them. The winds became variable and the ship was only making one-and-a-half to two knots as it crept up to the coast of Brazil.

McNeill wondered whether the winds would push them onto the coast so that they would be unable to round Cape Augustine (Cabo de Sao Roque). It took the ship thirty-five days to go from latitude 47° south/longitude 45° west to 11° south/32° west a distance of 2,800 miles. Then, at last, the southeast trades picked up the ship's speed and he writes in the journal: "Light winds from N.E. steering N.N.W. with topmast & top Galt steering set. I can now thank kind Providence in the North Atlantic Ocean & homeward bound after an absence of 40 months in good health."

The ship went across the equator from one trade wind to the next—no doldrums! In the last thirty-five days, the *Golden Farmer* covered 4,200 miles, arriving at Nantucket on 4 April 1828.

Matilda

Each guest to Matilda's "coming-of-age" potlatch, held in midsummer, was greeted with a long speech of welcome and an even longer reply that tried the patience of the young bucks eagerly awaiting the evening of feasting. There was a carnival atmosphere. Young Eagle hunters were sent out by their families to show off their skills in order to attract the attention of Matilda's chief father.

Who could outperform young Chief Sakau'an? Standing with his feet in the sea water his helpers splashed water on him before covering his body with white eagle feathers. In the fire, an iron hoop glowed red hot in the embers. His helpers spread the embers toward his feet. Chief Sakau'an closed his eyes in concentration and, with deliberation, walked to the hoop and lifted it above his head to display his hereditary gift of power over fire.

After this sterling performance, Sakau'an's uncle, Chief Mountain, was free to bargain with Matilda's father, unencumbered by competition. On Sakau'an's side there was wealth and status and this young chief already sported one ring on his hat. Matilda was strikingly handsome, talented and an heir to a chieftainship in her own right at the village of Gitradeen next to Sakau'an's own at Gitiks. Her mother passed on the crests emblazoned on Matilda's chest as well as the songs and dances of the Wolf Bearmother phratry (kinship group) at their village. She was a grand young lady, haughty, spirited and with a strong will of her own; she was destined to find life difficult under the command of Chief Mountain's lady in their big longhouse at Gitiks. The tactical endeavors of both chiefs were simple, Mountain needed sea otter skins for trade and Matilda's father needed shrowton. The strategy was another matter and the meeting between the chiefs lasted many hours into the night before the policies of trade and the extent of her dowry were settled.

After all the hoopla of her betrothal, Matilda's marriage took place after the salmon harvest in the fall. The bride's dowry of blankets and other valued goods were piled outside her house ready for loading onto Sakau'an's canoe. The two families gathered for a simple ceremony, a bench placed before them. Sakau'an sat on the bench and his eyes implored her to join him. A number of the groom's best friends gave speeches begging Matilda to sit with him. Matilda pretended resistance before she was persuaded to sit and they were wed.

McNeill

Boston captains took work from various merchants. Some of them were constantly employed by the same firm as with Captain McNeill who was with Marshall & Wilde, at least from 1818 to 1828. During that period he was nurtured by them for the northwest coast trade and was in favor with his employers.

On the *Golden Farmer*, McNeill was paid his salary by Marshall & Wilde and his account was paid off after his arrival. The journal, kept on board the brigantine *Burton*, gave no mention of the owner. His obstinacy over payment of his commission, his refusal to leave the *Convoy* and the blame he received for selling the blankets to the Russians at Sitka probably soured his relationship with his employer. His behavior may well have been a case of his head being ruled from between his legs! He was known to be stubborn, impetuous, obstinate and now there is evidence of a lusty nature! The hefty fees of $180 and $320, for bringing a girl to the Islands in the *Owhyee* and to the coast and back in the *Convoy*, charged to his account by the firm appeared, from the account book, to have been made in June, 1828, as an afterthought and were never charged to either the *Owhyee* or the *Convoy* accounts. It is known that many a Boston captain on the northwest coast took a female partner on board for their comfort. This was not frowned upon by the Native chiefs or by the merchants, because it enhanced trade. Before his final account was paid off, he was reimbursed with $158, because of an overcharge for bringing a girl from the coast!

In November, 1828, Captain McNeill commanded the brigantine *Burton* from Boston toward Salvador. This voyage was notable, as the log records: "...very hard severe gale. In fact I never knew it blow harder at sea in my life which I have constantly followed for 14 years to different seas it blows so at times that it brings the tops of the sea on board like a rain storm & makes everything tremble."

This storm brought what the log terms a "Cat Owl," when they were over one thousand miles from land and the resulting alteration in the currents in the north Atlantic baffled McNeill's navigation. This log notation included the fact that he had been at sea for fourteen years, confirming that he went to sea at eleven years of age. The effects of the storm lasted for three weeks and did much damage. McNeill opened the hold to get cordage: "...which we were much in want of as the greatest part of the rigging is dropping about our heads."

Llama was the official registered name and spelling of the vessel that McNeill was appointed to as master in October, 1830, although throughout the records the adopted spelling drops one 'L'. In the brigantine *Llama*, McNeill was employed by the owners of the vessel, the firm of Bryant & Sturgis.

Samuel Morison states in *Maritime History of Massachusetts*:

Quaint and interesting the ships of the Federalist period certainly were, with their varied coloring (bright, lemon or orange waist against black, blue or green topsides and a gay contrasting color for the inside of the bulwarks), their carved 'gingerbread work' on stern and quick-work about the bows; their few large well proportioned sails (royals seldom, and skysails never being carried) and their occasionally graceful sheer.' New England builders obeyed the ancient tradition that, 'ships require a spreading at the water's edge both fore and aft to support them from being plunged too

deep into the sea'. The appearance of a cut water bow a mere ornament to deceive or beautify. Their real bows were cod's head type,
bluff and full to buffet a passage through the sea. Rarely was the
length of the ship more than four times it's breadth.

The brigantine *Llama* was of the same ilk, only seventy-six feet
in length and twenty feet of beam, with two masts, the cabins did
not have access to galleries across the stern and a billet head
(carved scroll) of Boston.

The *Llama* was registered in Boston to Bryant and Sturgis.
However, the property on board was assigned by W. H. Boardman,
as the preface to the invoice shows: "Invoice of Cargo shipped by
W.H. Boardman on board the Brig Llama, W.H. McNeill Master
bound for the Sandwich Islands and N.W. Coast of America &
China being on account and risk of the owners of the said Brig as
per register who are all native citizens of the United States of
America residing & doing business in Boston and consigned to the
said master for sail." The total value of the goods on board from this
invoice was costed out at $17,641.01. The last word "sail" is proba-
bly misspelled.

"May God bless us with a safe and speedy passage," the first
mate, Mr. Selman, begs the log as the *Llama* passed Thatcher's Light.

Seventeen days out, the crew was put on a weekly bread
allowance of six pounds and twenty-five days out, on a daily beef
allowance of one and a half pounds with three quarts of water per
man per day. McNeill took over the log twenty-seven days out from
Boston as is evidenced by his characteristic, "occation," "hawl,"
and "thick harry weather" entering the daily accounts; the studding
sails became Steering Sails and in all mention of the 'Sea' the 'S'
capitalized. The log also takes on a more personal view of the voyage as he confides: "...for the last nine days we have experienced
nothing but head winds, here where I have always taken the trades
we have the wind S.W."

Three days later, his pessimistic pen records: "I think now we
shall do extremely well to cross the Equator in 60 days from
Boston." Ship board routine demanded a Saturday clean up in
preparation for the Sabbath and on one Saturday powder was burnt
in the Forecastle to rid it of vermin."

But not before McNeill records, "Trades at last!"

When they ran into the doldrums north of the equator the *Llama*
encounters: "...heavy squalls of wind & rain with thunder and light-

ning" which at least enabled them to catch two casks of fresh water. Now all pessimism left the account and they crossed the equator, forty-eight days out from Boston.

When McNeill reached the southern trade winds he was surprised by "…some of the heaviest squalls of wind attended with rain that I have ever experienced along here at times looks more like the weather off Cape Horn than the trade wind!"

Whale feed (krill), an albatross, rock weed and the greenish color to the sea told McNeill that he was approaching the soundings off Rio de la Plata and he reports: "…I byed for them at Meridian but could get no bottom with 100 Fathoms of line." In plotting his approach to Cape Horn he is dismayed by his progress: "…I have tried hard to get to the Westward of the Falklands but the S.W. winds have forced us to the Eastward of them."

Eighty-five days out the *Llama* at latitude 57°4' south, longitude 64°40' west, McNeill started his westward passage round Cape Horn and for the next thirty days there is not one sighting of land reported in the log. In spite of huge seas, he said that the ship made good weather, shipping but little water. In these seas Francis Grennell fell from the main top on deck and hurt himself badly; but survived to become one of the thorns in his officers' sides! As the *Llama* started north to enter the south Pacific, McNeill notes: "…hard gales, reduced Sail close reeft M top sail balanced reeft Main Sail reeft Spencer & fore Stay Sail. At 2 a.m. tremendous hard squalls of wind attended with rain & hail which split the main topsail & knocked the fore Staysail out of rope & brought us under bare poles. At 4 a.m. set balanced Try Sail. The Brig behaved well took no water on deck except what she lurched in."

When McNeill was 111 days out of Boston he confides to the log: "…ends the pleasantest day we have had for the last 40 days. We are now round Cape Horn which makes the Fifth time I have passed it & hope for the last time. Our Road ahead now begins to look more favourable."

This was the first written indication that William McNeill intended to remain on the Pacific side of the American continent. And indeed, favorable was the word, for the *Llama* sailed from 44°45' south/85°54 north to 20°18' north/152° west in 40 days, a distance of 6,000 miles, to arrive at the Sandwich Islands 152 days out of Boston without having to make a stop at Juan Fernandes for water.

Dixon Entrance from Captain George Vancouver's map, 1793.

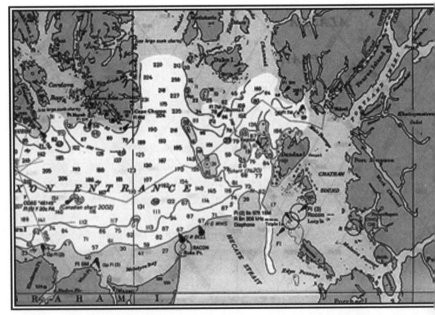

Dixon Entrance from United States marine chart 16016, 1993.

CHAPTER 6

The Brigantine *Llama* on the Coast

The men, at Columbia's River, are strait limb'd, fine looking fellows and the Women are very pretty. They are all in a state of nature, except the females, who wear a leaf apron — (perhaps t'was a fig leaf). But some of the gentlemen that examined them pretty close and near, both within and without reported that it was not a leaf, but a nice wove mat in resemblance!! and so we go — Thus, thus, — and no war!—!

          —John Boit, Diary 1792, at age 17 years

Bernard Barry is a cooper, "Bungs" to the forecastle crew. He went to sea at ten years old, a practical boy, good with his hands but not much given to school work, illiterate in fact. In the dull days of the war he apprenticed himself to a cooperage, but once the blockade was lifted and commerce opened again, he went back to sea with qualification as a cooper. Extra pay, no routine watch, only called up for "all hands ahoy." He was, in fact, an idler!

The brigantine that just arrived, called the *Llama*, needs a cooper. Barry rows out to inspect her. She's been kept smart and clean with her black hull and white bulwarks. He hails one of the crew to find out who came out as cooper, only to discover that the owners rated the ship as too small to need one on the voyage out. He asks if there was trouble on the outward stretch and hears of none.

Barry goes aboard the next day to take a walk round to inspect the condition of her rigging. Good seamen and tradesmen are in short supply, so he can be choosey! He sees Captain McNeill, learns that there will be no armorer and that he will have to do the iron work for the vessel in addition to forging his iron barrel. He approves the ship, preferring it to a stinking whaler anyway, and signs on at $25 a month.

In the captain's cabin, Barry notices that the apartments have been extended to give a separate sleeping quarter. The first mate is housed in a stateroom in steerage, an observation which piques his curiosity. He leaves the cabin but drops by the steward's pantry to chat about his new captain. He laughs as the steward mimes an exploding bomb but sees the steward's sloppy habits and assesses this to be bark rather than bite. He hopes the ship's cook is cleaner.

Barry reaches the waist of the *Llama* as two men, Francis Grennell and William Robinson leave the camboose with the forecastle dinner. The former carries the bucket of scouse and Barry learns that he's a bit soft in the head after taking a fall out of the main top coming around the Horn. Robinson carries the bread. He's a fighter, Barry hears over dinner, confirmed by his gap-toothed grin. Barry opens his sea-chest to take out his tin cup and jackknife, spears his share of the meat and dips his cup for some juice for the bread. A simple meal for a hungry crew. He observes several "noses to light candles at," and knows there'll be spile holes in his kegs before long. Dean and Rouch, short, tough, inseparable fellows with black hair and dark eyes, spell trouble in a dark street. Hurst and Hursey, full of blusterous courage and stories of self-congratulation, transform from stalwarts to cowards with one word from the first mate! Barry catches Stitches' eye. They know each other from a previous ship and Barry is aware that Stitches, although a supreme sailmaker, has a taste for rum in binges. Two lads, George Washington and Sam Ferguson, try for invisibility, the latter as easily led as a lamb to slaughter, Barry would bet. Old "Chips" holds sway in the forecastle, leads the scuttlebutt and sets the tone for his own comfort. The rest of the crew is on liberty; he'll assess them soon enough!

❧

The fur trade in the spring and summer of 1831 was different from McNeill's experience in 1822, 1823, 1825 and 1826. At that time the sea otter pelts were the primary object for a profitable voyage. But there is a telling alteration, in McNeill's hand writing, at the end of his description of Ennacanoe at the front of the *Convoy* log: "They are great Hunters and sell from one to two hundred Skins a season." McNeill crossed out the word 'hundred' and adds 'in 1831,' to become, 'from one to two skins a season in 1831!' After three months on the coast the log reports two casks of fur ready for shipping and we know from a later accounting these were not sea otter skins. In wintering on the coast he collected only 100 sea otter pelts.

There were three other ships also trading for fur; the *Griffin*, under Captain Taylor, and the *Active*, under Captain Raymond, were in opposition. The brigantine *Smyrna*, commanded by Captain Barker, out of Boston, was McNeill's supplier from the Sandwich Islands and allowed him to winter on the coast. On July 11, 1831, the *Llama* log reports McNeill's first meeting with the *Smyrna* in the inner harbor at Tamgass. He sent aboard the *Smyrna*, bars of iron, a chain anchor and two boxes of axes. In return, *Smyrna* restocked *Llama* with cloth, duffel, red flannel and check shirts, bales of blankets, casks of rum, all intended for trade with the Natives. In addition, *Llama* took on board tea, sugar, ten barrels of bread and a half barrel of paint oil.

Interwoven, but not recorded in the log directly, is another story. Soon after arriving on the coast at Kigarney in April, 1831, the log anticipates a cruise to Nass River. The weather did not cooperate and the *Llama* anchored in Clement Cittie (Harry Bay) prior to going south to Skidegate. Taking the southerly wind to advantage, McNeill planned to cruise up north to Henegea. Once more the wind changed and he was able to bear away for Nass.

While anchored in Kigarney the log records: "The Brig Griffin got underweigh & English Brig & Schooner in sight bound for Nass where they are to erect a Fort." He tried to follow them and got as far as Clement Cittie. There he was delayed again by the broken windlass and went into the inner harbor to effect repairs. At last, in mid-May, the log records: "Bore up for Clement City at 6 calm at noon took a breeze from Sd made all sail for Nass at 3 pm passed Pt Wales at 8 am came to anchor in the Harbor of Nass in 30 Fathoms water."

McNeill was then in territory that was under Chief Sakau'an, who was at the time married to Matilda, McNeill's future wife. The log also records that the *Llama* was boarded by Captain Simpson and Mr. Manson from the Hudson's Bay Company's barque, *Dryad*. They informed McNeill that they were about to build a fort for the Company to transact business with the Natives and that they had chosen this place from which to establish communication with the interior of the country.

Donald Manson was born 1796, joined the Company in 1817, and was promoted to Chief Trader in 1837. In 1832 he explored the Nass River, and in 1833, he established Fort McLoughlin at Millbanke Sound. He retired from the Company in 1857 and was not promoted to Chief Factor because, as Sir George told him: "...there is an impression in the minds of the gentlemen in the country that the value of your services has been a good deal neutralized by an unfortunate irritability of temper."

A few days later, another log entry states: "Capt Ryan & Mr Ogden of the English Schooner Vancouver came on board today."

Peter Skene Ogden was born in Quebec in 1790. He joined the Northwest Company and was bitterly opposed to the coalition with the Hudson's Bay Company. After two years he relented and joined the Company. He was promoted Chief Trader in 1824 and to Chief Factor in 1834. He took charge of building Old Fort Simpson (Nass) in 1831 and was instrumental in promoting the Company's coastal trade and driving the Boston traders from the coast.

Captain Simpson records the visit to Captain McNeill in the log of the *Dryad*. Neither of the logs suggest anything other than a cordial introduction. For the next year both vessels from the Company dogged the movement of all the American ships on the coast competing with them for furs.

Chief Factor Dr. John McLoughlin at Fort Vancouver and head of the Columbia department for the Hudson's Bay Company, had a recurring problem within his marine department. Governor Simpson wrote that it was highly important that any vessel coming on this voyage should be well officered. Yet in 1826, *Dryad* arrived at the Columbia River bar with Captain Davidson in command. In 1824, Governor George Simpson had assessed this officer: "...Captain Davidson's talent as a navigator I know nothing about, but his talent as a Grog Drinker is without paralell and I shall be agreeably surprised if he & his ship ever reach the Port of Destination."

In spite of this opinion, the Company continued to employ him.

In 1829, the Company's ship *Gannymede* arrived with Captain Hayne, a confirmed drunkard, who was also trading guns for furs with the Indians on the side. McLoughlin wrote to the governor and committee that it would be dangerous for this captain to be put in charge of one of their ships again. In 1830, another drunkard, Captain Minors, arrived in command of the *Dryad* and this tale of marine woes continued on into the 1850s.

In 1825, the brigantine *William and Ann*, under Captain Hanwell R.N., arrived on the coast and McLoughlin sent him on a mission to explore the Nass region for a large river that might form a conduit for furs coming to the coast from New Caledonia. Captain Hanwell was a slow, plodding commander and since McLoughlin had no power over him or his vessel he had to watch the *William and Ann*'s slow progress under "extensive repairs" before the voyage got underway on June 2, 1825, far too late in the season on the west coast. The purpose of the voyage was to assess the possibility of entering the coastal trade in opposition to the American vessels. To facilitate this objective he sent an experienced clerk, Alexander McKenzie, on board the *William and Ann* to negotiate with the Indian chiefs of the coast.

Alexander McKenzie had good knowledge of the Chinook language and took with him a Native with knowledge of the Nootka language. His instructions from McLoughlin were to assess the potential for the Company entering the coast fur trade. McLoughlin writes in his letter to the governor and committee on 6 October 1825: "In my instructions to Mr McKenzie you will observe that I direct him to consider himself under the directions of Captain Hanwell. But at the same time gave my opinion verbally to the Captain that in dealing with the Indians he ought to allow Mr McKenzie to act as he thought proper as from his knowledge of the Indian and the Nature of the Trade he was better able to deal with them than the Captain was to direct."

This voyage was a complete failure due to Captain Hanwell's mishandling of his opportunities to look for harbors that a vessel might use as a base from which to trade for fur with the Indians. He was wary of taking his ship into the rock-strewn coast and when he finally got to the Portland Inlet he failed to look for a major river and instead got locked in Observatory Inlet for twenty-seven days, due to bad weather. Even when he met the *Owhyee*, he declined Captain Kelly's invitation to go aboard to see a better way of fitting out a vessel for coastal trade. In short, Governor Simpson summed up Hanwell's performance of duty as: "...prudence of that voyage amounted to pusillanimity."

In spite of this failure, McLoughlin, who had a good nose for business, sniffed out some truth from McKenzie's account of the meeting with Captain Kelly and in his letter to Simpson writes: "There must be a good deal of business done on the Coast if there were six vessels this year on it as Captain Kelly informed our people, and if he could do business sufficient to pay the expense of his vessel and the expense of another bringing him supplies."

In October, 1825, in his letter to the governor and committee his view crystallizes into: "But to return to the communication with the Interior. By the Documents we have here Stating more Inland Furs are traded at Nass than any other place on the coast, from Captain Kelly's saying he traded one thousand Beaver Skins there last spring and from the Water being Muddy and fresh about that place I am certain there is some water communication as will answer our purpose."

In 1826, the new schooner, *Cadboro*, arrived on the coast with Lt. Aemelius Simpson R.N. in command. Simpson, a cousin of Governor George Simpson, was also appointed Superintendent of the Marine Department under McLoughlin. Although he was not liked by his contemporaries on a personal basis, there was no doubt that he was a superior sea captain and more importantly, sober! Furthermore, no enmity developed between McLoughlin and his new superintendent of marine.

In 1827, when Captain Hanwell refused McLoughlin's order to take the outfit for Fort Langley up the Fraser River (then known as Fraser's River), he sent the *Cadboro* instead. This was a ship of seventy tons with a low freeboard that made Chief Factor McMillan of Fort Langley shudder and comment that: "...the Cadboro is quite unfit for the Trade, there are hundreds of war canoes on the coast longer and higher out of the water than she is, carrying from forty to fifty men each."

It is hard for us in this age to conceive the comparative size of these war canoes or the ease with which the Indians moved around this thousand-mile coastline. These canoes carried enough men to outnumber the *Cadboro's* crew by more than three to one.

Soon after the *Cadboro* set out from the Columbia River in 1827, the *Owhyee*, under Captain Dominis, arrived in Baker's Bay. It remained a few days and when it left, William McNeill was on board as a passenger to the Sandwich Islands. Mr. McMillan went aboard the ship and was told by the mate that their sole intention was to get wood and water for their voyage. McMillan also found and reported to McLoughlin that the *Owhyee* was prepared to give twice as much as the Company in purchasing the furs. Even when the *Owhyee* with the *Convoy*, returned in 1829, they did not disrupt the Company's business, as Capt. Dominis' comments were reported by the *New York Gazette*: "He represents the Country as delightful, but that the Hudson's Bay Coy are too well established for citizens of the United States to expect to make any thing in the way of Fur Trade."

In September, 1830, Lt. Simpson wrote his report to McLoughlin on his exploratory voyage to the Nass country. He found the Nass River and sent a survey party up-river: "I was much disappointed by their reporting that a few miles up above our present anchorage the channel became quite narrow & shallow rendering the navigation for vessels of any draft very difficult."

He then set about surveying the land for a suitable site for a fort. He chose a place that: "...extends back from the banks of the river may be about three quarters of a mile where a range of rocky hills take their rise, its extent along the banks may be about one & a half miles with a good Southern exposure & appears a strong deep soil well calculated to produce vegetables."

He was particularly concerned with its position in and tactics for its defense against the large population of Indians of the Nass River and noted in his report that: "Vessels can lay at Anchor within Pistol shot of the shore, the Indians can be easily kept at check, the only thing to prevent this is ice in the event of its freezing during Winter months, this I was anxious to learn from the natives but could not make them understand me."

Lt. Simpson also assessed the opposition on the coast from the *Louisa*, under Captain Lambert, the *Griffin* with Captain Taylor and the *Convoy*, under Captain Dominis, noting that the *Griffin* had been sold in the Sandwich Islands and the purchasers had equipped her with a cargo to trade for fur on the coast. His only regret was that contrary winds had prevented him visiting ports for the purpose of trading. He also told McLoughlin that the Americans had goods that were more in demand on this part of the coast than those of the Hudson's Bay Company. Arms and ammunition were sold without limits, "with ardent spirits in great abundance." These articles, with the exception of blankets, he found in greatest demand at Nass. In 1830–31, McLoughlin was hit by a succession of tragedies. The new brigantine, *Isabella*, entered the Columbia River where Captain Ryan mistook Chinook Point for Cape Disappointment and went aground in the "southern breakers." Ryan abandoned ship in order to save the lives of his crew, an act much criticized later.

The "intermitting fever" (so called by Dr. McLaughlin, and which was possibly malaria) appeared at Fort Vancouver for the first time in the summer of 1830. The illness carried off three-quarters of the Indian population at the fort and when he wrote to the governor and committee in October, he reported that there were fifty-two people on the sick list. More trouble occurred with Captain Minors when he wanted to give Captain Simpson command of the *Dryad*. Captain Minors, another inebriate employee, refused to give up his command and incited the crew to side with him. James Douglas was called to the vessel to read the signed agreements to the crew and put the ship under Mr. Young, the first mate. McLoughlin writes in his letter to the governor and committee that: "…in the course of this discussion Capt Minors repeatedly said in the presence of his crew that he would not give up the command of his vessel as long as he could raise an arm."

Because of all these problems, not least of which was the "intermitting fever," McLoughlin was unable to send a large enough force back to the Nass to build the new fort until the spring of 1831. He had two good vessels, the brigantine *Dryad*, under Captain Simpson and the schooner *Vancouver*, under Captain Ryan. The schooner *Cadboro* was undergoing repairs in the spring of 1831. The two good vessels took the supplies and men to build the new fort at Nass. On May 9, 1831, McNeill records in the *Llama* log at Kygarney: "the English Brig and Schooner in sight were bound to Nass where they are to build a fort."

Captain McNeill impressed Ogden and Manson as a fur trader. He came from a long line of Boston men who had befriended the chiefs of Kaigani, Haida, Tlingit, Tsimshian and Nahwitti that went back forty years. He was a Boston man who, like his predecessors, made alliances with the chiefs, stayed in their houses and spoke their languages. He impressed Captain Simpson as an experienced captain who knew the harbors and whose experience reached back ten years although he was still only twenty-nine years old—a man who had spent more than four years in total on the coast. In the logs of *Llama* and *Dryad* there is no hint of armed aggression between them, despite the fact that the account of Capt. McNeill, given by his grandson in the British Columbia Archives, suggests that there was an armed conflict between the *Llama* and *Cadboro*. However, since there is no mention of this in the log of the *Llama*, it may well have been a tale spun by both McNeill and Ryan to entertain their grandchildren, using the 1821–22 armed conflict with the Russian man o'war, *Apollo*, when he was second mate in the *Owhyee*, to add drama to their story!

Over the next six months, two further disasters hit McLoughlin. In September, 1831, following a thirteen-day illness described as inflammation of the liver, Captain Simpson died at the new fort that was later named in his honor. McLoughlin's genuine anguish comes through his letter to the governor and committee: "…and I suffer the loss of an acquaintance whose Gentlemanlike conduct and zealous discharge of his duty entitled him to my Respect and Esteem, and though his death at all times would be a loss still in the present situation of our affairs it is particularly so."

The next disaster hit in January, 1832, when the schooner *Vancouver*, under Captain Kipling, was hit by a storm in Portland Inlet and disabled to the point of needing extensive repairs with little hope of being ready for service for up to one year. Even before this happened, McLoughlin wrote to Richard Charlton Esq in Oahu with this proposal: "In regard to Capt Cole's offer to sell us his Brig as we have as many vessels as we absolutely require, we cannot purchase his for Bills on London, but if it would suit Capt Cole to take payment in Deals we would take the *Griffin* at the price you would consider her worth and deliver him Deals at Wahoo at 25 per cent below our present invoice valuation."

McLoughlin also asked Charlton to engage Captain Taylor, or any other sober steady person. McLoughlin needed a responsible and knowledgeable captain to replace Captain Simpson, and was in fact, more in need of that than he was of another vessel!

Did McNeill have another reason to visit the Nass River, apart from trading furs or buying shrowton for trade? The affairs of the chiefs' wives or the Company's officers' wives are seldom mentioned in the Hudson's Bay Company or Boston traders' records at this time. In the log of the *Llama*, McNeill said he hoped it was his last time round Cape Horn.

His future wife was at that time married to Chief Sakau'an, who resided at Gitiks Indian village on the Nass River. While there is no written confirmation as to the identity of the girl he transported to and from the coast in both the *Owhyee* and the *Convoy*, the possibility exists that he came back here to claim her.

Every voyage seemed to have a recurring problem and in the prolonged time on the coast the *Llama* had three: the windlass, rum and mutiny. The windlass kept capsizing and needed repair on three occasions. Before and during this time McNeill had trouble with rum and mutiny. The first sign of disturbance came at the end of May, 1831: "…This day some of the people entered the Hole & took from thence rum & other goods & got drunk & then went to fighting. Put William Robinson in Irons & searched his chest & found things had been stole from the Arm Chest in it."

While the log does not indicate when William Robinson was released from irons, all remained quiet until late June: "At 6 PM while eating Supper hearing a noise on deck went up to see what occasioned it & found John Dean had been purchasing Rum of the Indians & got drunk & then attempted to shoot the 2nd Officer took the musket from him likewise all the arms out of the Forecastle & put him in irons Hands & Feet where he is to remain untill he gets to Oahu. His intention was to take the vessel & called on the rest of the crew to raise a mutiny."

This escalated and in mid-July the log records: "The men entered the Hole & took some Rum and got intoxicated and were attempting to take the Brig Samuel Ferguson, Joseph Hursey and William Robinson jumped overboard & swam onshore seized John Rouch in the rigging & gave him 2 Dozen lashes likewise Francis Grennell at 5 PM went onshore for the 3 men & brought them off onboard Put Samuel Ferguson in the rigging & gave him 2 Dozen lashes put John Rouch in Irons."

Now McNeill had two men in irons and no doubt a sullen belligerent group in the *Llama's* forecastle.

At this time the *Llama* sailed in company with the *Smyrna* until they reached Kyetes Cove in Millbanke Sound where they once more exchanged goods.

Llama left Kyetes Cove to sail to Sitka. McNeill wished to put the two men in irons ashore in care of the Russians as mutineers and on August 7, 1831, the *Llama* anchored in Sitka harbor.

Two days later the log records:

> Took our two prisoners John Rouch & John Dean that we had in Irons and put them onshore & put them under the Russians charge paying them off with a Dozen lashes apiece, crew employed various Jobs ships duty. Last night Milton Hurst William Robinson & Francis Grennell took the small boat & departed after searching we found they had taken all their dunnage 2 muskets 2 Cartridge Boxes filled with cartridges. Next day, Mr Selman & Mr Hanson with six hands & two Indians went on shore and searched for the men that ran away but did not retrieve them until the following day: At 4 am the Indians informed us that they had found the men that had run away the Officer & six hands went onshore & brought them off put them in the rigging & gave each one dozen lashes. paid the Indians 17 Blankets & 10 Fm Cotton for recovering the men & Boat.

This cooperation given by the Indians in returning deserters was a frequent occurrence. The payment for performing this service was generous and always made acceptable to the Indians to gain their future cooperation. McNeill already short two of his seamen could not afford to put any more men in irons, nor could he afford to make the punishment too injurious since he needed a crew to work the ship and man the defenses. There was no thought of ridding the ship of deserters, in contrast to mutineers.

This is one of the occasions when McNeill's disciplinary zeal got the better of him. Rouch had already received two dozen lashes at the time of his mutinous behavior. This punishment was not given on the spur of the moment under the stress of fear and the prospect of internment in a Russian prison was surely punishment enough! Very little trade was conducted on this trip to Sitka. The crew did salt down two barrels of salmon and after three days left for Coyou in Affleck Canal to trade for furs and then into Chatham Channel for Ennacanoe. After a two-week cruise, the *Llama* returned to Tamgass Harbor where they busied themselves and awaited the arrival of the *Smyrna*.

The *Smyrna* arrived on October 6, 1831, and they exchanged many items that gave *Llama* ample supplies to survive the winter.

The *Llama* delivered "644 deerskins, 40 Bear skins, 7 Bbls. of Mink skins and 9 Casks of Furs" The first mate, Mr. Selman, left the *Llama* to return to the Sandwich Islands in the *Smyrna* and Mr. Hanson was promoted to the position of first mate. The two ships left Tamgass in company, the *Smyrna* continued on to the Islands and the *Llama* went to Kigarney to spend the first part of winter at anchor there. Then, in company with the *Griffin*, moved to Tuxekan in November and remained there until mid-January, 1832.

⁘

Bernard Barry is heartily discouraged by the behavior in the fore-castle. He feels that the atmosphere is partly to blame for setting off poor Stitches on one of his binges that earns him a week in irons. As Barry puts them on his friend's hands and feet, he tries to show some sympathy for the sailmaker's plight, and yet knows Stitches will only dry out if absolutely denied further rum. Anyway, what else can a seaman do when under the captain's orders?

William Robinson, too, is a pain with his constant belligerence and wild schemes for getting at the hold to steal more rum. Barry doesn't know of his final success until the day he goes with the mate to the hold and the mate records in the log that they found the people had broached a cask of rum, " having 7 Spile Holes in the Head." No sooner is that sorted out and the hold made impregnable to the forecastle than Stitches goes wild again and Barry puts him back in his irons, which fortunately he had kept from last time!

Meanwhile, the carpenter is getting on with preparations for the captain's new "wife" to come on board with her little one. Barry knows, without orders, to keep a sharp watch out for reprisals from the Nass Natives, particularly Sakau'an, that double Eagle chief from Gitiks village!

Wintering on the coast is depressing with the long winter nights and little activity or exercise. The intermittent trouble in the fore-castle partly stems from this lethargy. But the days begin to length-en, snow turns to hail and the air becomes notably warmer. In the new year, Barry goes on shore to get a spar to build a deerskin press that will enable them to bale these skins. This is a bulky contraption that crowds the foredeck and gets in everyone's way. In late January the *Llama* leaves the winter anchorage to make a short cruise to various harbors in the south. They are short a second mate, and Barry hears that McNeill is expecting one when the *Smyrna* returns.

"No second mate," Barry notes, on arrival of the *Smyrna*. A month later, the captain calls him in and requests him to take the position. After Barry accepts, he passes the steward's pantry with a warning finger wagged in the steward's direction to indicate, "any more of your disgusting habits and you'll get your back flogged!" The first indication in the *Llama* log that something unusual was happening on board the ship occurred when it records: "sawing board logs for sheathing to cabin," on December 14, 1831. Then, on consecutive days, the carpenter is "set to work on berths in steerage," "work in steerage," "making a hatch for steerage." At the end of December, 1831, carpenter was "putting up a bulkhead in steerage" and next day, set to work on "a pantry in steerage."

The date of arrival of William McNeill Jr. suggests he was conceived in January, 1832, so that it is reasonable to deduce that the "marriage" of William and Matilda started at about this time. Matilda did not come aboard alone; her daughter Helen was three years old at the time and Matilda also brought her slave with her. Polite society might have called this slave her personal maid but at that time there was probably little practical difference.

On March 17, the *Llama* anchored outside Clement Cittie and next day warped into the inner harbor. A terse note in the log states: "...this day gave the Steward one dozen lashes for dirty cooking."

On March 28, 1832, the *Llama* came to anchor at Nass. The next day McNeill was visited by some of the Hudson's Bay Company. The *Llama* left Nass in company with the schooner *Cadboro* with Chief Trader P. S. Ogden on board. Perhaps it would be more accurate to say it was dogged by the schooner, since Ogden was making it his business to interfere with the trade of all American vessels. In this he did achieve some success and it was reported from Wrangell that Ogden collected 2,000 beaver, only a small number in competition to the 12,000 collected by the American ships. The two vessels sailed in company for nearly a month before the *Llama* went to Sitka to sell some of their trading goods. The log records his success: "...were visited by some Russians who bought considerable of our cargo." Perhaps there was another reason for going to Sitka in late April, a port that McNeill knew from previous visits. There was a Lutheran Ministry at Sitka and McNeill was a Christian gentleman. His first child was obviously "on the ways" and he may have wanted to take Matilda in Christian marriage.

In May, McNeill returned to Kigarney and off Forresters Island, made contact with Ogden who was on his way to Sitka on board the *Cadboro*. McNeill cruised to various ports, shadowed this time by the *Dryad*, ending up at Tamgass Harbor. *Cadboro* arrived back from Sitka in mid-May and Ogden gave McNeill two letters for delivery to McLoughlin. Did McNeill and his new wife take the sighting of a comet on May 25 as a good omen?

At Tamgass Harbor, McNeill readied the *Llama* for sea and a considerable quantity of goods changed vessels both to and from the *Smyrna* although the major direction was to the *Smyrna*. McNeill had the *Llama* up for sale and needed to transfer as much cargo as possible so that it was not included in the price of the sale. In all, he delivered 279 deerskins, twenty-five bearskins, twenty prime beaver and two casks of furs, probably containing beavers or martens. In return he received food, rigging stores, two six-pound guns and carriages, copper and a boatload of iron. In order to adjust the balance of the *Llama*, he took on a boatload of ballast. Two seamen transferred to the *Smyrna* for passage back to the Sandwich Islands. *Llama* continued to trade for furs, buying thirteen land furs and having natives alongside on a number of occasions. On June 27th the log closes its coastal trade with: "...this day ends 12 hours to commence Sea account."

v of Boston Bridge early nineteenth century.

otter, whose fur was prized by the Boston fur traders.

Photo: David Hancock

Hudson's Bay Company's schooner *Cadboro*.

Medicine chest similar to those carried on Boston brigantines.

Above: Interior of Haida Chief Weha's house (Masset 1884–1888).
Photo: Royal British Columbia Museum PN5324

Right: Kaigani Haida bear carving from Old Kasaan. An important figure in Kaigani Haida mythology.

Left: Indian berry basket similar to the berry basket worn by Peesunt in the Bearmother myth.
Photo: Curtis Collection

Below: Air drying male eulachon fish for candles.
Photo: Field Museum of Natural History, Chicago

Above left: John McLoughlin Sr.,
head of the Columbia Department at
Fort Vancouver.
Photo: British Columbia Archives H-80668

Above: Sir George Simpson, Governor
of the Hudson's Bay Company in
London.
Photo: British Columbia Archives A-02878

Left: John Muir Sr., overseer of the
Scottish miners sent to Fort Rupert to
mine coal.
Photo: British Columbia Archives B-03324

Sir James Douglas, chief trader and chief factor of the Hudson's Bay Company, was
made governor of the colony before becoming the first premier of British Columbia.
Photo: British Columbia Archives A-05698

Left: Governor Richard Blanshard, the first governor of Vancouver Island.
Photo: British Columbia Archives A-01112

Below: Dr. J. S. Helmcken (at left), the first European physician at Fort Rupert.
Photo: British Columbia Archives A-02841

Fort George (Astoria). McNeill first saw Fort George from the brigantine *Owhyee* in 1827.
Photo: British Columbia Archives

McNeill first visited Fort Vancouver on the Columbia River in 1832.
Photo: British Columbia Archives A-04355

Opposite: SS *Beaver*, Hudson's Bay Company ship off Fort Victoria, circa 1846.
Photo: Hudson's Bay Company Archives

Fort Simpson in 1873, painted by Charles Dudward. Fort Simpson was moved from Kincolith o
the Nass River to its present site at Port Simpson in 1835.

Fort Langley. McNeill took the *Llama* up the Fraser River to resupply old Fort Langley in 1833.
Photo: British Columbia Archives

Photo: British Columbia Archives PDP00037

Langley today. An original building showing the mode of construction.   Photo: David Hancock

Above: Hudson's Bay Company's establishment
Fort Rupert, on the northern side of Vancouver Isla
May 6, 1866. *Photo: Hudson's Bay Company Archives, Prov*
Archives of Manitoba P-111 (N6380)

Left and below: The second totem pole at Kwarh:
This pole was carved by Oyai for Matilda McNeill :
memorial to her brother Neeskinwaetk and raise
Angydae on the Nass River.

t: William McNeill Jr.
: British Columbia Archives
?36

w: Matilda Jesse (née
eill) daughter of Captain
H. McNeill between
ecca and Lucy.
: British Columbia Archives
'70

Above: Harriet McNeill.
Photo: British Columbia Archives G07869

Above right: Fanny McNeill.
Photo: British Columbia Archives I-60883

Right: Rebecca McNeill.
Photo: British Columbia Archives G-07866

126

Left:
Helen and George Blenkinsop.
Helen was the daughter of
Chief Sakau'an adopted by
McNeill and she was married
to George Blenkinsop at Fort
Stikine in 1846.
*Photo: British Columbia Archives
G-05201*

SS *Beaver*.

View of McNeill's farm from Gonzales Hill.

OUTLET of COLUMBIA RIVER

Scale

1 2 3 4 5 Miles

Astoria

Clatsop Indians

Chinnook Indians

Grays Bay

High Lands covered with Lofty

Country Low open & marshy interspersed with Pines Thick undergrowth

P.t William of Lewis & Clark

P.t George

Youngs R.

P.t Route of la Perouse P.t Adams of Vancouver

C. Disappointment *in N.Lat. 46°19'*
W.Lon. 46°54' from Wash.n
D.o 123°51 from London
Variation 21°30' E.
The Cape is a circular
knob about 150 f. high

J.Vallance Sc.

P A C I F I C   O C E A N

CHAPTER 7

The Hudson's Bay Company Brigantine *Llama*

I also engaged Captain McNeill to continue in command of her, as his experience on the coast, from cruising thereon for the past 12 years, will give our people an insight into the nature of trade & a knowledge of the Bays, Inlets, Harbours & trading stations of that coast, hitherto unknown to us & which cannot fail to give us a footing & promote our interest in that quarter.
—Duncan Finlayson to James Hargrave, February 1833

The brigantine *Llama* sailed to Kigarney from Tamgass Harbor and came to anchor just long enough to punish William Robinson with a dozen lashes for fighting, the second time in eight days. On July 1, 1832, the log records that the *Llama* sailed to the southwest and that "North Island bore S by E 1/2 E., fifteen miles," from which McNeill took his departure. The voyage to Columbia River took the *Llama* seven days and arrived on July 7, 1832. The following five days of extracts from the log attest to the unique difficulty of crossing the Columbia Bar in a sailing ship:

Light airs from the W.S.W. & thick foggy weather a large ground swell from the Westd Brig standing down the coast for the river at 10 P.M. moderate breezes from N.N.W. sounded in 25 Faths at midnight sounded 55 Faths soft bottom at 8 A.M. thick unsettled weather Cape Disappointment bore E.by.N. 6 miles Brig standing off & on at noon Cape Disappointment bore E.by.N. 8 miles Current setting to the Sd Closes thick cloudy weather.

"Strong breezes from N.W. all sail set standing off & on at (?) P.M. Cape Disappt bore S.E. 10 miles current setting strong to the Sd Middle Part light breezes & cloudy at 4A.M. Cape Disappt

130

bore E.by.S. at 10 A.M. anchored with the Kedge in 16 Faths water sandy bottom the Cape bearing East 5 miles Ends light airs from S.W. & cloudy. Calm with the current setting E.S.E. 2 knots p hour at 1 P.M. a light breeze from S.E. got underweigh & made sail off shore at 8 P.M. the Cape bore E by S.1/2 S. 10 miles Thro the night calm with light airs from all parts of the compass sounded every hour from 35 to 43 Fms sand till 8.30 P.M. current setting us onshore 2 Knots p hour anchored in 14 Faths sand Cape Disappointment bearing S.E. by S. 8 miles Ends with a light breeze from the Sd & cloudy pleasant weather.

Calm & pleasant at 1 P.M. current shifted to N.N.W at 3.30 P.M. got underweigh & stood on a wind to the Westd at 8 P.M. the Cape bore S.E. by.E. tacked to S.E. Middle & Latter Parts light winds from the Sd Brig still working to windward but the current runs so strong that we cannot make but little headway at noon the Cape bore E.by.S. 15 miles.

Midnight fresh breezes from the S.E. with light rain & cloudy weather tacked & stood to the E.N.E. at 2 A.M. tacked to the S.W. at 8 the Cape bore N.E. 15 miles dist at 9.30 crossed the Bar of the Columbia in 4 Faths the Cape bearing N.E. by N. at 10.30 A.M. anchored in Bakers Bay in 3 1/2 Fms water wind being too far to the Ed to proceed further up the River & tailed into 3 Fms hard bottom.

Mr. Birnie visited the *Llama* from Fort George and McNeill moved the *Llama* to anchor near the fort. He discharged four hogsheads of rum, only to find that one of the casks was half run out. Some member of the crew had put two spile holes in the head!

The log of the *Llama* indicates that McNeill initially tried to sail up river to Fort Vancouver from Fort George. He got only as far as Red Bluff before sending the ship back to Fort George. He and his entourage went by canoe up river to Fort Vancouver, a journey of three days.

Matilda stared through the fog toward a shadowy outline of Cape Disappointment. She could make out the bluff and wooded promontory with rolling country extending behind. Matilda looked over the side as the big swell raised and lowered the ship, leaving her belly in space and causing a momentary nausea reminiscent of her morning sickness. Helen hung tightly to the rail, her face turned up to smile and then back to look at the water's surface. Had she ever seen so many birds, their heads bobbing in and out of the rock-weed strewn water searching for krill?

Next morning, before sunrise, Matilda went up on deck, the light raindrops trickled down her oiled hair. McNeill reached to steady her arm against slipping on the slick deck. The Cape loomed closer with the *Llama* riding a moderate breeze and was sucked into the passage by the current. The middle ground sand bank was visible on the starboard beam as they slipped under the Cape into Baker's Bay. Matilda sensed a release of tension in the small crew before all hands were called to the bower and windlass.

Matilda began her trip up the river in late afternoon. The incoming tide, McNeill had told her, would give them a push. Indeed, she found the canoe made good progress under the direction of their stout voyageur, John More, a blue-eyed man whose long hair draped his shoulders. He was dressed in a blue capote, glazed hat and red belt, and he had with him, five Chinook Indians. The monotony of the banks was relieved by small sandy projections that were clothed in stunted trees and bushes of lighter green. A bald eagle, sitting on a tree stump, was no surprise to Helen but the large flocks of water birds still caught her excited attention; "geese and ducks," McNeill named them for her in English. They camped on an outcrop of rock just beyond the beach in late evening and Matilda settled Helen in her blanket.

At 4:00 A.M., Matilda was awoken by McNeill who brought her a cup of "water bewitched," a drink she had taken to on board the *Llama*, then she personally paddled upstream for five hours to the village of Kahelamit for breakfast. The village, of only a few shacks, did not impress Matilda. She could not conceive of such languor as that displayed by the people squatted outside their dwellings.

"No soap!" she exclaimed.

"Not clean," McNeill jerked his thumb at two youngsters who groomed and consumed each other's head lice, "Not Kaigani!"

Their journey took them through some beautiful islets with a channel not more than twenty yards wide, the trees forming an arch above as they glided on the river's surface. A canoe was tied to a tree branch, ashes of the dead in the bow of this sepulchre and she heard the whispering spirits of Neimlush Elihe, "the Place of the Dead."

When they entered the breadth of the river again, Matilda saw the wooded knoll of Oak Point and was greeted by Chief Yugher in the village of the same name. The chief had a droll appearance, with a square pit in the extremity of his nose, large enough for a pea and his front upper jaw lashed down to stumps, but he was a good man, who shared his venison. The second night, as they encamped on a small wooded islet, a blazing fire shone up against a ceiling of mist to disseminate the warm glow back onto Matilda's head. The light of the fire attracted two other canoes. Not until morning did she see the flattened heads of the Natives and their faces bedaubed with brown red pigment that lacked the vermillion shining through her own oiled face.

Matilda arrived for breakfast at Tawallish, a small lodge near where a party of Indians were camped. John greeted Chief Keisno and introduced the Great Chief of the River to McNeill. They too, were on a journey to Fort Vancouver. His men wore blue capotes or overcoats with hoods, providing a military presence. They even stacked their muskets in orderly fashion around the base of a tree.

The last night on the river passed under cloudy skies. Matilda awoke to rain spattering her face, no sunrise to greet them as they repaired to their canoe for the last leg of their journey. She recognized a renewal of enthusiasm in the paddlers, eager to get to the dry warmth of the fort. At last, the wharf was in sight, the road up to the stockades was visible and Matilda landed with Helen clinging to her, like a bear cub to a tree, scared and shivering at the unfamiliarity.

Dr. McLoughlin greeted Captain McNeill, his wife and daughter soon after their arrival and arranged accommodation for them. Matilda and Helen were taken under Marguerite McLoughlin's care, and leaving the men to breakfast alone, took their meal in the woman's dining hall, albeit from the same cookhouse.

The meeting of the men later at dinner was cordial and the food substantial. Soup was followed by a course of fish, ample bread made from their own milled wheat, and a main course of meat from the farm as well as vegetables and soft fruit from the kitchen garden.

Ogden had sent two letters to McLoughlin for delivery by McNeill. The first was a letter of introduction and recommendation, the second reviewed the coastal situation at Fort Simpson and his success fur trading from the *Cadboro* in opposition to the American coastal ships.

In October, McLoughlin replied to those letters thanking Ogden for his two favors. He congratulated Ogden on his very fair returns. He then explains: "Previous to Capt McNeil's arrival, say on 27th June, Mr Duncan Finlayson sailed on board the Eagle with a cargo of timber to Woahoo, to purchase a vessel if he found one to suit our purpose, & in consequence of this I would enter into no arrangement with Captain McNeil."

However, McNeill impressed McLoughlin at this social "interview" enough to give McNeill two letters for Finlayson to take to Oahu. The first letter informed Finlayson that McNeill had offered to sell his ship for $6,500. Finlayson was instructed to buy her but not to pay more than $5,000 if he had not already made a purchase. The second long letter opens: "As I have addressed you an open letter by Captain McNeil I will now only say that if you purchase the 'Lama' I think you ought to endeavour to get McNeil for the coast as he is well acquainted with the business."

McLoughlin relayed some of Ogden's other opinions that suggested Captain McNeill's first mate, Ephraim Hanson, be employed because he was a sober, steady man, well acquainted with the coast, and although illiterate, would answer well as second officer. McLoughlin told Finlayson that he disagreed with Ogden, arguing that if the first mate was good enough for McNeill he was good enough for them! However, these statements do not make sense since Mr. Hanson took over the log from Mr. Selman and neither one was illiterate. Ogden may have thought mistakenly that Bernard Barry was first mate. McNeill left Fort Vancouver promptly to return to the *Llama* at Fort George to hurry along the preparation for the voyage to the Sandwich Islands. On July 28, 1832, McNeill crossed over to Baker's Bay to await a favorable tide and weather that would allow him to cross the Columbia River bar. On August 1 he took his departure from Cape Disappointment and arrived in the outer harbor of Oahu in eighteen days. Upon arrival, Finlayson and Captain Kipling went aboard to examine the *Llama* for its condition and suitability for purchase.

McLoughlin writes to George Simpson on September 12, 1832, from Fort Vancouver:

On July 15th Capt McNeill of the Lama came here. He passed the Winter on the coast, where he was by himself. He said he collected, 4000 Beaver, 100 Sea Otters 1200 Martens and 300 Bear

Skins. He seems well satisfied with his returns, & the object of his visit was to sell his Brig, which he offered for 6,500 dollars; but as Mr Finlayson might have purchased a Vessel, of course I could not enter into a bargain with Capt McNeil; at the same time I told him we could not think of giving more than 5000 dollars, & from what he said I am of opinion he would have taken that price. He left this for Woahoo...

On Wednesday August 29, 1832, the log concludes: "Comes in clear pleasant weather at 11 am fire 3 salutes of seven guns ea & were answered by the brig Ivanhoe hald down the American colours & hoisted the English Middle light breezes & fine pleasant weather Ends light light variable airs & calm So Ends the Voyage."

The *Llama* was sold to the Hudson's Bay Company and returned to the Columbia River. The new Hudson's Bay Company brigantine *Llama*, under Captain McNeill, arrived at Fort George on 14 October 1832, to serve as a trading and supply vessel. McNeill set about preparing his ship for trading fur for the Company, but not before Matilda McNeill had presented him with a son, William Donald McNeill Jr.

Chief Factor Ogden was stationed at Fort Simpson at this time and was as determined as McLoughlin to rid the coast of American opposition. He ordered McNeill to dog the American vessels and outbid them for furs. Ogden supported McLoughlin's long-range plan for a chain of forts to trade with the Indians. In 1834, he sailed to the Stikine river to survey a site for a fort along the river. There, the Stikine chiefs made it clear that they did not want a fort along the river and Captain Zarembo ordered them out of Russian territory.

During 1833, the *Llama* was also used to transport supplies to and from Fort Langley. In the summer McNeill assisted in building both the new forts at Nisqually and Millbanke Sound.

An overland route from Fort Vancouver to Puget Sound used the Cowlitz River, then a portage to the Puyallop River that entered Puget's Sound near Nisqually Flats. The land in the area was deemed suitable for a farming center and the shore for an accessible shipping center. The Columbia River Bar, in spite of a new chart of the area, was still a hazard to shipping, not only because of the danger of shipwreck, but also for long delays in Baker's Bay waiting for the breakers over the bar to subside, a wait of up to two weeks. Millbanke Sound was chosen for a fort site because it was a center for the Bella Bella tribes and would attract furs from the numerous Indian villages of Dean Channel, Burke Channel and North and South Bentinck Arms. The wide entrance into the sound, relatively free of drying rocks, made it navigationally less hazardous than other passages into the archipelago of this rock-strewn coast.

In his correspondence, McLoughlin reasoned that forts were less expensive than vessels, were impressive to the Indians, and, as a result of his own experiences with ship's officers and crews, were easier to man. Beyond these forts, he was planning to extend this string of posts north, with forts at Stikine River and at Taco in Taku Inlet. Both of these were designed to intercept furs from New Caledonia before they reached the Russians. McNeill, in his first year, impressed McLoughlin with his energy and keenly justified McLoughlin's employment of the American officers as illustrated in McLoughlin's letter to Simpson on 12 March 1834: "I can give no proper proof of the propriety of the measure than that the opposition seeing us so decided on carrying on trade with vigour gave up the contest and Capt McNeill in the Lama collected one third of the furs traded on the coast, and he would have traded more but that he fell short of goods. I am sorry to see their honours disapprove of our purchase and of our engaging Captn McNeill and his two mates the fact is these men only fill the station of others and over and above are qualified to act as traders Pilots into the different harbours."

In his second year, 1834, McNeill took the spring outfit to Fort Langley. Intelligence received at Fort Vancouver told of a vessel wrecked at Cape Flattery and, because of a letter in Chinese characters delivered by the Indians, McLoughlin assumed it was from the Orient. He sent an overland party to try to rescue the crew from the Makah Indians, but they were unable to reach their destination. McLoughlin directed his ships to look into Neah Bay and try to rescue any survivors.

McNeill put into Neah Bay on his way to Fort Langley, and ascertained that the Makah Indians were holding three Japanese seamen. He invited a chief and his party aboard to trade furs and immediately took them as hostages against the release of the seamen. The three Japanese sailors were the only survivors of a fourteen-man crew. The vessel, a Japanese junk, had been on a voyage from Yahourage to Yiddo, then the capital of Japan, when a typhoon had driven them off course, unshipped their rudder, and in the process, broke their rudder irons. In spite of adequate supplies of rice and water, all but three of the crew died of sickness prior to the ship being wrecked.

The sailors were sent to England and in McLoughlin's words: "…that they might observe and report the grandeur and power of the British nation." He was also: "…in the hopes that this action might open communication with the Japanese Government."

McLoughlin, and particularly Duncan Finlayson, had been under censure by the governor and committee in London for purchasing the American brigantine *Llama* and even more so for hiring American officers to command a British vessel. Under British maritime law only a British subject could command a British vessel. However, by October, 1834, the governor and committee accepted McLoughlin's reason for his precipitate action and withdrew all censure against Finlayson who had, they now understood, acted under McLoughlin's orders. They were still concerned with getting rid of the American officers as soon as their contracts expired.

Chief Trader John Work went aboard the *Llama* on a voyage to Millbanke Sound that he recorded in his diary kept between December 11, 1834, and October 27, 1835. Born in Ireland, he joined the Company in 1814, was promoted to chief trader in 1830 and chief factor in 1857. He was described by Sir George Simpson as: "…a queer looking fellow of Clownish manner and address, nevertheless he is a shrewd sensible man."

They left from Fort George after the new year and Work expressed surprise at how long it took to prepare the *Llama* for sea. Then they were held up in Baker's Bay waiting for the westerly gale to blow itself out. John Work went on shore with the mate, Mr. Scarborough, to observe the state of the breakers over the Columbia Bar, and assessed that it would take many days for the sea to settle enough to let them over the bar. Two days later the *Llama* crossed the bar and headed north before a good southeast wind, making 160 miles in twenty-four hours. Eight days later they were standing off and on in Millbanke Sound. Dr. Tolmie reported the presence of the *Llama* in his diary and that he took a canoe with an Indian crew to meet the *Llama*. However, as they neared the ship, a blinding snow storm made the ship turn out to sea and Tolmie turned back to shore to camp on a gravelly beach. At the time, he was a prudish man of twenty-two years and writes that he: "…passed a most uncomfortable night under inverted canoe, where red man and Whites were all promiscuously huddled as closely as herrings in a cask!"

When McNeill eventually came to anchor off Fort McLoughlin, Manson sent a canoe to invite him to dinner at the fort. McNeill found the establishment in good order and nearly finished. The land around the stockades was cleared up to a hundred yards all around to give good sightings for defense and also to allow for a garden to be planted in the spring.

The chatter over dinner included the matter of John Work's failure that morning in trying to get the men to re-engage at the fort. They all wanted to return home from this damp and dreary spot! They objected to their diet that was 80 percent salmon bought from the Indians, for they did not like the way it was cured. Even the fresh salmon taken in the river was of poor quality and they discussed the possibility of netting the salmon earlier next year. McNeill knew Manson from before, but this was his first meeting with Dr. Tolmie whom he found to be religious, well educated, a little too fastidious for his liking and annoying with his use of Latin medical jargon when he recounted the story of the Indian attack. A party of men had gone outside the stockade to collect water and wood when they were rushed by the Indians, caught in, "their calls of nature," or as Dr. Tolmie put it, "sacrificing to the Goddess Cloacina." McNeill preferred the straight talk of "caught with their pants down!" No doubt about it, the doctor was a bit of a prig!

From Fort McLoughlin, they continued their journey north to the new Fort Simpson (Port Simpson). Here the stockades were completed, the Indian shop open but the men's houses were only partly finished. John Work stayed on board the *Llama* when the ship left for its trading voyage and he was glad to give Chief Eligigh's son passage to Kigarney so that he might deliver a message of peace to the Kaigani Haida. As always, the interests of the Company were uppermost in deciding to give this assistance. Peace among the Indians would bring a greater concentration on collecting furs, as well as fresh provisions, for trade.

John Work saw at first hand the difficulty of getting the Indians to part with their furs early in the season in case the American competition arrived and drove the prices up. His diary gives a good account of many of the problems: uncharted rocks, rigging repairs, crew discontent, lack of fresh provisions and possibility of Indian attack, that McNeill needed to overcome during his trading voyages into the various harbors. During a slow period of trading, Work learned of the Haida treachery at Rose Spit where the schooner *Vancouver* went aground and broke up on shore the previous year. Her captain abandoned her because he was outnumbered by the Indians on shore. The *Vancouver* was plundered by the Haida. During this voyage, Work discovered that there were only eight Indians on shore and that they had lit fires along the beach to give the illusion of a great force.

Three American ships appeared on the coast to compete for furs: *Bolivar Liberator*, with Captain Dominis at the helm; *Convoy* under Captain Bancroft; and *Europa*, commanded by Captain Allan. It was the *Europa* that needed to be dogged since it had the advantage of superior blankets set against the *Llama*'s better rum and tobacco! This competitive trading reached a climax on May 17, 1835, at Nass Old Fort. Captain Allan came aboard the *Llama* to inquire of the prices being given for beaver pelts. When McNeill told him, Captain Allan "…got into a violent passion & declared he would do his utmost to rise the price." He then turned to the Indians and said he would give four gallons of rum and eight heads of tobacco with one large blanket per beaver. The Indians cheered at this news and left the *Llama* for the *Europa* only to be encouraged back by a counter offer of five gallons of mixed rum, ten heads of tobacco with a blanket per beaver! Captain Allan left Nass, and McNeill followed him into Portland Inlet knowing that any unsold furs would be traded at Fort Simpson. All in all, quite a grudge match developed between the two captains.

As the two ships beat out of Portland Inlet they came together in a minor collision that carried away *Llama*'s martingale and board netting chains with minor damage to the *Europa*. At the time of this incident the *Europa* was on a larboard tack and, as McNeill pointed out to Work, Captain Allan was under an obligation to give way to the *Llama* on the starboard tack. In July, McNeill returned to Fort Simpson and John Work stayed at the fort while McNeill continued to dog the opposition in all the harbors. He had orders from Work to return by September 1 to load aboard the returns for the year. The year was successful for the *Llama* was loaded with 144 sea otter furs and 3,500 other furs, not including 1,000 rabbit skins.

The *Llama* left Fort Simpson on September 8 with John Work on board. They left Fort McLoughlin on September 13 and sailed on the west side of Vancouver Island (then known as Vancouver's Island) to anchor in Neah Bay on 20 September. They entered Juan de Fuca Strait next day and took passage up Rosario Strait to anchor at Point Roberts on 25 September. Here, John Work took the longboat up river and by land to Fort Langley hoping to be able to have Indian canoes loaded with the 1835 returns and brought to the *Llama*. However, damage to the longboat forced Work to send it back and order the *Llama* to sail up the river. The ship arrived on October 2, loaded and returned to Puget Sound where John Work took the overland route to Fort Vancouver and the *Llama* continued on to the Columbia River where McLoughlin sent a canoe to order it up the river to the fort. So ended this ten-month trading voyage.

In 1836, McNeill made his last trading voyage in the *Llama* and for five months from April the fur trade log shows that he visited, often several times, Kigarney, Nass Old Fort, Clement City, Cossack Harbour, Seal Harbour, (Calamity Bay) McLoughlin's Bay, Millbanke Sound, Actives Cove (Kyumpt Harbour) and Nahwitti and in total purchased 1,574 furs.

A new era was ushered in with the arrival of the SS *Beaver* at Columbia River on March 19, 1836, under the command of Captain Home. This steam vessel was built by Green, Wigram and Green at Blackwall Yards. She was 100 feet long and 20 feet wide, a paddle steamer and powered by two 35-horsepower Boulton and Wall steam engines. For the voyage out, the steamer was rigged to sail out round the Horn with its paddles stowed on board. It took three months to convert the *Beaver* to a steamer before it left on June 18 on her maiden voyage on the coast, with Duncan Finlayson on board. She had a long and distinguished career until 1888 when she went aground under Prospect Point. If Dr. John McLoughlin was the first to suggest a steamer for the Columbia department, he later became adamantly opposed to it and considered it to be uneconomic, compared to the forts.

Finlayson reported back to McLoughlin in a letter dated 26 September 1836. He said of the returns at Fort Simpson that in spite of American and Russian opposition, they were double the previous year. He graded the tribes contribution in the following way: "The Pearl Harbour and Skeenah Indian called the Chimmesyan tribe, The

140

An observatory telescope of the kind that Captain Vancouver used on land for the accurate measurement of latitude.

Nass, The Stikine, Tongass, Sebassa, and the Queen Charlotte Island tribes: and it is now confidently expected that the Kygarnie Indians who have commenced to negotiate a treaty of peace with the natives of this place will, if it be concluded, occasionally trade here."

Of the returns of the *Llama*, he stated they were lower, due to the task imposed on McNeill of watching closely the American opposition of *Peabody*, under Captain Moore and *Lagrange*, under Captain Snow: "Having from his intimate knowledge of the harbours, and trading stations on the coast, on many occasions given them the slip and secured all the skins before their appearance at such harbours, and when they happened to be together the Llama generally collected the best share of what ever was to be gleaned."

On the maiden voyage of the SS *Beaver*, Finlayson examined the coal deposits on the east side of Vancouver Island. The mine was situated about latitude 50°30' north and longitude 126°35' west and he reports to McLoughlin: "The mine appears to stretch along the beach for some distance and where the sea washed against the bank

141

we could perceive that there was a considerable deposit of Sandstone over it."

He described the deposit at Suquash Creek and concludes: "I do not think a mine can be built without building an Establishment at it, there being a very populous village of Quaquill Indians, consisting of 50 to 60 houses within 2 1/2 miles of it. The mine, without the protection of a Fort would be useless to us."

When Finlayson visited Sitka on board the *Beaver* during the summer and before the new governor had arrived, he ran into the same problem with Captain Zarembo that Ogden had encountered with this Captain at Stikine in 1834. In spite of Zarembo's warning to Finlayson not to use the inland waterway, the *Beaver* did as it pleased and navigated through Cross Sound into Clarence Strait.

Finlayson disembarked from the *Beaver* in late August at Fort Simpson and set sail in the *Llama* for Sitka on September 4, 1836. This time the meeting with the newly arrived governor, Baron Wrangell, was cordial and he received apologies for the inconvenience that he had been put to by his officials. This was the beginning of negotiations that, in 1840, James Douglas was to finalize and Sir George Simpson was to seal in 1841.

McNeill, in the *Llama*, returned to Fort Simpson and then to Fort Vancouver on the last voyage that he was to take in this small brigantine. Captain Brotchie sailed the *Llama* to Oahu where she was sold to Captain John Bancroft for $5,000 on behalf of Eliah Grimes in Honolulu, for sea otter hunting off the coast of California. Captain Bancroft's endeavor in the *Llama* was short-lived. In late 1838 he took the *Llama* to Kigarney where twenty-five Kaigani Haida hunters were hired to go to California. He sailed down the coast with his hunters, canoes and provisions of fish and oil.

There was trouble from the outset. On the one hand, there was a captain addicted to drinking and harsh treatment, with his amorous Kanaka wife, harboring strong racial antagonism toward the wild Kaigani hunters and on the other hand, quarrelsome Indian hunters who liked to work where and when they pleased, who were incensed by the slim rations handed out to them as a matter of discipline when the hunt was unsuccessful. All of this was bound to cause friction.

Back in Oahu, the second mate, J. Molteno reports to Eliah Grimes:

...at 11.00 a.m. they were all on board, and Captain Bancroft began to find fault with them, and they came to very high words, all in N.W. language so that we could not understand what was said. At last it appeared to be all settled, and the Captain went down to dinner, all the Indians remaining on the forecastle talking together. When he came up the row began again, and by what we could understand, very bad language passed between them. On a sudden the Indians began to pass their muskets up out of their canoes and had got them nearly all up before any notice was taken of it. Capt B saw it, he told Mr Robinson not to let any more come up, and he stopped them. Captain then went on the forecastle amongst them, but Yeltenow now shoved him away, and he ran off and jumped up on the rail, saying something which was supposed to be, "fire if you dare," for they immediately fired, and he fell down in the waist. Trying to protect her husband, Mrs Bancroft was seriously wounded and he was killed. One of the white crew was shot in the head. Armed with boarding pikes and knives, the Indians took command of the arms chest and they forced Mr Robinson to return them to Kigarney where the hunters disembarked on 26th December 1838.

East side of Vancouver Island from Captain George Vancouver's map, 1793.

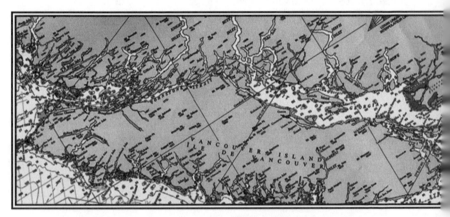

East side of Vancouver Island from Canadian Hydrographic Service
chart L/C-3000, 1994.

CHAPTER 8

Fighting With Property

The Steamer's Crew and Engineers recently mutinied and refused
to serve under Capt McNeill, (who is the most active serviceable
Capt ever we had on the coast, notwithstanding he is a Yankie).
—John Work to James Hargrave, 1837

Hladerh is a fine carver from the village of Gitiks on the Nass
River and a friend from youth of Chief Sakau'an of the Double
Eagle and Chief of the Salmon Eaters. He sees Chief Sispagut taunt
his friend and Chief Sakau'an leave in anger. He follows him along
the path up to the high cliffs that overlook the river. He feels his
friend's dejection at Chief Sispagut's inquiry about his wife and
daughter's desertion for a white-face tribesman. Sakau'an's bravado
at first counters all the jibes of his enemies, but recently the people
of his village lower their eyes as their chief passes them and even
his own kin are silent on the subject of his shame. Hladerh, his
friend, is one of a few who know just how deep are his wounds.

Sakau'an stops ahead of Hladerh, turns to his left and teeters on
the edge of the cliff with the river too many feet below. He raises his
head to call on the spirit of the Double Eagle to give him courage.
Hladerh quickens his pace and his stealth allows him within an arms
reach before Sakau'an feels his presence. In that quick glance
Hladerh sees the tears course down Sakau'an's cheeks. His friend's
face shows not sadness or melancholy, but anger, deep and bitter
and hunger for revenge. Hladerh, still uncertain of his friend's intentions, puts his hand on Sakua'an's shoulder, and applies pressure to
ease him back from the edge.

"Come," Hladerh insists and guides him to a rock seat, "you
must disgrace her, not punish yourself."

"A ridicule carving?" Sakau'an asks wiping his cheeks, as he considers raising a totem pole to degrade his former wife.

"No, a great feast, a new song and a present for your flighty one!"

"Stop sending shrowton to Cogwealth?" Sakau'an suggests. This breaking of a treaty would be seen as an act of aggression.

"War, you mean!" Hladerh expresses surprise that he would go to war and deprive himself of the trade.

"If he challenges me," Sakau'an narrows his eyes in a bitter-faced sneer, "and kill McNeill!"

In the spring Hladerh carves the Double Eagle on the cedar bent box that will contain the twelve pure white ermine skins, those with the black spots on their tails to make them exceptional. He carves the eagle's talons striking deep into the snarling wolf's head and that pleases Sakau'an. This spring the little fish arrive in greater abundance than ever before to fill the cedar boxes for trade and for the gifts sent out with the invitations for a Great Potlatch Feast. Those invitations arrive at Skedans, Cumshewa, Kiusta, Masset, Cape Fox, Stikine, Tongas, Sebassa's and all the Nass River villages save one; no invitation to the neighboring village of Gitradeen, home of the Wolf-Bearmother phratry of the Raven Clan for 'she' is chief in common with her brother Neeskinwaetk. All their people will hear, but not participate!

As the days grow shorter and shorter, the anticipation rises to fever pitch, Hladerh is certain that Sakau'an will triumph. The canoes arrive, from Cape Fox and Tongas, across the water from all the Haida villages, but not one Kaigani Haida is welcomed. Each chief, greeted with long speeches of welcome, answered with longer orations of the honor bestowed. The people of Gitradeen lie low in the face of such power and prepare for their defense against possible armed retribution.

On the day of the Great Feast, Sakau'an hands out his gifts to all his people and his guests. Then he accepts the talking stick to tell the audience the story of his tribe's creation. The climax of this feast is approaching, Hladerh feels it from the crowd as once more the drums beat and Sakau'an's voice in a low haunting register gives the first verse of the song he composed for his friend.

> Wait and see what a chief can do!
> Wait, O Sweetheart, that you may learn how,
> After my humiliation because of you,
> I have again raised my head.

Sakau'an pushes his chin forward in a gesture of defiance for this august assembly and above his eagle nose, his brow of scorn.

> Wait, O flighty one,
> Before you send me word
> Of how you have failed
> In your foolish escapade
> And pine once more for my love!

Sakau'an's hands beat his chest in time with the drums to accentuate her foolish fancy for so inferior a being from the whiteface tribe and he spits on the ground.

> Time is now ripe, O woman,
> Who would rather belong to the whiteface tribe,
> For you to send me a bottle of old Tom.
> For my part I dispatch to you
> This small handful of mere beaver skins!

Percussive words staccato from Sakau'an's mouth before he holds the twelve white ermine skins high above his head for all to see the perfection of his gift and he hears, then grins at the scornful laughter from his people who understand, raise their heads and look him in the eye to restore their chief's dignity and pride, for he has truly disgraced his wife forever; there will be war!

147

Matilda received the gift from Sakau'an, accepted the skins as an insult to disgrace her in the eyes of her people at Gitradeen. She must fight him or lose all her credibility. She raised enough blankets and other goods to pay her brother Neeskinwaetk, the great carver, to carve a huge trading canoe for her answering gift.

Neeskinwaetk went into the forest to select the great red cedar for his purpose, shaped its high prowed form and dug out the center of this forty-foot vessel. It took a labor of nearly two years to make this gift fully answer Matilda's troubled pride and return her stature.

Matilda wanted Wolf on the prow, with snarling teeth and piercing eyes of disdain to reflect her fury. Rising up out the bottom forward section was the back of Bearmother as if a sleeping giant and two Ravens one on each side to represent the sun and moon that always rise again!

Matilda traveled north on board the *Llama* to arrange for the delivery of her gift to Sakau'an in the fall of 1836. She was pleased to return to her land and looked forward to a visit with her people at the village of Gitradeen. This was the first time she had seen the trading canoe that Neeskinwaetk had carved. Its realism and beauty made her regret that it was going to that miserable chief!

This great trading canoe was delivered to Sakau'an, paddled into Pearl Harbor by the men and women of Gitradeen. Chief Tsebassa, true friend of Neeskinwaetk, and his villagers swept alongside the canoe to give added protection to the renegade gifters. After her people had delivered it, Matilda's honor was restored, she could hold her head up high and accept their renewed loyalty.

Matilda stayed the summer at Fort Simpson, her growing family, two sons and two daughters, around her. Helen was eight years old and in line to be hereditary chief of the Wolf-Bearmother phratry. Helen must stay at the village to learn the ways of her people and Neeskinwaetk's family took her in to educate her. In the fall of 1837, the whole family returned south in SS *Beaver*. Mr. and Mrs. Manson were on board with her, returning to Fort Vancouver in October, 1837.

Donald Manson was most unwell and was sent to recover under Dr. McLoughlin's care. Mrs. Manson and Matilda kept company on the voyage to Nahwitti, where that old roue, chief of the Kwakiutl came on board for passage to McNeill Harbor after his visit to Chief Nancy of the Nahwitti tribe.

The old chief, ardent in the chase of the fair sex, demanded of McNeill that he take payment in furs for his intended pleasure from Matilda. She flattered him, teased him with innuendo, but she would have none of it so he turned his attention on Mrs. Manson, much to the amusement of the two women. Such prowess declined! He did not understand the wiles of these two women, who made him return his attention to his new young wife.

കൃ

The SS *Beaver* wintered at Fort Simpson in early 1837 and when it left on 10 March 1837, it was under the command of Captain McNeill.

McNeill started his trading voyage at Old Fort Nass and then proceeded down the coast. He spent four months trading for furs and with the steamer was able to add a number of new trading harbors southeast of Nahwitti at Beaver Harbor, Nimkish River and McNeill Harbor, all inhabited by Kwakiutl tribes. By the time he returned to Fort Simpson he had on board 2,346 pelts. During the time spent trading, the six axmen aboard went to shore to cut wood for the steamer's boilers. It took the axmen two days to cut that wood and the steamer one day to use it and go ninety miles, limiting the vessel to thirty miles a day.

In early September, McNeill received orders from Chief Factor James Douglas to survey the east coast of Vancouver Island for possible sites for a new fort that would move the Columbia department further north and out of possible United States territory. In London, closer to diplomatic rumor and influence, the governor and committee were aware that the Columbia River at best would be the new border and the forty-ninth parallel may well be the preferred settlement of the dispute. Vancouver Island was undisputed British territory and chosen for the new center.

McNeill started his survey at Nahwitti and worked his way down the Johnstone Strait and into the Gulf of Georgia. He commented on the forbidding nature of the geography that continued all the way down the coast until he reached the south end of the Island. He reported to Douglas that there were three good harbors west of Point Gonzales and that at two of them he had passed a few days.

The land around the harbors was covered with wood to the extent of half a mile. In the interior, the forest was replaced by a more open and beautifully diversified country presenting a succession of plains with groves of oaks and pine trees for a distance of fifteen to twenty miles. Two of the harbors he referred to were Camosoon and Esquimalt and he suggested that the former was preferable. McNeill called in at Fort Nisqually to send his report and then steamed north. On December 10 he was in McNeill Harbor and the Fort Simpson Journal entry for December 22, 1837, notes: "At 1 P.M. the Steamer Beaver Capn McNeill arrived last from Fort McLoughlin. She left Nisqually on the.... and touched at Fort Langley and Fort McLoughlin and stopped at the different trading stations in Queen Charlotte's Sound. The York Express was very late arriving this season and occasioned their detention at Fort Vancouver much longer than was expected."

The York Express was the overland communication with York Factory that left Fort Vancouver in the spring and returned to Fort Vancouver in the fall.

On the trip up north from Fort Nisqually, McNeill continued to trade and collected furs in addition to the 2,346 purchased during the summer and fall. He had over a thousand assorted furs including 343 beaver pelts that were collected in Queen Charlotte Sound.

Christmas was celebrated at Fort Simpson by both officers and servants, who were allowed extra rations and a pint of rum and enjoyed themselves. They had a few fights by way of enlivening the scene but did each other little mischief except a few black eyes and scratched faces.

In the new year, the Fort Simpson journal comments that: "30 Beaver and 30 Martens traded from the Indians who arrived yesterday and the day before. A considerable number of the above furs were traded for rum. It seems that Sebassa and his people are invited to a grand feast by the Chimsyans and that the liquor is wanted for the occasion."

The *Beaver* was under repair during the first two weeks of 1838. One of the main beams over the boiler was found to be rotten more than halfway through, and John Work was in no doubt that it was so when it was put in. He thought that this was a gross piece of knavery on the part of the builders. To repair this beam the crew had to remove stores and cargo from the steamer and raise some of the decking in order to get at it. A new beam had to be cut and squared before it was installed above the boilers. The *Beaver*'s paddles were damaged by driftwood. (This may come as a surprise to those who think that driftwood is a modern problem due to our logging practices.) To repair them, Work supplied two men to saw wood for the paddle blades: "...since none of her own people could saw such wide 19 inches straight planks."

On Sunday 14 January 1838, Captain McNeill was taken very ill with a violent griping and vomiting. The journal reports next day that Captain McNeill still continues very bad. No one else was reported sick before or after this time. The next day he was still very ill and it was three more days before the journal recorded that Captain McNeill was getting better but slowly. Although pure conjecture, it is valid to ask whether this was this an attempt on his life.

The next day Tsebassa and his brother arrived from Pearl Harbor with a party after attending a great feast given by the Tsimshians. It was to a feast such as this that Matilda sent the trading canoe in answer to Sakau'an's ridicule present and potlatch feast. The date of delivery of the trading canoe is uncertain, although it was known that Matilda was in Fort Simpson 1836 to 1837. A few days later the journal reports: "A canoe of Tongas Indians and two canoes of Chatseeny people & tribe of Kygarney Indians also arrived. These latter never were here before we have not learned what quantity of furs they have with them."

The village of Chatsina at Chucknahoo is where Chief Cogwealth lived.

In June, 1837, McNeill had given in his resignation to McLoughlin. He wished to return to his home in Boston to put some family affairs in order. It was a year before he received news of the Company's offer to make him a chief trader.

In the dispatch from the governor and committee of the Hudson's Bay Company to McLoughlin of November 15, 1837, paragraph two states: "Captain McNeil has been so useful and conducted himself so well while in the service that we should feel disposed to make our approbation of his conduct by promoting him to the rank of a Chief Trader in the concern if the difficulty of being a Citizen of the United States could be overcome by his coming a British subject this you will be pleased to communicate to that

Gentleman and if willing to change his allegiance an early oppertunity will be taken of enabling him to do so."

Even before McLoughlin received this dispatch, he had written to Chief Trader Work in November, 1837, that: "As Captain McNeill is not a British born subject… if he falls in with an English Cruiser while in command of the Steamer it would expose her to seizure; you will please make out the Papers in the name of Mr Scarborough, for which his pay will be raised to Eighty Pounds p. annum from 1st June 37, and perfectly understood, that command is still with Captain McNeill, and on falling in with any British Cruiser, Mr Scarborough may step forward, and declare himself Master, and be fully justified in Calling upon the Crew to defend the Company's property, and resist seizure."

This letter, which traveled with McNeill to Fort Simpson and Work, following his instructions, apprised Mr. Scarborough of his appointment. At the end of January, McNeill was busy getting the *Beaver* ready for sea when the fort journal records the start of the mutiny: "Capt McNeill had some of the Seamen employed drawing off rum to send aboard in small casks, the blagguards took advantage of his turning his back a moment and two of them Wm. Wilson & J. Starling made themselves drunk. As a punishment the Captain told them that their grog would be stopped for a month. When ordered repeatedly to go off aboard they would not go like all drunken sailors had a great deal to say on different matters till finally they provoked the Capt so far that he gave the pair of them a good caning, they brought it on themselves for they had been repeatedly told quietly to be off aboard and would not go."

The next day, January 29, 1838, the journal continues its description of events: "Captain McNeill ordered the Steamers people to carry wood down to the waters edge to be ready to take on board tomorrow and sent an order to Mr Arthur to send the stokers to assist. They refused on the plea of it not being their duty but two of them J. McLennan and R. Slacum on the impropriety of their conduct being pointed out, eventually went, but the other two Wm Gullion and D. McDonald persisted in refusing Capt McNeill tied them up and gave each 2 dozen lashes for disobedience of orders after which they said they would go tomorrow."

The following extract from the Fort Simpson journal, kept by John Work, is reproduced with all events not pertaining to the mutiny edited out to allow for a continual narrative:

In the morning the sailors sent me a letter signed by Mr Burns the Steward, George Gordon, Wm Wilson, Wm Philips, Wm Gray, Thos Locky and James Starling Seamen, stating the illegality of having a Foreigner commanding a British vessel and enclosed what they called Abstract of an act of Parliament to that effect, and pointing out that the vessel was liable to seizure. They requested a reply as their further steps would be regulated by it. I have sent them none, I have sent them no reply, as considering that the vessel being subject to seizure that they have nothing to do with it. The whole drift of their letter is requesting to be placed under the commander who is a British subject, in short to have Capt McNeill unshipped.

30th Jan 1838. A note came ashore this morning from Mr Scarboro to Capt McNeill that the seamen who sent me the letter yesterday and the stokers had refused duty. At the same time a letter came to me signed by the mutinous Sailors and Stokers repeating their request of yesterday to be placed under a British Captain and urging the legality of their demand and pointing out the law on the subject. I replied to it and the one sent yesterday that I was aware of the laws that the Articles which they signed did not state who was to be their Captain but that they were bound to obey him. And that as to the liability of this vessel it was our business and no affair of their's; And that when they knew the laws so well how come they to overlook that relative to mutiny, and commanded them to return to their duty on their peril or stand by the consequences, And finally that their request would not be granted. To this I received a reply nearly in the same strain as the other two letters and urging the legality of their claim and requesting an interview with me on board. At the same time a note came to me signed by the Engineers stating that they could not go on with their duty under Capt McNeill.

After this I went aboard accompanied by Mr Manson, ordered the men aft where the whole seven man by man absolutely refused to sail under Capt McNeill. The Engineers persisted in adhering to the purport of their note that they could not continue their duty under Capt McNeill but would not say that they would not do it. So the matter rests. The Engineers are our only difficulty. We could soon manage the rest but when the Engineers refuse the vessel is at a stand still.

31st Jan 1838. I sent a note to the Engineers directing them to come ashore which they did, and on being questioned still persisted in what they had stated in their note that they could not go on with their duty under Captain McNeill's command and held forth a great many arguments in support of what they said. After they went aboard I sent another note directing them to send me an explicit reply in writing whether they would work the engines under Captain McNeill's orders provided the Stokers were made to do their duty or others put in their place and to give me an explicit answer yes or no; to which they returned each a note stating that after they seriously considered the matter they would no more work the Engines under Capt McNeill's command, but offered no pleas like the sailors as to his not being a British Subject.

It was now clear that there is a complete combination among the whole gang not to serve under Captain McNeill. We think ourselves strong enough to put the whole of them in irons though bloodshed might be the consequence of the attempt, but by so doing the vessel would be stopped for, there is no knowing how long, and as it is essential to have communication with Fort Vancouver before the express starts we determined that the only step we could take to effect that object was for me to go and take the command of the vessel and Capt McNeill to accompany me as passenger to Nisqually and thence to Fort Vancouver where it would be determined what further steps to take I accordingly went on board accompanied by Mr Manson and stated to the people that they were now to consider me as their commander and ordered them to resume their duty which they said they were ready to do, I at the same time told them that they would have to answer for their conduct, this they said they were aware of and that they have weighed all the consequences.

It is mortifying in the extreme to have to yield thus far to these mutinous scoundrels. But when the Engineers are also in the fold (though they disclaim having any connection with the men,) we have no other alternative but at the almost certainty of losing the use of the vessel where perhaps an opposition may come on and have everything their own way without her, and all the trouble and expense we have been at in getting rid of them have been incurred to no purpose. By this arrangement of taking the command myself should any danger occur I will be sure of Capt McNeill's assistance so that there is little danger of any accident happening. I might have given the command to Mr Scarboro the first Officer but there are circumstances which render doing so not advisable at present. Of the whole crew Mr Scarboro the mate,

Peter Duncan the carpenter, Jake McIntire the cook and six lands-men wood cutters remained neutral or at least did not join openly in the affair, Much credit is due to the Carpenter and the Cook and they ought to be remembered for it.

Chief Trader John Work took command of the steamer and left Fort Simpson on 5 February 1838. The *Beaver* arrived at Fort Nisqually in late February. Work, McNeill with the chief engineer, Mr. Arthur, went by the Cowlitz route to Fort Vancouver, arriving in early March, where McLoughlin appointed Chief Trader James Douglas to head an inquiry into the mutiny.

The report of McNeill's impetuous loss of temper, leading to the use of his cane, albeit provoked by the two intoxicated seamen, and the flogging of the two recalcitrant stokers was not expected to be well received by the governor and committee in London. William Brown, who left Fort Langley without taking his Indian wife and child and refused the order to return to Fort Langley to bring them out, was flogged over the cannon at Fort Vancouver for disobedi-ence of the command. On arrival in England he wrote a letter of complaint to the governor and committee in London. In their dis-patch of November, 1837, they observed that: "...we have to impress on your mind that we cannot sanction violence or the infliction of Corporal Punishment on any of our Servants."

Douglas accepted Work's version of events, determined that McNeill must be reappointed and issued a severe reprimand to Mr. Arthur. The chief engineer agreed to serve under McNeill again. Mr Work and his party returned to Nisqually, boarded the *Beaver* and informed the crew that McNeill was reinstated as captain. All the crew, save Wilson, Starling, Burris and Gordon, signed back on board the steamer and agreed to the authority of Captain McNeill. Those four who still refused, were sent to Fort Vancouver, put in irons for a day by Douglas before being sent to outposts as prison-ers at large. When the barque *Columbia* arrived, the seamen were sent home to face legal action in England.

⟨≈⌐⟩

Chief Sakau'an of Gitiks was once more on the horns of a dilemma. His former wife, by sending such a significant gift, had regained her stature in the eyes of her people in the village of Gitradeen. The women of his own people were starting to doubt his virility with the

155

fair sex. To counter Matilda's gift he set about collecting blankets and goods for another potlatch to disgrace her name and restore his own within the village of Gitiks. Once more at the height of the ceremonies he sung a song to his people that was composed to regain his honor.

> Hush, stop your idle chatter!
> Why do you gossip about me?
> Why do you point your finger at me?
> I speak to you, Women of the Salmon-Weirs!
> Hush stop your idle chatter!
>
> Why do you single me out as the only black sheep?
> For this alone I must admit I'm lost?
> Oh stop your idle chatter!
> I speak to you Women of the Place of Scalps!
> Hush stop your idle chatter!
>
> You waste your breath over my love affairs.
> Why should I mind you when my heart pines away?
> I have not seen my young sweet heart for one moon,
> The hutsinee beauty who has made a Christian of me!
> Hush stop your idle chatter!
>
> Why do you mind my private affairs?
> Hush stop your idle chatter!

Chief Sakau'an sent no property as a gift to Matilda, but news of his largesse at this potlatch reached Matilda and obligated her to respond or lose face.

◦৯৽

The November 15 dispatch, offering McNeill promotion to Chief Trader, reached Douglas in June, 1838, and when he reported back to the governor and committee on 18th October 1838, he was able to tell them that McNeill accepted their offer. Indeed, McNeill accepted the offer with alacrity and set about taking the *Beaver* on the annual fur trading with renewed enthusiasm. Douglas also reported to the governor and committee that Captain McNeill found time to visit "Butes, Knight and Rivers Canals, the two former in Johnstone Strait and the latter in Queen Charlotte Sound." McNeill reported their desolate appearance as consisting of almost unbroken chains of rocky precipitate mountains, whose loftiest snow-capped summits fed innumerable streams of water that rush over their declivities into the quiet strait beneath. Douglas observed that the geography indicated a country unfavorable for the resort of beaver. There were, however, rivers at the heads of these inlets that promised to contain a population of beavers. He also states: "Not a single Indian was found in Butes Canal, the population having been destroyed by the murderous "You-cul-taws", who are deservedly the terror of the surrounding tribes."

The fur returns were excellent for the season with 5,645 furs collected: 72 sea otter and 35 tails, over 2,000 mink, over 1,000 marten and 937 beaver skins. The steamer's boilers were nearing the end of their usefulness and new ones were ordered. However, the engines were running with the same ease and power as when first set in motion. At the end of August, McNeill took the *Beaver* up both Gardner and Douglas Canals to trade with the Kete-mart and Kit-loope tribes at the heads of the canals, where he obtained forty large beaver pelts and other skins in proportion.

The good returns of sea otter pelts in 1839 resulted in part from a visit to Fort Simpson of the Kaigani hunters who highjacked the *Llama* and killed Captain Bancroft. That these Kaigani were the hunters was confirmed by Matilda's sister who visited Fort Simpson at the same time. On arrival at Kigarney, these hunters took their California sea otter skins for sale at Fort Simpson. In the journal, John Work writes: "...from the way these skins were come by, I regret seeing them come here and traded them with reluctance. But what can we do if we don't take them, not only them but all the other furs the whole tribe might have would be taken by our opponents, the Russians, not only this year, but probably years to come." Such comment brings an image of the Irish Catholic, John Work, kneeling at his bedside in prayer, "We know, Oh God, that it is a sin, but really we cannot afford not to do it!"

The year 1840 presented the *Beaver* with a change of pace. On April 26 at Nisqually, James Douglas with a party of thirty-three men, went on board. Their purpose was to take over Fort Stikine on Wrangell Island and build Fort Taco after Douglas had negotiated the lease of the Alaska panhandle with the new governor at Sitka. They visited Fort Langley to assist Mr. Yale in erecting the bastions for the new fort. They traded in the Johnstone Strait from May 9–11 and visited Fort McLoughlin and Fort Simpson before proceeding to Sitka. They arrived at Fort Stikine on May 31 to take over the fort. They left William Glen Rae in charge with John McLoughlin Jr., his assistant.

While at Fort Stikine, the first mate, William Heath, got into a fracas with James Douglas over whom should give him his orders. Already Douglas had contravened the ship's rules by ordering the men to bring wood aboard after 6:00 P.M. The next day, a Sunday, with Captain McNeill on shore until night, he organized prayers between one and two o'clock. After the service he ordered the men to take in wood. According to ship's etiquette both orders upset the first mate.

Next morning, McNeill was sulky and informed Douglas in an agitated tone that he would leave the steamer at Fort Simpson if he interfered again with the duties of the ship.

"In what instance, sir, have I interfered with the ship's duties?" Douglas asked.

"In ways which I cannot exactly remember, but still you have done so," McNeill replied weakly, intimidated by his senior's direct approach.

"You would oblige me, sir, by more explicit information, it was never my intention to do anything on board this ship to diminish the respect due to you, however in my ignorance of naval routine I may have inadvertently trespassed on some point of etiquette that I wish you to point out, in order to avoid it in the future."

"Why the mate an hour ago inquired of me, whose orders am I to obey, yours or Mr. Douglas!" McNeill blurted back.

"Aye, call him," Douglas said with agitation.

When the mate arrived and Douglas explained the situation, he asked: "Mr Heath, why did you put such a question to the captain?"

"Because, sir, you gave me several orders yesterday when the captain was on shore; you told me to furl and unfurl the awning and to send the men for wood."

"Did I ever tell you, sir, to disobey the captain's orders?"

"No, sir, well sir, you have acted very improperly in a manner more becoming an inmate of the forecastle than a gentleman and officer."

"I have supported you, sir," Douglas' irritation from this insult rising to anger, "against the wishes of others when no one would have you, perhaps to the prejudice of more deserving men."

"Well, Captain McNeill, I refuse duty, sir!"

With this pert remark, Mr. Heath turned on his heel and left the cabin. Douglas, more incensed than ever, hurried after him onto the deck and shouted after him, "Get back to the cabin, sir!"

Since the mate agreed only reluctantly, Douglas seized him by the jacket collar.

"You lay violent hands on me," Mr. Heath hissed.

Shocked by his action, Douglas immediately let go and the mate followed him back to the cabin. Back in the privacy of the cabin, Douglas made it clear to the captain and the mate that he was their superior in all ways and would be obeyed. He then turned to the mate and hauled him over the coals to sign off with a statement only Douglas could have devised, "and truly in the person at the head of affairs, who bears the weight of responsibility and whose mind is on the rack devising ways and means to expedite our over backward operations, methinks such trifles, light as air, are like feathers in the balance."

The *Beaver* went north up to Taco Inlet to establish and build Fort Taco (also spelt Tacow or Taku, the fort's official name was Fort Durham). This operation took until August before the steamer was able to head south again. At the new fort, Douglas left Dr. John Kennedy with twenty-two men under his charge. During the building of the fort, McNeill explored Lynn Canal in the steamer in order to invite the Chilkat of Chuckanuck and Tlingit of Hood's Bay to trade at this new post.

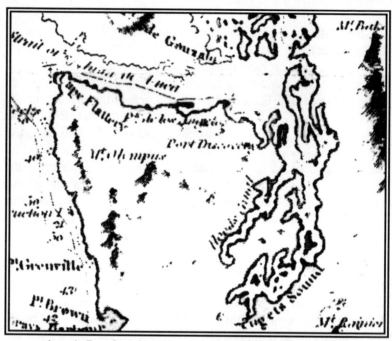

Juan de Fuca Strait from Captain George Vancouver's map, 1793.

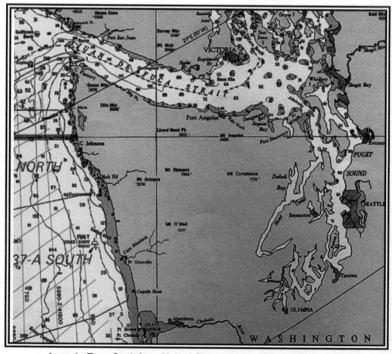

Juan de Fuca Strait from United States marine chart 16016, 1993.

CHAPTER 9

Citizenship

At Fort McLoughlin, when the ladies fair come to blows as they always do when drunk, and sometimes when sober, each pounces on her antagonist's lower lip as at once being the most vulnerable region, and furnishing the best hold.

—Sir George Simpson, *Voyage Round the World,* 1841

In late 1839, the governor and committee sent confirmation of Captain McNeill's promotion to Chief Trader, which prompted him to write his first private letter to George Simpson.

Hon'ble H.B.Co's Steamer Beaver
Frasers River Dec 25th 1840.

My Dear Sir.

With much joy I received your respected and kind favor from London of Decr 30th 1839, you will suppose Sir it was not the less acceptable to me now on your informing that I had been pro-moted to a Chief Trader in the concern and was much flattered by your observing that my promotion had arrisen by merit. I have to thank you Sir for complying with the wishes of my friends for friends I must have or I should not have been recommended to your kind notice. I came among you an entire stranger you have taken me by the hand and brought me forward, this act of itself shows your kindness, if you think my actions and services merit it I assure you I feel most grateful to you and those who recom-mended me.

I hope Sir that you will never regret the confidence placed in me and sincerely wish that my knowledge of the coast and ships may be of service to all concerned, at all events you may rely upon my remaining true to my word. You mention that you intend paying us a visit next year in the Columbia, I have heard also that

161

you will visit all the Forts on the coast, of course you will honour me with your company on board the Beaver for I still command her, you will meet with a hearty welcome it will gratify me much to become personally acquainted with you. I start tomorrow for the North touching at all the posts to collect the 2000 otters that is to be sold to the Russians. I have now on board the 3000 otters from the East side and a beautiful lot they are and in fine order, also 2000 more from Vancouver that is intended to pay the rent for our newly acquired territory. In my opinion Forts Taco and Stikine will turn out very well so far as regards Fur, I should say the two posts will have 3000 Beaver and otter per year at least, also Foxes, Martens, Lynx & many fine Black Bear. Provisions at Taco will be scarce at times, however while lying there last summer as guard ship I traded from five to fifteen Deer a day but at other times for a week we obtained nothing fresh. Stikine is our, if not the best place for provisions on the coast it abounds in fine fat Deer and excellent Salmon. The Indians here are numerous and very turbulent and will give much trouble if not closely watched. Fort Taco lies Lat 59°4' N and is in the immediate neighbourhood of the Glaciers I got in among the floating ice last summer with the Bark Vancouver in tow and broke a number of our paddle Blades I should think the cold would be severe there in Winter. I should think Potatoes would thrive there in summer as the soil is good, and a few acres can be cleared of trees in course of time.

We were most kindly treated by the Russians last summer on visiting Sitka and Stikine they were very obliging and offered to assist in anything. We visited Cross Sound & Lynns Canal last August and invited the Indians to Taco with their Fur many Sea Otter will be obtained from the Sound and Beaver from the Canal.

If a Fort is built at Newitty which I understand is in contemplation it will I think turn out more Beaver and Sea Otter than any one post on the coast I should say 3000 Beaver & otter and 100 Sea Otter and many small Fur. Hiqua could be obtained here cheap and in sufficient quantity to supply the whole country, in fact this is the place where they are obtained. A Fort at this place should be strongly built and well manned as the tribes who visit here are numerous and daring I have had 2000 round the Steamer at one time and mostly armed.

I gave Mr Work a census of nearly twenty thousand souls that inhabit the inland canals and Vancouver's Island and these are people which would visit the Fort, as we shall visit these places forward on our route to Sitka you can see for yourself and I shall be happy to give all the information in my power.

I am sorry to inform you that our Boilers are getting the worse for wear they are giving way fast and have been patched in many places new Boilers have been ordered for us but in my opinion if the Beaver could be disposed of or converted into a Sailing vessel the best plan would be to procure a Steamer of 600 tons as the beaver carrys no cargo, a large Steamer would do away with keeping a ship in the country, the yearly vessels from London could take a cargo of plank &c to Oahu and be back in time to take the Fur home. The Steamer could take all the Outfit to the coast in the spring and would be at leisure to go to the Islands or California and on her return go to the coast for the Fur in the fall, I merely hint these things to you but you can judge best how to determine when you are on the spot.

Arthur and Donald have gone home in the Vancouver, Mr Carless and wife are on board and seem well contented he appears to know his business well and seems interested and everything is going on well and quietly on board.

> I remain my Dear Sir
> mo resply Your Obt Sert
> W.H.McNeill.

In 1834, Mr William Kittson, a clerk in the Hudson's Bay Company, was appointed officer in charge of Fort Nisqually from the time of its inception. In 1840, he became too ill to work and he was replaced by Captain McNeill who was put in charge of marine affairs while still master of the SS *Beaver* and A. C. Anderson in charge of the farming center. A letter from the Russian governor, Adolpe Etoline, on 15 February 1841, acknowledged the receipt of the 2,000 otter skins from Captain McNeill, "a bord du vaisseau-a-vapeur Beaver," the rent for Fort Stikine, and other articles delivered according to their agreement, which included a supply of butter.

McNeill left Sitka on February 20, arrived to trade at Nahwitti on March 4 and took passage for Nisqually. He was at Fort Vancouver and as McLoughlin reported in his May 24, 1841 letter to the governor and committee, was instructed to re-examine the boilers of the steamer and report back.

McNeill wrote to McLoughlin on May 2, 1841: "Mr Carless says he can be ready by June 15th if the *Cadboro* arrives here in time with the white Lead which he must have to make the joints Steam worthy, In that case I can proceed with the Steamer and secure the Northern Fur, and be back here again in twenty days at most."

McNeill was obviously concerned about the boilers and in this letter to McLoughlin warns that: "Possibly the Boilers will take us to Sitika and back again to this place after performing the trading voyage, but will not be answerable for what may happen, after arriving here from the Quacolts, we will still have two months to overhaul and paint the Engine, and finish many other jobs before Govr Simpson and yourself will be ready to proceed to Sitika, I think we can risk to make both before mentioned trips, but no human knowledge can foretell, the consequence."

A week later McNeill sends a second letter to McLoughlin: "Since I wrote you, nothing of importance has occurred as concerns the Company's affairs the repairs of the Beaver are going on well as our means admit, The last patch was finished the 8 Inst, one on the bottom of the flue, it is the first time we have discovered any flaw in the bottom of the Boilers or Flues."

McLoughlin instructed McNeill to do the best he could with his repairs and assisted him by relieving him of all trading responsibility by sending the schooner *Cadboro* to the coast for the season. McLoughlin favored the use of forts rather than ships in the conduct of the fur trade. He developed a particular dislike of the *Beaver* because he felt it was too expensive and unreliable. His opinion was not shared by other officers on the coast. A. C. Anderson at this time writes privately to Simpson: "...it is, I know, become quite general to decry the merits of that valuable craft, and her utility in the past affairs of the coast; but, with deference to the judgment of others, my own partial experience induced me to conclude that it is the Steamer, chiefly, that we are indebted for the recent absence of competition in that direction."

The Charles Wilkes expedition was surveying Puget Sound for the U.S. government during this time and Wilkes' diary records several meetings with McNeill and Anderson. McNeill sent Mr. Heath to pilot Wilkes' vessel, Peacock, into Puget Sound. Mr. William Heath was first mate of the *Beaver* and his brother, Joseph, was an agronomist at Nisqually. Wilkes was not the first to get the Heath brothers muddled as indicated when his diary shows some concern as to an agronomist being sent to pilot his vessel. When he was first introduced to McNeill and Anderson he writes: "They took tea with me and appear desirous of affording us all assistance in their power, at least such was their offer, a few days will show the extent of it."

When McNeill wrote about progress with the repairs to the steamer he mentioned that he was giving all assistance he could to Charles Wilkes. Later, Wilkes acknowledged the help that both McNeill and Anderson had cordially given to himself and his officers by inviting them to a party at which an ox was roasted, a cooking process that started on the evening of July 4, although the meat was not ready to eat until the next afternoon! Wilkes also honored both men by naming the two islands south of Nisqually Flats after them.

The repairs to the SS *Beaver* were not made without difficulty and McNeill, in his letters to McLoughlin, tells of their anxiety over moving the six-ton boilers. The steamer, however, was ready for Sir George Simpson and his party by the end of August, 1841. Sir George had been knighted by the Queen before leaving London.

The *Beaver* left Fort Nisqually on 6 September, with James Douglas, Mr. and Mrs. Rowand and Sir George Simpson on board and Point Roberts was their first destination. They anchored there for the woodcutters to go ashore and Sir George gave his opinion in his diary describing "Fraser's River as being of little or no use to England as a channel of communication with the interior." In 1829, he had come down this river by canoe from Fort Kamloops and knew of the difficulties encountered.

Their next port of call was Beware Bay (Blubber Bay) at the north end of Fevada (now Texada) Island. Sir George described the bay as a snug little harbor, and noted that Captain McNeill preferred halting there on account of the superiority of the fuel, which was both close grained and resinous. On the route from Beware Bay to Port Neville, Sir George said that Natives from the three villages of "Comoucs" opposite Cape Mudge, came off in their canoes to visit the *Beaver*. He writes:

> The Ladies, who obviously appreciated their own beauty, attempted by a liberal display of their charms, and every winning way

that they could devise to obtain permission to come on board. We did allow a chief of the Quakeolths to embark, along with his wife and child, as he was desirous of obtaining passage to his village, about seventy miles distant, while his canoe, a pretty little craft of about 12 paddles, was taken in tow. This was not this grandee's first trip in the Beaver. On one former occasion, he had made love to the Captain's wife, who was accompanying her husband; and, when he found her obdurate he transferred his attentions to Mrs Manson, who happened to be on board along with her husband, he gravely backed his application by offering a bundle of furs. On the present occasion, also, this ardent admirer of the fair sex was true to his system, for he took a great fancy to an English woman on board, while, at the same time, with more generosity than justice, he recommended his own Princess, not to the woman's husband, but to myself."

Sir George referred to this chief as "this Lothario!" They arrived at his Indian village in McNeill Harbor and discharged their passenger before putting up their boarding nettings in readiness for trading. McNeill allowed just half a dozen Natives on board at any one time. Sir George's diary gives a graphic description of his manner of trade:

Stationing himself at the steerage hatchway Captain McNeill threw down each skin, as he examined it, with its price chalked on it, the equivalents being handed up from below by 2 or 3 men that were in charge of the store. The natives, now that they no longer dare employ force against the whites, still occasionally resort to fraud, practicing every trick and devise to cheat their trader. One favourite artifice is to stretch tails of land otters into those of Sea Otters. Again, when a skin is rejected as being insufficient in size, or defective in quality, it is immediately, according to circumstances, enlarged or coloured or pressed to order, and is then submitted, as a virgin article, to the buyer's criticism by a different customer. In short, these artists of the Northwest could dye a horse with any jockey in the civilised world, or "freshen-up" a faded sole with the most ingenious and unscrupulous of fishmongers. As he has neither mayor or alderman to invoke in such cases, Captain McNeill dispenses summary justice on his own account, commissioning his Boatswain to take the law, and the rope's end as its emblem into his own hand.

While anchored in Beaver Harbor, Sir George comments further:

Generally speaking, the natives were tiresome in their bargaining, and they were ever ready to suspend business for a moment in order to enjoy a passing joke. They appeared, however, to understand the precise length to which they might go in teasing Captain McNeill. They made sad work, by and by, of his name; for, whenever his head showed itself above the bulwarks young and old, male and female, vociferated from every canoe, Ma-ta-hell, Ma-ta-hell, Ma-ta-hell, a word which, with comparative indistinctness of its first syllable, sounded very like a request that their trader might go a great way beyond the engineer's furnace.

In Shushartie Bay, one of the axemen's capotes was stolen and McNeill managed to grab a chief's ax and with possession nine parts of the law, held onto it against the return of the capote. The young chief, whose name was Looking-glass, immediately informed against Chief Nancy as the real culprit and when McNeill refused to return his ax, he went into a long harangue in Chinook jargon. In his diary, Sir George Simpson records verbatim a translation from Chinook jargon of the chief's speech:

The white men are pitiful, since they have stolen my axe. My axe must have been very good indeed, otherwise the ship would not have stolen it. If an Indian steals anything, he is ashamed and hides his face; but the great ship-chief Matahell steals my axe and is not ashamed, but stands there scolding and laughing at me, whom he has robbed. It is good to be a white chief, because he can steal, and, at the same time, show his face. If he was not strong with a large ship and long guns, he would not be so brave. I am weak now, but I may be strong by and by, and then perhaps I will take payment for my axe. But it is very good to be a white chief in a large ship with big guns; he can steal from a poor Indian who is here alone in his canoe, with his wife and child, and no big guns to protect him.

His speech was pronounced with provoking coolness, supported by the disdaining blank look of his spouse. Simpson ends with: "…to detain his axe was impossible after so rich a treat!"

The rest of the voyage to Sitka was uneventful, calling at Forts McLoughlin and Simpson. Over dinner at Fort Simpson, Sir George sought out opinions about the coastal trade from John Work, James Douglas, Captain McNeill and others around the table and found considerable agreement with his proposed change of emphasis from forts to shipping in carrying on the coastal trade. The die was cast during these weeks of travel, much to McLoughlin's chagrin in the years ahead.

On November 25, 1841, Simpson, in his letter to the governor and committee from Fort Vancouver after he returned from Sitka and Fort Simpson, writes:

> The trade of the coast, cannot with any hope of making it a profitable business, afford maintenance of so many establishments as are now occupied for its protection, together with the shipping required for its transport, nor does it appear to me that such is necessary, as I am of opinion that the establishments of Fort McLoughlin, Stikine & Tacow, might be abandoned without any injury to the trade, and that the establishment of Fort Simpson alone, with the Beaver steamer, will answer every necessary & useful purpose, in watching and collecting the trade of the whole of that line of the Coast, the transport of supplies and returns to be accomplished in one trip of a sailing vessel from Fort Vancouver to Fort Simpson. Under this arrangement, the steamer would be constantly employed, in visiting the principal trading stations between the Quakeolth village in about Lat 50°30', to the Northward of Johnston's Straits & Cape Spencer, the Northern entrance of Cross Sound.

Simpson went on to estimate a saving of £4,000 a year, stressed the importance of the steamer and records: "...would strongly recommend (notwithstanding a difference of opinion on this subject with Gentlemen, for whose opinion I have very high regard) that another steamer should be provided with as little delay as possible."

Simpson was referring to McLoughlin, for whom the proposal was tantamount to blasphemy!

Simpson was also proposing the removal of the major trading center at Fort Vancouver out of the Columbia to Puget Sound or Juan de Fuca Strait, a proposal McLoughlin had fought against since 1837. All this apart from the rising antagonism between them over Simpson handling of the inquiry into the murder of John McLoughlin, Jr. at Fort Stikine. This meeting, more than any other, decided Sir George that the northern forts should be closed and a new one built at Nahwitti and the *Beaver* provided with a barge to carry supplies. Two years later, Douglas writes to Simpson: "The opinion I gave in reference to the change in measures on the coast, I have at all times firmly supported, but it is certain that some of the parties present when the question was discussed at Fort Simpson, have since embraced views at variance with those they professed."

McNeill, however, remained in agreement with Sir George and James Douglas. At Sitka, the barque *Cowlitz* awaited the arrival of Sir George and took charge of their honored guest for the voyage to Russia. Before they set sail for Kamchatka, the *Cowlitz* was towed by the Russian steamer to Fort Stikine where the silence of their greeting gave Sir George a foreboding—a feeling not misplaced when they saw the flags at half mast and discovered that John McLoughlin, Jr. had been murdered by one of the servants. Simpson writes: "I placed the establishment under charge of Mr Dodd, chief mate of the Cowlitz, a young man in whom I had much confidence, giving him as an assistant, one Blenkinsop, who, though merely a common sailor, was of regular habits, and possessed a good education."

Sir George's cursory investigation and poorly supported conclusions of the cause and perpetrators of this murder were to blemish his relations with John McLoughlin Sr. for the rest of his life. The murder, and his change in policy without any consultation with McLoughlin over the question of the forts, would prejudice all their correspondence in the future.

McLoughlin was furious with Sir George Simpson for his conclusion that implied that his son, John, was as much responsible for his own murder as the perpetrators of it. He appointed Douglas to head an inquiry into the murder. Douglas, with McNeill and the Rev. Jason Lee, convened the inquiry at Fort Nisqually. New depositions from the servants at Fort Stikine contradicted those on which Sir George had based his conclusions. Douglas, no doubt, hoped that his inquiry would put an end to McLoughlin's single-minded quest. However, that was a forlorn hope as McLoughlin continued his endless dispute with Sir George on both the murder and the proposed closure of Forts McLoughlin, Stikine and Taco until 1848.

In 1841, Sir George Simpson wrote a letter to McNeill offering him passage on the *Cowlitz* as supercargo to London, which prompted the following reply:

Fort Nisqually
4th Decr 1841

Honord Sir.

I received your two kind communications of 24th Inst and
return my sincere thanks for the kind, and prompt manner you
have taken in complying with my requests to visit Boston, I shall
ever feel under many obligations to you for the interest you have
taken in my welfare. Had I ten days more time or had my family
been at Fort Vancouver or Simpson it would have given me much
pleasure to have accepted of your offer and taken the Columbia
Home, and as the Columbia has been for somedays at the Cape I
might not arrive there in time to relieve Capt Humphrys of the
command, I think it best to remain untill next year, and take the
Cowlitz home as you have been pleased to grant me that favour.
If I should leave my family at only one days notice I am fearful
of the consequences, the old Wife being a stranger in this part of
the world. Be assured Sir nothing would afford me greater pleasure than seeing you in England or America and relate our pleasures and troubles, during the voyage to the North on board the
Beaver. I must mention again Sir that I never was more vexed
than I was the whole of that voyage to be so completely knocked
over the entire trip.

As to the flattering way you have been pleased to value my
humble services which in the country, you may suppose I feel not
a little proud coming from such a source and as I have said before
you have only to command, and your own and all my superiors
orders shall be executed, I did not come among you to give or
make trouble. I should have been pleased to acertain concerning
my interest in the concern the year you were pleased to give me a
commission but am satisfied that all is as it should be. I am building Mrs Carless a House on the side of the Hill abreast the
Steamer a delightful situation she has not been very well for some
time and thinks a turn on shore will do her good it will answer
famously when we commence putting the Boilers in which by the
way will not be for a long time and I do not know what I shall do
to kill time. You tell me to write you fully on all occations, and
take advantage of it to mention that C.T. McLoughlin told me
after I had obtained my Commission I should have to overlook all
the Shipping in the country, so far from that being the case I
scarcely have the control of my own, neither do I wish it, but I
want you Sir and all the Gentlemen both at home and in the country to understand the matter perfectly. I presume I know the reason why my opinion is not asked concerning the Ships, if it was,

no one should be concerned that I should take advantage of it as I wish to be generally useful on Sea or Land.

I hope you will not be detained long at the Cape as it is very tedious and lonesome. Wishing you every enjoyment, success and pleasant voyage.

I remain, my Dear Sir
To Sir George Simpson Yr mo Obt Hum Sert
WHMcNeill

From this letter, McNeill makes it clear that his wife did not want to stay at Nisqually while he was absent. The family was closest to Fort Vancouver and Matilda spent part of her time there. She and the family were taken up to Fort Simpson on the *Cowlitz* after McNeill's return. At some point, Mrs. McNeill and Mrs. Work had a falling-out, and there was also another reason for Matilda to spend time at Fort Simpson before or after McNeill sailed for England. Matilda's brother, Neeskinwaetk had died and she wanted to raise a memorial totem to him at her village of Angydae on the Nass River. She employed the great Nishga carver Oyai, to carve this monument to her brother and planned to give a great potlatch feast at the village at its raising. That would once more establish her esteem and put down her former husband.

This totem pole, identified in Marius Barbeau's *Totem Poles* as the second pole of Kwarhsuh, starts with a figure atop the pole who sits on the head of the "Grizzly of winter or snow." This bear is sitting erect with a smaller part-human figure in front of the bear's abdomen. The bear's feet rest on the "People of the Smoke Hole," three part-human figures standing in a circle. They, in turn, are standing on the head of Bearmother who also has a part-human bear cub in her lap.

In 1929, Lazarus Moody, who was seventy years old at the time, told Barbeau that it was a very old pole when he was a boy. Barbeau purchased this pole for the Canadian National railways when under the presidency of Sir Henry Thornton who in turn presented it to the French. It now resides in the Musee de l'Homme in Paris. The magnificence of Oyai's work can be seen at the Royal Ontario Museum in Toronto, where Chief Sakau'an's totem pole is confined in the stairwell. To place it in the confinement of a stairwell was "a good idea at the time!" Unfortunately, you cannot really see it to admire it. It surely needs the beautiful treatment of those lesser carvings in the Museum of Man in Hull, Quebec.

The raising of her pole at Angydae was the last act in Matilda's fight with property that she waged with Chief Sakau'an from the time she left him to marry Captain McNeill in 1831.

McNeill stayed at Fort Nisqually until November, 1842. Sir George arranged for the barque *Cowlitz* to be commanded by first mate Heath with McNeill as supercargo, in name only, as with Scarborough on the *Beaver*. McNeill's journal of this passage in the *Cowlitz* exists in a small notebook he kept during the voyage. The *Cowlitz* left the Columbia river on November 18, 1842, and arrived at the Sandwich Islands nineteen days out. The ship stayed just one day before continuing on its voyage to London. McNeill notes: "...found a lad, 'Peter Copp' stowed himself on board." On December 26 they passed Christmas Island, and in the New Year he: "...spoke a missionary, off Aitutaki and went ashore on Rarotonga."

The rounding of the Horn was uneventful and the only event of note for the rest of the voyage, was the loss, overboard, of Seaman Tubb in the English Channel. McNeill arrived 152 days out from Oahu at Gravesend and stayed in London. His notebook recorded Captain Brotchie's address as if he intended to stay there. His stay was brief, as he had been granted a one year furlough to visit Boston.

McNeill's attempt to change his citizenship back to that of his forebears was not a success. He arrived in London and visited both Archibald Barclay and Sir John Pelly at Norway House, the headquarters of the Hudson's Bay Company. On June 1, 1843, Archibald Barclay writes in his letter to to Sir George Simpson: "I have had frequent interviews with McNeill who seems a sharp intelligent fellow and well acquainted with matters of all kinds on the NW coast. He goes on a visit to his family in Boston but is to be back in time to take out the Cowlitz."

McNeill called on Sir John Pelly, who was governor of the Company at that time. Sir John distinctly told him that he was to be appointed the superintendent of marine in the Columbia department. The next dispatch from the governor clearly ordered this position for him. McNeill saw him a second time when Sir John asked him to cut short his furlough and return to London in time to take the *Cowlitz* back to the Columbia via Sitka. Once more he showed his willingness to put aside his own affairs in preference of the Company's and once more the Company made him supercargo in name and captain in fact. McNeill, even though he failed to gain the purpose of his visit, obviously enjoyed London immensely, although he was disappointed that he did not get to meet Lady Simpson. As he took his departure from the English Channel he writes in the journal that he kept of the voyage: "Saturday 14 October. At 8 Start light bore E by N 1/2 N dist 14 miles from which I take my departure being the last we shall see of old England for many years. I will at this time remark that I never enjoyed myself in any part of the world so much as I have in England, and never saw Women I loved better than the full bosomed daughters of England, they are Noble, Generous and Free — God bless them."

What draws a sailor back onto the deserted oceans, or into the womb of cabin or forecastle? There is a sense of grandeur and freedom for a sailor as he moves away from the troubles of society on land. For the landsman, the sea holds many terrors, but for the sailor there is no terror, just tranquillity of a calm and excitement of the challenge of a storm. What then of William Henry McNeill, what drew him to the sea? At the front of the journal that he kept on the voyage, he wrote out this poem as representative of his feelings for the ocean.

Alone with God upon the boundless sea,
No spot of earth in view, no sombre cloud,
The glittering stars and gentle move to shroud,
On rides the Bark in calm tranquillity.
Quiet the autumn breeze, while in the lee
The billows past without a sign of life
Silent the mighty ocean vast and free
Seeming to herald some portentous strife
Alone with God! how unlimited the power
Of man the creature here to shield or save
For few the bounds that part the yawning grave:
Most awful thought at this most solemn hour
Alone with God! alone to worship him
Before whose throne all worldly thoughts grow dim.
W.B.*

*Possibly William C. Bryant

Although this journal is not like a ship's log and reads more like a diary, McNeill complained in it that the ship steered very badly:

"...owing, I think to her being 4 inches by the head but she will be better as we near the Horn as all the water and salt provisions will be used from the fore storeroom."

He also recorded the inevitable case of the venereal that routinely occurred following a ship leaving port.

Two events disturbed McNeill early in the passage. The potatoes were found to be rotting and they all had to be picked through, a tedious process that took two days. They threw out all the rotten ones, losing a quarter of their supply as a result. He then found that the water tanks in the magazin had not been properly secured and that the deck above had never been caulked.

After crossing the equator, McNeill put the boatswain in the second officer's watch to: "...assist in the Ship duty, the 2nd Officer not being competent to have charge of the watch in night during the boisterous weather we may soon expect."

When the starboard watch refused to obey the boatswain, McNeill persuaded them back to work by threatening them with transfer to a man o'war at Valparaiso! Their passage around the Horn lived up to its reputation: "Noon, Cape Horn bore by compass N by W 45 miles we are now in the same position as last night at 8, of course we have had a N.E. current and are but six hours run from where we was 13 days since."

The death of Mr. Carrick, the second officer, who threw himself overboard, came as a surprise to McNeill even though he knew he was not a competent fellow. McNeill in his captain's cabin, was kept isolated from the crew and did not realise that Mr. Carrick suffered from depression and had an alcohol problem until it was too late. Investigation revealed:

> Mr Carrick 2nd Officer threw himself overboard. The whale boat was lowered immediately, the ship hove too with all Stud'g Sails set but unhappily without effect as the boat returned without seeing the body. The deceased had been to work in the lazarrett and by evidence of the Carpenter, Boatswain & Birch apptce it appears that he had been drinking spirits gave some to the Carpenter who was very intoxicated and offered some to Seaman Bigmore. There is also every reason to believe that the deceased had not been in a sound state of mind since leaving England.

Sunday 4th February. This day Leonard Birch told me that Mr Carrick was in the habit of drinking spirits every time that he went to the Lazarrett, and that he had seen him take a half pint mug at one time of pure spirits.

A few days later McNeill sold the effects of the late Mr. Carrick to the crew for the benefit of his poor mother. Young Leonard Birch was a midshipman and McNeill approved of this sober young man. Apart from this tragedy, there were only minor disciplinary problems on the long, nonstop voyage to Sitka. He avoided a stop at Juan Fernandes, sending a boat ashore for knees to repair the longboat. On 24 March 1844 he records their arrival at Sitka and this remarkable fact: "I shall make the remark that we came from Cape Horn and sighted Edgecombe without making one tack which may never be done again, 159 days from the Channel of England and were 162 days to an anchor at Sitka."

CHAPTER 10

Fort Stikine

To any other being less qualified the vapid monotony of an inland
trading Post, would be perfectly insufferable, while habit makes it
familiar to us, softened as it is by many tender ties, which find a
way to the heart.
                                    —James Douglas to James Hargrave, 1842

From the time that McNeill was posted to Fort Stikine in 1844 to
the abandonment of the fort in 1849, he wrote six private letters
to Sir George Simpson, from which this picture of his family and
life at Fort Stikine is drawn. The private letters from all the chief
traders and chief factors had a real influence on the policies that
Simpson presented to the governor and committee. Today, the
weather in Wrangell records annual precipitation of 105 inches and
in no month does it rain less than fifteen days in the month. If living in this isolated post on an island, close to the mouth of the
Stikine River with its climate of inclement rainy weather was a challenge, it was preceded by a nightmare of getting transport to the
place! After arriving from London at Sitka, McNeill continued to
command the barque *Cowlitz*.

McNeill was given a cordial greeting by Governor Etholin of
the Russian American Company at Sitka who was gratified by his
early arrival in the *Cowlitz* on March 25, 1844. He discharged
£3,900 sterling worth of Russian cargo, sent it ashore and after only
a few days the *Cowlitz* set sail for Fort Simpson. McNeill took on
board 4,000 beaver pelts at Fort Simpson for transport to Fort
Vancouver. These pelts came partly from trade with the Indians and
partly from exchange with the Russians at Sitka. In the agreement
with the Russian American Company, the Hudson's Bay Company

undertook to deliver wheat, flour, pease, barley, salt beef, butter and pork; further, there was a clause covering the exchange of Russian American Company beaver pelts for the Hudson's Bay Company land otter skins.

The *Cowlitz* sailed for the Columbia River in mid-April and crossed the bar of the river in early May. The vessel proceeded up the river to the mouth of the Cowlitz River and anchored. Here, McNeill sent the beaver pelts and other skins to Fort Vancouver by canoe. He then prepared the ship's holds for a cargo of 6,000 bushels of wheat for delivery to Sitka. Six small boats ferried the wheat from Fort Vancouver to the ship with forty-two men employed to achieve the loading of this cargo. During this time McNeill was reunited with his wife and family at Fort Vancouver, after an absence of nineteen months.

On arrival at the Fort, McNeill found HMS *Modeste*, an eighteen-gun frigate commanded by Captain Baillie, lying at anchor. This vessel was sent to show the British flag during the border negotiations because of the new settlers arriving at the Willamette River in large numbers that threatened the Company's interests in the territory. McNeill accompanied James Douglas, Captain Baillie and a group of his officers on a visit to inspect the crops and they seemed much pleased with the country; the crops were ripe and standing and would be abundant. McNeill reported to Sir George Simpson in his second letter that the captain's party were much entertained, took notes and intended to publish their findings.

McNeill opens his first letter to Sir George Simpson from Sitka:

I was much disappointed at not seeing you on my arrival in England, I hoped to have had the pleasure to talk over and given you an account of my proceedings since your departure from this side of the world. I was much pleased with my reception in London at the H.B. House and with England and Englishmen I must say they are more frank than my own countrymen. I was exceedingly sorry that I had no one to introduce me to your Lady in London. Sir Henry Pelly gave me permission when I first arrived to remain in the States for one year and go out with the express. A few days after he sent for me and told me that I must come to London again and take the Ship out to the Columbia and Sitka. He also told me that I was to take charge of and Superintend the Shipping in the Columbia and that he should write the Doctor to that effect which I hear he did no one ever told me or said anything to me on the subject on my arrival at Vancouver and as I wished to quit the Sea asked for the charge of a Fort and was appointed to Stikine and Dodd to take the Steamer. At all events as you must be aware I could not do justice to the Shipping without being stationed at Vancouver.

McNeill was upset by McLoughlin's failure to even mention this directive from the governor and committee. However, he gives the same reason as McLoughlin for not being appointed that McLoughlin gave the governor and committee. Then in 1846 he writes to Simpson: "My being appointed Superintendent of the Shipping seems to have created some jealousy at Vancouver, sooner than it should create any bad feeling I am perfectly willing to give up the Appointment, it was not of my seeking neither am I making a fortune by it."

In his first letter to Simpson from New Archangel in November, 1844, McNeill tells him that it took six weeks to load the wheat onto the *Cowlitz* and suggested that had it been stored at the entrance of the Cowlitz River, it would have taken six days to load. This private letter arrived on Simpson's desk at the Red River Settlement on 6 June 1845.

Ten days later Simpson wrote to McLoughlin, Douglas and Ogden, in which he berated them for allowing the operations of the barque *Cowlitz* to be of a ruinous character. He pointed out that the vessel only performed a single voyage to Sitka between 6 June 1844 and 11 March 1845 and that he thought this loss of time might have been avoided by having a small granary at the mouth of the Cowlitz River for the reception of the grain as it might be brought down gradually from the farm, instead of making a granary of the ship. This letter from Simpson, written at the height of the dispute between McLoughlin and Simpson, also rebuked the officers at Fort Vancouver on a number of other issues.

The barque *Cowlitz* was ready to sail two days after *Modeste* passed them down the river. When McNeill arrived at Fort George he found the *Modeste* at anchor after the frigate had gone aground on the "south breakers" and in refloating her, had to drain all her water to lighten the ship, lost two anchors in warping her off and unhinged her rudder. With Mr. Birnie from Fort George, McNeill piloted the *Modeste* to the anchorage in Bakers Bay. There, the two vessels were anchored for fourteen days to repair the *Modeste*'s rudder, restock the water casks and await a break in the weather that would allow them to cross the Columbia River Bar. The *Cowlitz* led the way over the bar and once the two ships headed north, the *Modeste* drew alongside *Cowlitz*, mustered her whole crew on deck and publicly thanked McNeill for his assistance.

Both vessels entered Juan de Fuca Strait to visit the new establishment on Vancouver Island known at that time as Camosoon. In 1837, before the death of King William IV, the new establishment was to be given the name Fort Adelaide, after his consort, Queen Adelaide. Later, the establishment was named Fort Albert before finally settling on the name, Fort Victoria. HMS *Modeste* was hauled out for repairs and the *Cowlitz* went north to Fort Simpson. Originally the *Cowlitz* planned to go to Fort Nisqually where McNeill and his family would transfer to the SS *Beaver*, give Captain Duncan charge of the *Cowlitz* and proceed to Fort Stikine in the steamer. At Stikine, McNeill would relieve Charles Dodd who was to take command of the steamer. However, the delay in the river made the *Cowlitz* late for this appointment and the *Beaver* had already steamed.

McNeill now planned to stay at Fort Simpson until the steamer arrived to take him to Fort Stikine. When he requested the two spare rooms in the large house at Fort Simpson for his wife and family, he was denied them by John Work, as he reports to Sir George in his letter from New Archangel: "I came here to wait because Mr Work could not afford me accomodations or rather the two spare rooms in the Large House at F.S." As a result, McNeill packed his family back on board the *Cowlitz* and sailed to Sitka to deliver the cargo of wheat where Governor Etholin was more generous in his reception.

McNeill and family spent Christmas at Sitka and he dispatched the *Cowlitz* to the Columbia River under Mr. Heath's command.

The *Beaver* was due at Sitka early in the New Year on its annual visit to deliver the rent of 2,000 land otter skins. Unfortunately, Captain Humphries now had command of the vessel and during her passage up Wrangell Strait, struck a rock and damaged her forefoot (fore section of the keel). McNeill did not approach Humphries directly but applied to him by letter requesting passage for himself and family to Fort Stikine. Captain Humphries refused McNeill who learned later from Governor Etholin that Humphries had run on at a terrible rate, acting the "big man!" Humphries also told Etholin that Dodd at Fort Stikine would not receive McNeill.

Once more, Etholin came to McNeill's rescue and ordered Captain Zarembo to go to Fort Stikine on a tour of inspection of their leased property and take McNeill and his family in the Russian steamer. McNeill, now obviously in a depressed state of mind, worried that Dodd would not receive him, as he tells Simpson in his letter from Sitka before he set out for the fort:

> If this is the case and I am to be passed about in this manner by every officer in the service that has a little authority I see no other way for me to proceede than to abandon my family and leave the service. Mr Work would not give myself lodgings in the two spare rooms at his Fort but wished me and my family to stow away in the single room or Indian Hall where the Stikine Provisions were put which I would not consent to. he afterwards said that we could occupy the two said rooms so long as my Ship lay there, after her departure the family must go into the Indian Hall but to be brief this is all about the women which I may have to refer to hereafter. I wrote Mr Work that if women were to arrange the H.B.C's affairs it was high time for me to be out of this service.

McNeill need not have worried, when he and his family arrived at Fort Stikine in the Russian steamer, they were welcomed by Charles Dodd and George Blenkinsop. For the next four years Fort Stikine was to be home for him and his increasing family. Before McNeill's command of Fort Stikine, the murder of John McLoughlin, Jr. had cast a pall of uneasiness over the fort. Among the servants were two trouble makers and they had tried to entice Charles Dodd into an act that might justify their attacking him with their life preservers (like knuckle dusters, used for self defense) and killing both Dodd and Blenkinsop. This misfortune was only averted by Bottineau giving timely warning. McNeill, in a postscript to the first letter before he arrived at the fort, tells Sir George Simpson: "I am sorry to inform you that there has been another disturbance at Stikine, some of the men there threatened to shoot Dodd, they came to him in a mutinous manner. He succeeded in putting the two ring leaders in irons kept them on bread and water for a while and has sent them to Vancouver by the Steamer in October last. It will be my turn next I hope to get on without many rows, the men will not talk too loud about shooting me as they are sure to get the first shot themselves."

Sir George Simpson used this incident to stir up the controversy with McLoughlin once more when he took sides with the mutineers: "As to the life preservers we learn by a letter from C.T. Manson that, they were prepared by the men, with that gentn's knowledge & approbation while he was at Stikine, for the purpose of defending themselves against attacks from the Indians while employed in the woods, not being provided with arms and Collette and Savard, instead of being the dangerous characters they are represented, appear, by Mr Manson's letter, to have been victims of Bottineau's revenge, arising out of some previous quarrel."

The removal of the two trouble makers from the fort seems to have settled the problem of mutiny. Bazil (sometimes Baptiste) Bottineau became a trusted servant in the fort. He married a Stikine Indian woman and McNeill allowed him to go with her family to explore the Stikine river:

> I allowed "Bazil Bottineau" to go Inland with his wife's rela-
> tions last summer when all the Indians went to trade fur with the
> Interior people, he told me on his return (they were gone thirty
> days) that after they had ascended the River about 60 miles they
> came to a beautiful plain country, the ground ready for the
> Plough, and a fine situation for a Fort, the River however has
> rapids in it, but he thinks our Batteaux could go up in five days
> time, and come down in one. The land otter from that country
> (we get a very few here) are equally as good as those from the
> East side, but owing to some superstition the Natives will not
> kill them.

The Kaigani Haida and Tlingit thought that the land otter was able to steal the wits of a person and turn that person into an idiot or *gogiid* in their language.

McNeill tells Simpson in his 1845 letter, before he arrived at Stikine: "The Russian vessel that took you from this place to Ochotsk arrived about two months since from Sta Francisco with 2000 Fanyas (Fanegas) of Wheat all she could obtain the crops had failed, and Suter did not pay them our Bushels on a/c of his debt. Suter is in debt to Rae $6000 and Rae put in his claim to be paid first and it was left out to reference Capt Baillie of the Modeste was our and the Consul at Monterey the other and they decided against Rae. Business was dull there and Rae was not doing much, or very little in the business way."

In the 1846 letter McNeill tells Simpson: "...poor Rae died a horrible death, cards and Brandy I learn was partly the cause of it."

McNeill knew William Glen Rae at both Fort Vancouver and Fort Stikine before Rae was sent to California in charge of the Hudson's Bay Company business there. Rae was married to Dr. McLoughlin's daughter Eloisa in 1838.

This was indeed a particularly horrible incident for Eloisa Rae. She was confined to bed after the birth of their third child. She saw her husband make his first attempt by holding a pistol to his forehead, which failed to fire. She dragged herself out of bed to grab the six-barrel pistol from him only after it had failed to fire in three attempts. A short time later he left her and she noticed another pistol in his pocket. This time the pistol that he held to his forehead fired before she could prevent it and he died instantly.

If there was failure on McLoughlin's part to appoint McNeill Head of the Marine Department immediately, it did not stop McNeill from taking considerable interest in the marine affairs and he wrote his ideas in his letters to Simpson. He urged Simpson to make seamen and officers sign agreements that covered their conduct and terms of service. Fresh provisions on board ship and at forts were often scarce and he suggests that: "...our seamen should sign an agreement in London to live on Deer and Fish in this country when it can be procured, it was formerly the case on American ships."

McNeill applauded Captain Fitzroy's work in parliament that would require British registered ships to carry a written agreement with every man on board. In 1845 the Board of Trade instituted voluntary examinations of competency for men intending to become masters and mates on ships making foreign voyages, and these became compulsory in 1850. However, these regulations were of little account in redressing current problems in the Hudson's Bay Company vessels on the coast. When Captain Humphries struck a rock in Wrangell Strait, McNeill writes: "... he should have hawled on shore and repaired the damage but no, off he went without looking at it I really think the man is a little touched in the head."

McNeill also noted that Latter (Alexander Lattie) was on shore at Fort Simpson, "turned out of the steamer for habitual drunkenness, Captain Sangster was pulling hard on the bottle and that his first mate on the *Cowlitz*, Wm. Heath, was much given to it of late."

In 1846, McNeill sums up his opinion of Humphries who was on his passage to London as master of the barque *Cowlitz*:

> What a scamp Humphreys turned out to be setting to one side the manner he behaved to Work and myself, the man was constantly drunk, Never!! Sober, always slept with a bottle under his pillow. One was found there when Work took the command from him, all those fine speeches and independant airs &c that he assumed was under the influence of Spirits. Why he constantly held con-sultations at night in his Cabin with his crew or rather with three of them Green was always one of the special ones. I shall feel anxious about the Cowlitz until I hear of her safe arrival in England for I think so badly of Humphreys now that I think he would cause a Mutiny on board, all the men that joined her from the Steamer are his creatures, and he has too much art for Heath, and they have no great regard for each other, but we must hope for the best.

The *Cowlitz* did arrive safely in London. However, McNeill once more gets onto Humphries' case:

> Young Birch who came out with me from London in the Cowlitz was so disgusted with the conduct of Heath and Humphreys on the homeward voyage that he left the Service, his friends writes me that they are grateful for all that was done for him during my command. It is really surprising the forebearance the Company have shown to those two men as well as other officers in the Naval Department. Humphreys is a bad man in principle and the example he sets would ruin any officer or man on board of his Ship. Heaths fault is, that he cannot keep sober when Brandy is comatable. he in particular has been forgiven for his bad conduct very many times.

The American whalers were a problem for the Russian American Company and the Hudson's Bay Company. They poached on the fur trade, and were so numerous that they forced the cost of labor and provisions to exorbitant levels. At the height of the whal-ing industry, between 1847 and 1860, there were 600 American whalers on the oceans of the world and the discovery of the bow-head whales in the western Arctic attracted a high proportion of these vessels to the north Pacific. McNeill was ambivalent about these vessels, on the one hand he suggested attracting them to

Victoria for the sale of provisions and on the other applauds Governor Etholin for asking for two men-o'-war to keep them out of the Russian fur trade territory. He tells Simpson in his 1847 letter: "The American Whalers literally speaking, cover this Northern Sea some 400 Sail of them visit the islands in one year. They obtain from 1000 to 2900 Bbls !!! of oil in one Season of Six months many of them visit Kamtchatka during the Summer and as any of them have large quantity of goods on board they find a ready sale for them and in my opinion they are encouraged to visit that place, on account of the cheap goods they throw into the market there."

McNeill was indignant about the American whaler that anchored in Shushartie Bay to catch whales and trade for furs on the side and may have forgotten his enthusiastic suggestion in the log of the *Convoy* when sailing in Chatham Strait in 1825: "I have been up and down this Strait several times and always saw from 40 to 50 Whales. A Whaler to visit here, might lay to an anchor in one of the Harbours and fill a ship in two months at the farthest and purchase furs at the same time. It is smooth water and Pleasant Weather in the Summer Season."

McNeill was impressed with the marine community at Sitka and when it was clear that the *Beaver* needed repairs to her hull, recommended that this refit be done at Sitka. In 1848 he writes in his letter to Simpson:

> The Steamer is still very useful, and Dodd takes excellent care of her, and I think she will run very well without any very great repairs untill the New Boilers are put in, which may not be 'till 1851. The Engineer told me the other day, that he would make the old or present ones last till that time 1851, "so that he would get clear of putting the new ones in." I should by all means say that Sitka would be the most preferable place to repair the Hull it will be done for a very small expense, and the Vessel will be soon on her cruising ground. At Victoria or Nisqually many things would be required that those places cannot furnish, at Sitka they have a large force of men and all of them are Carpenters, for Govr Etolin told me that he never asked a man if he could do so & so, but told him to do a job and it was done. Little or no rot can be seen in the vessel except in the cealing, some of which will no doubt be replaced when the general repair takes place, No doubt the Board will inform you more particularly on this subject, as the reports will be sent into them concerning Vessel and Boilers.

In 1841, McNeill recommended to Simpson that the *Beaver* be converted to a sailing vessel and a new 600-ton steamer be sent out. At Fort Simpson, when discussing the change of policy from forts to ships, they discussed the building of a barge to be towed by the *Beaver*. In the first letter from Sitka, he suggests that the *Cadboro* was only fit for river work and recommended that a 210-ton brigantine should be sent out that could take the Fort Langley salmon in one trip instead of the *Cadboro* that did the job in three trips.

McNeill had a number of ideas for improving the Company's success in the Pacific with greater use of the Company's vessels. In his 1848 letter he sounds envious at the success in business of some of his contempories from Boston. Captain Peirce of the brigantine *Griffin* is not the same Pierce who was a clerk in 1826, and who with Brewer had been successful in business at Oahu. Charles Brewer went to school in Boston with McNeill.

McNeill writes:

Business at Sandh Islands must be paying as yet to my countrymen. Several new houses have been established, a Mr Williams, has Pierce and Brewers old stand. Brewer went to the States and came out last year in his New Ship of 700 tons with an Investment of $90,000, Charles Brewer 2nd came out with him, and established himself at the Islands. I do not know how our establishment at Oahu pays, but report sayes not much, I should fancy with our means that it would or should, pay better than any other house at the place, our Ships are constantly going and returning from England and the River, and will afford an oppty to bring any quantity or quality of goods that would be required for that market.

I have always understood also that the Company stands No 1 with Sandh Island Govt, which is an advantage also. Captain Grimes has his farm on California and the establishment at Oahu, and is rich, would you believe it Sir, that Brewer in 1831, was Second officer of a Brig, and Pierce in 1826 a Clerk on this coast? such is the case. And they made all their money at the Islands.

In my opinion If some other speculation does not occur to us besides the Fur Trade, and that very soon, I am of opinion that C.T. Emoluments, will be reduced very much. In fact they can but be small for the last two years, Beaver the main stay, and now they are a drug, and Martens are also very low in price. I hope some new investment can and will be made to assist us to obtain the needful. When I write in this manner Sir, perhaps you will say, he is a real Yankee, always wishing to "speculate", I wish to do and act to the best of my knowledge for all concerned, and am ready to put my shoulder to the wheel to assist. I hope you will not think me disrespectful for writing as I have, for I shall never do anything to hurt your feelings on the contrary, rest assured Sir that I am ready to do anything, that I can to promote your interest or comfort.

The Doctor has sent David (McLoughlin's son) two or three voyages to California and the Islands as Supercargo, and has done tolerable well, so I hear, Couch and Crosby, have gone to China as passengers, to purchase goods for the Wallamitt, therefore we might suppose, that they have prospects of realising some profit. Dominis has been lost, together with a Brig's crew on a passage to Canton from Oahu, the vessel was supposed to have gone down in a Typhoon.

He Dominis was building a house at Oahu to cost without furniture, $14,000, he was sailmaker when I was second Officer "in the same vessel." Dudoit has been superceeded as French Consul, he had the Order of "Legion of Honor," confered on him, for his long and valuable Service at the Islands by the French Govt. California has been a good market for flour from the River, the Company I believe, made a good sale of some that was sent by the Columbia. It was required for the American Sailors and Troops. If California is ceeded to the U.S. Govt, It must become one of the greatest places of trade in the Pacific. It will take a part of the trade away from the Islands. Already a large number of the Whaling fleet go there for refreshments, Again they have taken off all charges that formerly was paid on ships at Oahu they do not even charge pilotage. the Govt pays it themselves. Your old acquaintance Revd Mr Richards is dead, he died at Oahu. Mr (George) Pelly also had been very sick had lost the use of his eyes for a time does not go down to the store often, he however is recovering.

The fort officers and servants eagerly anticipated the arrival of any ship that would bring them letters or news of the world outside. McNeill's letters display surprisingly up-to-date knowledge of affairs in Oahu. He derived this from newspapers sent from Oahu and in his 1847 letter to Simpson, writes: "I have thought proper to enclose to you a few Oahu Papers that you may see what the Press says concerning matters and things in the Pacific." He mentioned on other occasions news gleaned from Boston and New York papers:

By the way Sir I have seen in an American paper that Sir George Simpson had left in the H.B.Coys Canoes from Lachine, and intended to cross the Rocky Mountains, and visit Vancouvers Island, I hope this may turn out to be true as we should be honord with your presence at this place I hope. If you do come and see, and hear for yourself, something may possibly be done to benefit the Company in many ways. Things in general look rather squally as we Sailors say, at present in this quarter, in particular the want of men to man the forts and to carry on the duty required in various ways and places, but I will conclude, as I am well aware that your numerous correspondents will give any information that I may have neglected to mention.

McNeill's comment about "the want of men" is the first comment to forewarn of the difficulties the Company was to face once the California gold rush got into high gear. Later in his letter of 1847, McNeill expands on the problem.

You also must have seen by accounts from California that most valuable mines of Quick Silver. Gold. Copper & Iron are about to be worked the Quick Silver mine is worked at the present moment, and pay's well. There is two Quick Silver Mines one on the North & one the South side of Santo Francisco Bay. The American Army & Navy at present in California demand large quantities of Provisions of all kinds and I hear that the Company's vessels have taken Flour &c to California for sale I presume it must with a good market. Darcie McLoughlin sold some flour there for $12 per Bbl & an American Capt Crosby for $14. to the Am' Commodore.

Even today, the small town of Wrangell can be bleak and forbidding when the wind blows and the rain pelts down on the roofs of the houses. The fort was on relatively flat land above a wharf where the visiting Russian and Hudson's Bay steamers could moor to discharge their cargoes. The Indians were more aggressive than most and this kept the officers, servants and children confined within the stockade. Not surprisingly, McNeill blamed life at the fort for his lack of well-being and soon after settling in 1846, he was asking Sir George Simpson for relief.

I have been very much out of health for the last Ten months at this place, and this Summer for a long time was confined to the house and a part of the time to my bed I presume it is the close

187

confinement that causes it, I am fearful that if I stay here over one year more that my health will be seriously injured and shall apply to the Board of Management to be pleased to remove me to any other post they may think me qualified to take charge of. As I have always be accustomed to an active life and plenty of exercise I am certain that remaining at Stikine over another year will injure me for life, I know or am aware that I have no right to ask to be removed or expect such a request if I was healthy, as it is, I hope the Board will think favourably of my request. In fact if it cannot be complied with I must although (very reluctantly) give up my Commission, I do not say so to talk Big, I merely think that it is the only way to preserve my health. The Honble Company have dealt justly & kindly towards me and I wish still to serve them.

In the first two letters, McNeill says that he has been given to understand that John Work, who was supposed to have cancer of his tongue, was going to leave Fort Simpson and that he was to take over at Fort Simpson. He warned Simpson that the state of the buildings at Fort Simpson would need a great deal of labor to bring them up to standard. However, John Work did not leave Fort Simpson and McNeill was stuck at Fort Stikine.

The following winter was extremely severe with McNeill expressing a wish that he had not invested fifty pounds sterling in the Puget Sound Agricultural Company. Horses, cows and sheep were lost from freezing to death at both Nisqually, Fort Vancouver and the Willamette farms of the new settlers on the Willamette River. Fort Stikine experienced a long hard winter and McNeill reports: "…our water was frozen up for three months, and this summer the Indians find Deer lying dead in large numbers in the woods."

McNeill's threats to resign his commission and leave the service occurred so frequently that they had little effect on Sir George Simpson. Every letter from Fort Stikine implies that he might leave the service if he is not transferred. In the 1847 letter, McNeill resigns again.

Now my Dear Sir, And Friend, I must inform you that I have sent my resignation to the Board of Management and I presume you have seen it. I did so to get clear of this post. I wrote you last Autumn that I wished to be relieved from this charge, likewise to the Board of Management, They wrote me that there was no one at Vancouver of sufficient experience to take charge of Stikine &c

Knowing that I should not receive an answer from you 'till March Proximo, which would be too late for me, "even if you were pleased to order my removal to another place" I thought it for my interest to give in my resignation. I have made the proviso however, that I would remain in the Service to be put in charge of any other post. But do not expect that the Board will listen to my proposal, as they no doubt would think it a bad precedent, and others would be asking the same favour, The confinement to me here is most annoying and erksom the trouble or work is a secondary consideration with those things I am familiar with and must expect both through life. If I do go shall in all probability go to California or Sandh Islands and try my luck there a steady moral man must do well at either place, why not? look at my School mate Brewer at Oahu he has made a large fortune and is going home in one of his own Ships. Two others have made fortunes at the same stand, Viz, Hunnewell and Pierce Old & Young Grimes have made money by Bags full at the Islands so Reynoulds writes me. they also have a farm on the Sacramento near Suters it is now worth $30,000 including stock, houses, land &c

Sir George did respond to this plea and offered McNeill a leave of absence to go to the United States by the Rocky Mountains, but this offer was cancelled by the decision to abandon Fort Stikine.

Life at Fort Stikine for McNeill and his growing family was not without event. During the eight months they were together at the fort, McNeill became firm friends with Charles Dodd, who he described as "this steady correct man." He recommended Dodd to Sir George Simpson in nearly all the letters he wrote after their first acquaintance: "...he has done well at this place I found it in famous order and the returns are better than any year since we rented it from the Russians."

George Blenkinsop stayed on as McNeill's second when Dodd left in November, 1845. The arrival of Helen, aged seventeen years, turned George's head, and heart! McNeill recommended Blenkinsop for promotion to clerk in the first letter from Stikine, even before he knew that Blenkinsop was to be his son-in-law. He writes of him: "I can say that I do not think there is a Young Gentleman at Vancouver that would give more satisfaction than himself."

In 1846, he tells Simpson with tongue-in-cheek: "Blenkinsop is still here, and this summer was married to my Daughter Hellen by the Lutheran Parson who came here in the Russian Steamer, when she brought (a part) of our Supplies, he had been deeply in love with her for a long time which I finaly saw, in fact it was affecting his health, (at least I thought so) he applied to me asking if I would consent to his taking her for better or for worse I told him that I was willing, at the same time told the trouble of having a Wife &c all to no purpose, as you may as well attempt to convince a horse as a man in love."

By 1847 McNeill's family was growing up. There were no schools for the children at this time. McNeill and Blenkinsop were the only two people in the fort who were literate in English, where French was the most prevalent language, so that the responsibility for teaching their children fell on their shoulders. Not until 1849 were the children sent to The Reverend Staines school in Fort Victoria. William was fifteen years old and by Boston standards should have been well on his way to being self-sufficient. Douglas suggested that William work with Blenkinsop who should train him as an Indian trader. McNeill wanted him: "...removed from myself, as he would do better away from me, there is always a certain restraint in boys under the immediate inspection of the parent."

A year later McNeill thanks Simpson for helping him solve his problem:

Blenkinsop is still active and clever as ever, no Clerk in the Service deserves more praise or credit and I am certain none are more capable. We will have an addition to his family soon, if we can judge by "appearances", my Wife also seems inclined to make more legs for stockings. My son William is now at Nisqually, or Victoria, as apptice Postmaster. Mr Douglas wrote me on the 27th October last to send him down in the Spring to assist Doctor Tolmie which I did, as Mr D did not write before, I concluded that William would not be required, or wanted, for the Service, and I wrote you to that effect in my last letter, I have again to thank you for this act of kindness and will feel grateful always, for Williams wages will always find him clothes and of course not lighten my purse as heretofore. I only hope he will earn his salary and please his Master and Employers, he had a good lesson and advice before leaving here, his education is not the best of course he however writes a tolerable hand, and has been as far as the Rule of Three in Arithmetic.

McNeill told Simpson in a postscript to this letter that his wife had presented him with another son on the 27 August 1848 and that she had been near going for it herself during childbirth. Matilda had brought eleven children into the world: William (1832), Alfred (1834), Lucy (1835), Matilda (1842), Fanny (1843) and Henry (1848) are the known children of McNeill at this time and Helen was born in 1828, the daughter of Chief Sakau'an and adopted by McNeill. By the time of McNeill's death in 1875, he bequeathed his estate to William, Lucy, Matilda, Fanny, the twin girls born at Fort Rupert, Rebecca and Harriet. Helen died before McNeill in 1869. Alfred and Henry were not traced. The other two children likely died in infancy or childhood, although he says there were ten children in 1851.

In 1848, McNeill tells Simpson: "...I have received accounts of the death of my beloved, and much respected Mother, she was a sincere Christian, well educated, and clever, her society was courted by the first Families in the land of her birth, and several poor people will miss her, although her means are limited."

His sister, Sarah, continued to keep house in Charleston for a year and then moved to live with a cousin in Boston. His brother, a captain in the Marine Corps was stationed in Philadelphia.

On March 18, 1842, Sir George Simpson writes to the governor and committee:

> In the final adjustment of the Boundary Question, it is more than probable a line drawn through the Straits of de Fuca, till it strikes the Mainland South of Whidbey's Island, will become the Coast Boundary between Great Britain & the United States in the Northern Pacific: I say so because I am of opinion the Government of the United States will insist on having a Port on the North West coast, and that Gt Britain will, for the sake of peace, accept the Straits of de Fuca as a boundary on the Coast, & thereby give up Puget Sound & Hood's Canal, together with the country situated between those inlets & the lower parts of the Columbia. In that case, I presume the line would be continued from the Southern end of Whidbey Island [i.e., at approximately 48], in an easterly direction, till it struck the Lewis River, and following up that River till it struck the Rocky Mountains. It is exceedingly desirable however for the British interests in this quarter & for the national honor, that Her Majesty's Government should not submit to such degrading conditions; but I think it is nevertheless well to be prepared for the worst.

The Hudson's Bay Company officers were suspicious of the motives of the Methodist missionaries from the time they opened their establishment in 1836. In 1844, Simpson summed up the situation with the terse comment that in spite of the many favours done them, they appeared to be "our most implacable enemies."

McNeill had observed the missionaries in Hawaii and mistrusted them as much as Mr. J. C. Jones expressed his dislike of them in his letters to Josiah Marshall in the 1820s. In his 1844 letter, he tells Simpson: "The Society at home have just now found out that all was not going on right with their Bretheren, I knew long since that most of them were scamps."

However, by the time he wrote this, the problem for the Company was no longer the missionaries but the large influx of settlers. He tells Simpson: "…about 600 Americans came to the Wallamette last fall and I hear that 4000 are expected in this fall, if so and the Wallamett continues to fill up will it not alter the present state of things in the Columbia, no less than four Shops are now opened by the Americans in the Wallamette, one of them belongs to the Doctor, which the Americans will hardly believe they say it belongs to the Company."

This barb, aimed at the doctor, refers to an incident in McLoughlin's career that is as muddy as the Fraser River. It is still unclear whether McLoughlin bought the property at Willamette for himself or on behalf of the Hudson's Bay Company. All through the letters McNeill has a tendency to show McLoughlin in a bad light to gain favor with Simpson. However, James Douglas and Peter Ogden were getting a little tired of the constant war of words between Simpson and McLoughlin.

With regard to the settlers at the Willamette River and the emigration of settlers to the Oregon territory, McNeill was in an ambivalent position. For the settlers and their leaders who emigrated west along the trails from Washington and Louisiana, there was general loathing for the Hudson's Bay Company and its monopoly. McNeill had traveled to England in an attempt to be given British citizenship, which was not granted by the British parliament. He had served the Hudson's Bay Company loyally and devoted considerable energy to driving his countrymen out of the coastal fur trade. Yet, he was still an American citizen in a territory that was increasingly under the influence of United States expansionism. The influx of so many settlers, even before the boundary question was concluded, made it obvious to the occupants of Fort Vancouver that whatever happened, this population would demand American rule of law. McNeill writes to Simpson in 1846:

> ...my countrymen are getting to be numerous in the Wallatt and saucy as they gain strength. They i.e. the Missionarys and Emigrants have been very ungrateful to the Company after what has been done for them and still is done. We have been most shamefully represented in congress. I for one think it is high time something is done to let the world know we have been better Christians and done more in every respect to assist and civilize Indians than all the Missionarys together in fact we well know that the Mission in the Wallamitte have done only for themselves. In my opinion we should defend ourselves in the American papers. I as an American would cheerfully inform the world how my countrymen and my-self have been treated by the Honble Company.

Later in the same letter, McNeill voices his opinion on the boundary: "presume it is still very doubtful which of the contending powers will eventually obtain possession of Oregon but in my opinion Britain will not relinquish her right without a hard struggle."

McNeill, as an American citizen, was concerned that war could ensue over the boundary question and in 1847 writes in his letter to Simpson: "...it seems to me by last account that the Oregon Question may cause trouble yet, it seems that Mr Polk offered as far as 49° which was refused by Mr Packingham and as the War party in the States are stubborn. War may ensue, time will determine but for the sake of the Civilised world, it is to be hoped that some friendly power will make all right, I think however that England has as good a right to the North side of the Columbia as the States Government."

McNeill was in a no-win situation. If the issue was not settled peacefully, he would have been distrusted by the American settlers for working for British interests and by the British in the Company as a possible informer for the enemy.

McNeill was able to express his relief in his 1848 letter to Simpson: "We are all well pleased that the Oregon Question is settled without bloodshed, I however think that the Columbia should have been the boundary, but the difference was not worth fighting for. It is hard to tell how or what manner matters and things will go on in Oregon. but I am inclined to think, by what I hear from various sources that ere long the Americans will be giving annoyance at Vancouver and wheresoever the Coy have land contiguous to theirs. Of course the Gentlemen at Vancouver can inform you more correctly as regards such matters."

The fur trade with the Indians was still the mainstay of the Hudson's Bay Company. McNeill, like all fur traders, complained of the quality and quantity of the trade goods provided to them from England. He complained that too much of the regatta cotton was being sold to the settlers on the Willamette, popular for its current fashion. But the Indians too were subject to fashion and liked this cotton, leaving the traders short of this popular item. Fashion on the other side of the world was creating havoc in the beaver skin trade. In 1825, the silk hat was introduced in Paris and by 1845 had swept the beaver hats off the markets of Europe. The Company's warehouses were full of unpurchased beaver pelts in a diminishing market. McNeill encouraged the Indians to bring him bear skins and marten skins. He also tried in vain to convince them to trap the land otters. He was unable to overcome the Indian prejudice against these animals that in their superstitious belief were able to steal the wits of their people.

To the Kwakiutl, the land otter was a weather charm. An Indian informed Franz Boas that when the southeast wind blew strongly, he would look for an otter slide, pick up a handful of soil, turn to the right and throw it into the water. At the same time he prayed to the otter to bring him a northwest wind.

The Indians around the Stikine River mouth were more feisty than those further south. Trouble began in 1846 when Governor Etholin was appointed Director of the Russian American Company in St. Petersberg and was replaced by Governor Trebenkoff. In 1846 McNeill tells Sir George Simpson:

> We have had a serious rebellion with our Indians this Summer, such an outbreak I never saw among Indians and they did nearly all that they threatened to do. It was caused by the Russians giving a Great feast at Sitka, to all the neighbouring tribes of Indians and giving Rum!!! also. (some Kako people brought some here on two occations) I saw about one pint myself in the fort, they

excited our Indians to such a degree that they said if I did not do likewise, that we should not cut another stick of wood, that they would not trade either Fur or Provisions for Twelve months (to commence with) I refused of course, and they would not come near the fort, but used threats, and actually drove our men from cutting some wood we had on the Wharf. I thought as the Russians had brought us into trouble that they might just as well come here and take a share of it. In fact if things remained as they were I concluded that that we would be obliged to abandon the place to them, and wrote Mr Work and Govr Trebenkoff to that effect. "I presume a copy of my letter will be forwarded to your Honour." I also desired the Governor to send his Steward here and some Gentleman in here to arrange matters, he did so, and when they came & saw the state the Indians were in were quite surprised, and felt guilty of giving Rum to the Indians in violation of the Treaty made with yourself and Govr Etholing. However they did all in their power to settle the differences between the Indians, and ourselves and succeeded in doing so in a conciliatory way however, invited the Chiefs on board feasted and talked to them, and finally the scamps came to terms, and commenced trade again.

In August 1847, Chief Factor Work ordered the tariff for beaver pelts to be cut from one three-and-a-half point to one two-and-a-half point blanket or other goods in proportion. As a result, no furs were traded at Stikine. McNeill reports:

The Indians are very troublesome and threaten every thing base, say that no more Beaver will ever be traded, and that they must have a 3 pt Best Blanket for 7 Martens &c. They have given the hunters Tw days to hunt Deer for us, and then no more provisions of any kind will be brought to the fort, and say that we shall cut no more wood &c. "I gave them from the 16th to 26th Augt to trade what Furs they have procured in the Interior previous to the alteration in the tariff, as they pay a 3 pt Best Blkt there for a Beaver, They start for the Interior again say 10th inst and return about 10th October, and then we shall have trouble if ever, I cannot say to a certainty how it will end, but think that but few fur if any Beaver will be obtained here, after this date, we have now 600 Martens and 200 Beaver per Outfit 1848.

The relationship with the Indian chiefs at Fort Stikine were never easy. They were quite aggressive in their dealings with McNeill, who reported his ambivalence about his policy of noninterference in their tribal affairs. In his letter McNeill writes: "We were shocked at this place the other day. Eight poor slaves were put to death, 'with daggers', close to our pickets. this was done at what we would term a house warming, I tried to stop it to no purpose, the Chief said it was their fashion, or custom, when a new house was finished."

In 1847, McNeill makes first mention of the coal deposits in the Johnstone Straits: "...the Cormorant, H.M.B.S.. Sloop; visited the coal mine in Johnstone Strait during her visit to this part of the world, Sangster was on board as Pilot, they found the coal to answer admirably well for steam Navigation and they welded immense Bars of Iron with it also. they blew up the coal with powder and by that process obtained good coals. these coals may be worth a fortune to some one hereafter."

On the first voyage of the *Beaver* on the coast and before McNeill took command, Duncan Finlayson surveyed the area between McNeill Harbour and Beaver Harbour for the surface coal seams reported there and made the point that there would be need to build a fort nearby to protect a mine. The growth of steam engines for ship and shore work made these coal deposits of value.

In McNeill's 1848 letter he complains again to Simpson:

I very much wish to be relieved of the charge of Stikine, I very well know that we have no right to pick and chuse, nor ask to be relieved &c, but my health is suffering owing to the close confinement at Stikine. "Four" months together I have never been once outside the fort, "which has impair'd my health at times, though at present am in good condition. Mr Douglas gave me some hopes in Winter, that I would be relieved by the Ship in Summer when she came with our Supplies as she is now more than a month over her time, we are inclined to think that some accident has occured to her. If that unfortunately be the case, I shall be detained here one year more, You very kindly Sir have offered me a leave of absence to go to the States by the Rocky Mountains and to pay you a visit. for which please accept my grateful thanks, If I cannot get clear of Stikine otherwise I will accept your offer and start so soon as possible, I should prefer a more active life than Stikine affords for I still feel young, but this place will ere long take that feeling out of me.

When the *Beaver* arrived, it brought instructions on the abandonment of the fort. When the time came to abandon the fort in 1849, McNeill and his servants were careful to keep these intentions a secret from the chiefs. In late March, 1849, John Work and a party from Fort Simpson arrived to assist in the move. They came in the leased Russian brigantine *Constantine* that would take all the fort members south to a new establishment they were to build at Beaver Harbour at the north end of Vancouver Island. After his arrival he writes to Simpson:

We abandoned my old quarters "Fort Stikine" on the 15th April last and arrived here on the 11th May. The Stikine people did not relish the idea that the place was to be abandoned so soon, the rascals were taken by surprise, and made up their minds to attack us, were very saucy, but finding that we put on a bold front, and mustered a good force, they thought better of it. they would have rued the day that they fired a shot at us, as we were perfectly prepared for a row, we mustered about thirty guns in the fort, as Messrs Work & Beardmore with a party of men from Fort Simpson were with us and rendered us much assistance. The Russian American Coy's Brig Constantine, was Chartered by us, to remove the men and families, property &c from Stikine at $1000 per month, she had 53 souls on board and was full, even the deck was crowded.

Queen Charlotte Strait from Captain George Vancouver's map, 1793.

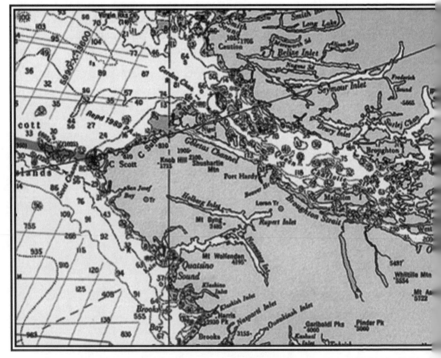

Queen Charlotte Strait from Canadian Hydrographic Service chart L/C-3000, 1994.

CHAPTER 11

Building Fort Rupert

I see a man is King at sea, but he is quite a common man ashore.
—The Diary of Andrew Muir, Thursday 29 March 1849

In late 1848, John Muir Sr. signed a contract with the Hudson's Bay Company to oversee the sinking of a coal mine shaft and the subsequent mining of the seam of coal at a new fort to be built at Beaver Harbor. He signed on his three sons, Andrew, Robert and John Jr., his nephew Archibald Muir together with John MacGregor and John Smith, as miners. The Company provided a blacksmith, Charles Jobb, to travel with them. His wife, Mary, Mrs. Turner, his daughter and Michael, his ten-year-old son, made up the rest of the party. They met with Archibald Barclay at Norway House before proceeding to the docks to go aboard the Hudson's Bay Company vessel *Harpooner*, under Captain Lewis Morice. Andrew, John Muir's eldest son, began to keep a diary at the time they all boarded the train in Manchester. The early pages of the diary are full of optimism. They little knew, however, that they were on a collision course with Chief Trader Captain William Henry McNeill!

Andrew was outspoken, arrogant and self-opinionated. Later, his character was summed up in the Fort Rupert journal: "...he (Andrew) being a meddling impudent fellow leading others to do as he bid them." His father, Mr. John Muir Sr: "...allowed that he was impudent and forward saying it was his failure &c."

Andrew records in his diary that he took umbrage at other passengers and crossed swords with the first mate and doctor over matters of supplies. Early in the voyage he records that he had: "...a little spree after dinner, John Smith being displeased with the cooking, I commenced to cook after got watch for tea ready at 5 O.C. gave it out and had a fine coollyshangie of our company of the name of "Yeats James" he may be a man but he has not the common principles even of a man about him. He says he is above cooking. I must confess it is too good a job for him or any one of his stamp I need say no further it is no use wasting paper on him."

Andrew spells James Yates' name wrongly although the 'coollyshangie' would not have been entirely Andrew's fault. Mr. Yates was hired by the Company as a ship's carpenter and Doctor Helmcken described him as: "...a powerful cantankerous being, a dark coloured Scotchman."

James Yates was later in the British Columbia legislature and a street in Victoria is named after him.

One of the major contentions on the voyage was a firm belief of the Muirs that the beef put on board for them was of superior quality, but was being eaten by the cabin set. Nearing the equator Andrew writes: "A regular row with Doctor and Capt. about our allowance of provisions being too little being less than we ought to get from the list of stores laid in for us which we saw but we got no redress, they are not willing to do justice it seems to me they know not the term justice. I hope one day I shall be able to see justice done to its full extent, and that aggressor may be punished. Why should one man rob another fellow man of his right due to him except it be for his own aggrandizement nothing else time must be the opener up of all these events."

The next day he continued his row: "...had another row or two with the Doctor today about provisions by himself, but he was too proud he could not stand to speak to us contented we must wait our time although it should be hard to bear."

One of the few times that he approved of the captain of the *Harpooner* was on Sunday: "After that we had worship altogether went to worship on deck but I must really say few attended which says very little in their favour The Capt. mustered all hands and gave them a very severe reprimand about not coming aft to service which negligence he deprecated in very severe tones."

Not many days passed before Andrew was back on his hobbyhorse:

We refused to take our beef it was so bad we went to the Doctor about it and could get no redress but we must either take it or want so we are going to want it is the ship Coys Stores they having consumed all ours first which was good now we must either take the bad or none Gedion the storekeeper gave us the information that ours was all used if we ask to get our own stores served out to us, we are told they are whatever is served out to us, such is Mr Wright's statement the first Mate he is what I call a man of no principle as he told me one day when I tried to reason with him he said he should listen to no reason from that and other cases in which I have seen him I have no difficulty in coming to a conclusion.

John Muir Sr. was a covenanter and preacher and Andrew too, was a zealot for attendance at divine service. However, he was not so puritan that it prevented a drunken spree on Saturday nights.

The Muirs were not the only people to complain. Soon after this incident, the crew made complaints backed by action that Andrew, perhaps gloatingly, records, unable to hide his indignation at the authorities aboard:

It got dark and threatening like the wind got up till it became necessary to reef topsails again all hands was called to reef which they refused to do till they got a cask of good beef opened for them they having been for several days without beef the one opened being bad they complained saying they were weak and could not work day and night without meat, which caused the following row, the Mate (Mr Wright) went to the fore castle and ordered the hands to turn out they told him they could not work night and day without meat but if they would open another cask of beef and if it was good give it out to them and they would work and if it was all bad they should bear with it till they came to the first port the mate said they should open no other beef and should have struck one of the men had not another got between them, The Capt. came forward to see what was ado when he heard he asked them to turn out they told him the same that if he opened a cask of beef and if good serve it out to them and if bad should work the vessel to the first port namely Valparaiso he the Captain said the beef they had was good and he should open no more about 10 O.C. open hostilities commenced with the captain and men we were all down below and saw nothing of it fortunately it did not last long otherwise the consequences might have been very serious. Some of the men seemed worse for drink after matters were quieted again we passengers were called aft and divided into two watches 8 in each to work the vessel into Valparaiso but fortunately for our good and sake of the vessel they agreed to open another cask of beef and the men resumed work.

Andrew, like many sailors, was enchanted by Juan Fernandes and records in his diary: "…a glorious sight when understood it was our watering place, the island on which poor unfortunate Robinson Crusoe was cast."

On the second day in the harbor he was in a party granted liberty ashore for a full day's outing. He gives a detailed account of his day of liberty on land when he climbed the mountain to look down on the bay. He describes the event: "…. we very soon found our descent to be both easier and quicker than our ascent halting every now and taking a repast from the peach trees which was spread in rich abundance both on hills and valley then the luxuriant fragrance arising from the mint in the valley below one might have said he was in perfect paradise, oh it was truly delicious, in fact we were just in the same predicament as Adam was all we seem to want was a help-mate, human pleasures are all short lived."

In August, 1848, Douglas wrote to McNeill to tell him of the arrangements with the hire of the Russian brigantine *Constantine*, because the HBC vessel *Mary Dare* was under repair in Oahu and the *Beaver* was having new boilers fitted. Two months later, Douglas wrote to Mr. Trebenkoff, governor of the Russian American Company, of the Hudson Bay Company's intention to abandon the post at Stikine. In October, 1848, Simpson writes to the Board of Management at Victoria: "A headsman and six miners were to sail from London in October, however, since the coal might be required before the miners arrived the board was to use its utmost endeavours to provide 500 - 1000 tons by employing Indians."

Even before this letter was received at Fort Victoria, Douglas had made plans for the move and in December, 1848, writes to the governor and committee: "Our plans in regard to that object are as follows. To establish a Post at a convenient point for working coals, about McNeill's harbour, near the north east end of Vancouver's Island. Withdrawing for that purpose the men and Officers on the present establishment of Fort Stekine."

Chief Factor John Work arrived at Fort Stikine to oversee the move and the *Constantine* sailed on 15 April 1849. They stopped at Fort Simpson to load prefabricated parts for the two bastions that would be erected at the new fort on Beaver Harbor. The ship was so heavy-laden that there was little room below or on deck for the fifty-three passengers on board. The SS *Beaver* towed the *Constantine* into Beaver Harbor on 11 May 1849 and construction of Fort Rupert began next day.

Charley Beardmore, Indian trader from Fort Simpson, is assigned to open the Indian trading store at the new fort at Beaver Harbor. He is good-natured, energetic and tall, with a shock of curly red hair. Apart from his height and red hair, everyone identifies him from a distance by the shillelagh in his hand. People ask its purpose, and he replies, "Good against Indians and bears!" then grins, like an overgrown schoolboy.

Charley goes ashore with the other officers and a few armed men to select a site to be cleared for the new fort. He's jovial with young John Simpson, Sir George's half-breed son; John will have little influence in the Company as he is all too keen to get to the California gold! Next morning, assisted by Simpson and a couple of men, Charley starts on the construction of a small hut, a round one with no windows but with an opening in the roof to let out smoke and let in light and rain! He keeps it simple and light, for it will have to be carried inside the fort pickets later. For the present, it has a stout door, no furniture and just two bunks. Two refinements, an altar for the fire and clay between the logs, will have to wait until it is moved inside the stockade.

Six chopping axes sound like myriad giant woodpeckers and a creaking, wrenching sound announces the falling of another tree. Crackling fires around the tree stumps add to the cacophony. A band of Indians cut eighteen-foot pickets and add the small branches to the fires. They are friendly people, Charley observes, who have welcomed them to this wild place. Their village of sixty solid houses is decorated with carved posts, crests to mark a chief's abode: salmon, suns, double-headed snakes or that big-lipped man, Tsonoqoa. They erect no tall carved poles like the Nishga or Haida chiefs at Fort Simpson or Skidegate. The men and women are darker-skinned than the Haida, Tshimsian or Tlingit and are in a state of nature under their three-and-a-half-point blankets; blankets are both covering and currency. The children too, huddle under blankets, not playing today in the cold, biting northwest wind. "Can these children be trusted to play with the McNeill, Blenkinsop, Bottineau or Cedras youngsters so quaintly dressed as miniature Victorians?" he wonders.

Day after day, Charley leads the men to clear the ground. At last he assists Mr. Work in setting up the prefabricated bastions at opposite corners of what will be the rectangle of pickets. On the fifth

Friday, June 6, in the early morning, he holds his dram of grog to toast the hoisting of the flag, which was accompanied by the roar of a seven-gun salute echoed back in triplicate by the three vessels at anchor in the bay. "That should impress the natives of this place," he declares to John Simpson.

All during this time the Indians have made pickets, removed stumps, levelled the fort's yard, brought tons of coal and piled it in front of the new fort. The *Mary Dare* arrives a week before they raised the flag, to deliver planks and filling-up pieces for the bastion. Now the *Mary Dare* waits for a succession of canoes to haul aboard 130 tons of black gold. All this labor is given in return for tobacco.

After ten weeks of hack and hew, Charley supervises the removal of his house from the beach to within the stockade. Next evening Captain McNeill drives the last picket and furnishes each man with a half pint of grog in celebration. All the houses are now within the pickets, the Indian trading houses planned for each side of the main gate will form an alley. He stops to admire his future offices and store house. Two sets of gates will prevent the Indians from entering the court yard, with the exception of ladies, vouched as wives to the men. The six Kanakas are housed separately within the pickets and fend for themselves.

The Indian village does not disturb Charley. He walks freely and is constantly greeted by the dark brown robust men with their hair top-knotted on their heads, brown spaniel eyes gazing at him from their painted faces. The women too, paint their faces, which are partly hidden under their cedar bark hats, their oolachan-oiled bodies covered by their blankets. But that aroma does not reach his nostrils through the smell of fish offal strewn over the clam shells on the ground—air to cut with an ax! The young women, now, they are different. Their long black hair flows from flattened heads, as they sit painting their faces with vermillion and red earth, a small round mirror to ensure symmetry to their patterns. They are coy too, with eyes that flirt and attract, attract him to lie with one sated on some private bower. These are natural, joyous women enough to make Ovid blush; and Charley will have a daughter 'ere long!

Charley admires the industry of the Native Indians and there has been no trouble until the fractious Nahwitti Indians spread an ugly rumor that the white people of the fort intend to poison the Kwakiutl village for stealing tools. At 3:00 P.M., with dinner just commenced, there is a kerfuffle at the gates and McNeill sends Charley to investigate. The 400 irritated Indians milling around sends him back to report to McNeill. Club in one hand, musket in the other, he covers McNeill and Bottineau as they parley with the chiefs, explain that the rumor is false, pernicious even. McNeill calls him over and asks him to fetch tobacco from the store, which he distributes to the chiefs for their work-gangs in a show of good faith.

"He's good with these Indians; they trust him," Charley says to himself as he sees their smiles and hears their cries of Ma-ta-hell.

In August, the weather fine and hot, as Charley is working on the upper flooring of the trade house, sounds of voices bring him to the window to watch a gang of fifty-two Indians haul the foundation of the men's houses past the gates and into the yard, after which they will slot the wall timbers and build a stone chimney before the roofs are constructed. Later that evening Bazil Bottineau reports that the Indians have been heard talking of taking the fort.

Captain McNeill calls all the men together and sets watchmen at both front and back gates. He orders Charley to draw up a roster and informs the men that indolent watch-keeping will be punished as if sleeping on watch at sea. No mercy or excuses will be accepted or leniency afforded any man who disobeys. Next morning Charley is called to witness punishment. Cabana left his watch for six minutes unattended, putting all their lives in jeopardy. No room for courts or appeals, he receives a dozen across his back from McNeill's cane.

Blenkinsop, the Canadian servants and the Kanakas were sailors at heart and accepted the law of the sea that stretched back to the medieval Rules of Oleron, which describe a seaman's obligation that binds him to the ship for the length of the voyage and accepts the absolute authority of the captain. Even though they are on land, these officers and servants of the Company showed a fierce loyalty to this Company that nurtured and paid them. They accepted as necessary the kind of discipline that ensured their safety as a minority in this hostile foreign land of the Native Indians.

The clash between the fort's officers and the miners was inevitable. The Muir family, in particular Andrew, were fully conversant with the contract signed to mine coal and Andrew was articulate in presenting his rights. He expected the rule of law, not the arbitrary execution of a sentence for a crime he perceived to have been committed by another party. His father, the titular overseer of the miners, was chivvied by his oldest son and the diary reads as if Andrew made the decisions. Already Andrew had expressed his disgust with the authority of the captain and first mate at sea and fort-life differed but little from ship-life.

During the time that Andrew spent at Fort Victoria he did not keep a daily diary, he obviously summarizes his impression of the fort at a later date:

1 Jun 1849: remained at Fort Victoria until later end of August before we got an opportunity of going to our destination the Island at this Fort is capable of cultivation to a large extent a good space of it being clear and here the Company have 2 dairies with upward of 150 Milch Cows and an abundance of wild ones they also grow wheat, corn potatoes and other vegetables, the only thing wanted at this place is Moisture in the Summer season for want of which the crops are greatly hurt the ground being so burnt up by the long drought, this Fort consists of a square formed of wood 18 feet high and at the 2 angular corners are Bastions mounting 14 Guns, this is now the head Fort of the Company where all vessels land their goods from England we remained at Fort Victoria nearly 3 months when I left along with our party in the Coys Brig Mary Dare for our destination the Coal Mines and after a very tedious (voyage), during my stay at Fort Victoria I was employed along with the rest of the party blasting rock for dockyard and digging well, during that Period we wrote 9 hours per day to hasten completion of the dockyard before we should leave. I along with the others had also a conversation with Mr Douglas concerning our ration when he agreed to give us 14lbs Flour 10 1/2lbs beef or Venison or in lieu as much salmon fresh as should be equivalent 1lb. sugar 4oz - Tea. 3 Gills of Rum per week, which he said was as much as any man could destroy. we were for taking the shilling per day in lieu of our rations, but from the statements made to us of the prices of articles it should not keep us in flour as their prices for goods got today were moderate and get the same goods out of the store tomorrow they were exhorbitant in Prices, so that a person here is as it were in a dilemma, with everything he gets and they cannot give you an explanation. Mr Douglas told us we should be as well to take the scale of rations which I have mentioned before as it should save all further trouble and that anything produced on the Island should

be served out to us and not charged such as potatoes &ct. all these things settled we left Fort Victoria on the 27th of August 1849 in the Coy Brig Mary Dare and after a very tedious passage arrived at our destination Beaver harbour 24th September.

Andrew did not record that they made a formal complaint against Captain Morice about their beef aboard. Douglas sent the sample to the doctor who said that it was well cured and of "perfectly inexceptional quality." Douglas only mentions this because the Muirs appeared to consider their grievances of greatest importance to themselves and other parties. In an ironic note, Douglas goes on to suggest to the governor and committee: "It appeared to me, that these passengers who are chiefly from North Britain, and accustomed from infancy to an oat meal diet would have preferred it, to any other kind of food; and I am of opinion, that in future shipment of Scottish emigrants for this country, the stock of preserved meats which were not relished by those who arrived this year, might be reduced and replaced by an additional supply of oatmeal, equally to the advantage of the Company and of the emigrants."

While the *Beaver* took the inside route to Fort Rupert, the *Mary Dare* went to the west of Vancouver Island out of the Juan de Fuca Strait and around Cape Scott into Queen Charlotte Sound. The distance covered was about 400 sea miles by dead reckoning. However, at this time of year southerly winds occurred about 40 percent of the time and westerly to northwesterly winds about 40 percent of the time, while for the rest, calm prevailed. Progress tacking against a northwest wind, hindered by a strong current flowing southeast on the outside of Vancouver Island, made for a long voyage. Once around Cape Scott a sailing vessel was faced with a difficult passage, impossible against a headwind down either Gordon Channel or Goletas Channel. Any modern-day sailor knows the frustration of tacking against the strong currents in both of these channels or finding the wind die at the change of tide and drifting back to their starting point, with the water too deep to drop an anchor.

Chief Factor John Work accompanied the miners on board the *Mary Dare*. On the 26 September, the fort journal records: "Mr Work started this afternoon with Mr Muir and two of the miners also Bottineau and five Indians to examine the coalgrounds."

Andrew records in his diary that he was one of the miners, with McGregor the other. They headed south toward McNeill Bay to inspect the Suquash area as well as other possible sites. Before the *Mary Dare* departed with Mr. Work on 3 October, McNeill wrote a long letter to Sir George Simpson from the new establishment at Beaver Harbor. In this letter, McNeill tells Sir George Simpson of their arrival at the harbor in the *Constantine* towed by the steamer *Beaver* down the difficult stretch of Gordon Channel. McNeill reports on the progress at the fort; the pickets, Indian shop, and bastions were completed and the men's house well advanced with part of the house to be fitted out for the miners. He mentions that there were 2,000 Indians encamped in the harbor who worked well and were friendly people. There were some problems obtaining fresh provisions: "Deers meat, is very scarce, we have as yet procured but few Salmon, they however are of a good quality, the Indians obtain so much property for labour and Coals that they will never hunt, and if this place is to be kept up, we must live mostly on salt provisions, Potatoes are not to be had of the Natives, we may get some planted next Spring at the place."

McNeill tells Simpson that they had already collected 950 tons of coal and stored it at the fort. This surface coal had been mined from Suquash, about six miles south of Beaver Harbor and carved out in blocks with axes by the Indians. From the Indians' viewpoint this was an easier way to obtain tobacco for trade than hunting deer for fresh provisions at the fort. The major difficulty of the times, the 1849 California gold rush to San Francisco, had already started to plague the Hudson's Bay Company on the coast. McNeill tells Simpson that he did not expect any vessels to come for coal until the next spring because sailors were not to be had to man the ships for less than $150 per month:

> One of the American Steamers some few months since left Sta Francisco, with all her crew, and some of the Engineers in Irons, a Sloop of War accompanied her out over the Bar, with her Guns double shotted, this is the way they do things in the Pacific. Our Sailors and Landsmen are running away every opportunity 5 from the Steamer and 4 from the Mary Dare took french leave a short time since, and expect to hear that many more have gone, no men will re-engage for any of the Forts on the Coast, and how we are to keep up this place and Fort Simpson is a mystery to me. We have offer'd our men whose times have expired £40. per annum, ie we offered them the same as the New hands say that they agreed for in Canada, and they would not take the offer. As regards the Gold regions, it is impossible to say what may be done

208

there hereafter, some of the men obtain $5000 in one day others not more than $10 I hear however that they average abt one ounce of Gold per diem, The Speculators in California are reaping all the benefit however as they purchase the Gold at $10 the ounce at least the papers say so and the Gold's worth $17 per ounce in Oahu!! This of itself is a good speculation and many are making fortunes. We have been afraid to send a vessel to Sta Francisco with goods or provisions for fear the Crew running away, some Vessels have been laid up there for months with no crew on board, Murders and Roberies are the order of the day at the Mines, a great deal of sickness has prevailed there and carried off many. I think a good business could be done there at present, in fact a steady person cannot help making money, mechanics obtain $16 per diem other labourers $10. Sailors from $100 to 150 per month, In Wallamitt I hear that $10 is paid per diem for men of course this must be paid in produce. I also have heard that Doctr McLoughlin is likely to obtain $200,000 for his place on the Banks of the Wallamitte.

If the cost of labor had risen, it was nothing compared to the cost of provisions, and McNeill reports: "I hear by Mr Work that flour sells at the Gold mines for $400!!! per Bbl I mean four hundred dollars per barrel & other articles in the same ratio, I fear that we may be short of flour and other provisions in the Columbia District, as most of the settlers have gone to the mines and besides provisions bring such a price in California that many Vessels have loaded in the Columbia and sold in California."

Not only private companies were having trouble as he tells Simpson: "The soldiers from the American force and Sailors from the Men O'War on California desert every opportunity, 60 from the Ohio, and 15 from the Constance deserted and some of General Leane's Dragoons were missing at roll call one morning."

McNeill reports on business and trade at the Sandwich Islands again. These two passages in the letter may have added another doubt in Simpson's mind about McNeill's reliability:

A good bargain I think is to be made at the Islands at this time as nearly all the Foreign residents have gone from there to California, The Govt is very anxious now, to sell lands and invite settlers to reside there, as they have lost about $300,000 per annum already, by the Foreign residents giving up business and going to California. If California prospers, and it must, The Islands will come in for their share of the Cakes and Ale ere long, and in my opinion is the time to purchase lands and to extend the

Honble Companys Trade not at the Islands, but in the Pacific Throughout the next Ten years should if properly conducted, put Ten millions into the pocket of the Hudsons Bay Coy, there is a piece of land in St Francisco that was bought three years since for $40 - sold the other day for $10,000!!! no one on the east side of of the mountains can have no idea of the excitement in the Pacific caused by the immense quantity of Gold Silver & Quick Silver obtained in California.

Now Sir I will say a little on my own affairs, you very kindly "by letter" from Norway House 1st July 1847 offered me a leave of absence I have applied to the Board of Management for such "and sent an extract of your letter", They have refused it, and say that they have not the power to grant it &c, I am indeed much out of health caused by the constant and continual confinement inside of the Pickets both at Stikine and now at this place, I require open air, "and must have it". If I cannot obtain a leave of absence, I must and shall send in my resignation, this time to the Governor and Council, I have no doubt Sir but you will readily grant it, but I cannot get away from this in less than Eighteen months, and before that may lay my bones outside the Pickets. Blenkinsop is here with me together with Beardmore, your son John was here for a short time, his engagement expired, and he would not re-engage again, he went with Mr Work to Victoria. Blenkinsop is also very much out of health, and it will be years before he recovers his health.

Now Sir I hope you will not think it wrong or out of place for me to say that both of us are determined to retire if we cannot be removed from this place, we have had more confinement than any two officers in the Service and I think it no more than right that we should now be retired, and have a little of the civilised life now so near us as well as other people. We can do our duty to the South, as well as to the North. If our Service cannot be dispensed with why we should have more remuneration, but we both wish to get from what is termed the coast, and as I have said that much is to be done at the Islands and California, and in the Pacific and China. I have no objection to head and do any business for the Company at either place. Blenkinsop is willing to second me, and I do not know any two on this side the mountains that can do more, or better than we two can, for the Company. As I believe I know also the merits and capability of all the Gents on this side. If I should serve as agent for the Company at the Islands or California or China I shall of course expect more than a Chief Traders pay for our emoluents now a days is mere nothing for what we do, or rather suffer.

I hope Sir you will not think me getting vain or, that I am talking Big. I am writing as a businessman, and saying what I know, and think may be done in the Pacific Ocean, And as time has come for me to better myself and the Company. I have taken the liberty to write as I have done, and I really think that the Company can, and should do more business in the Pacific, the Fur Trade seems to be a secondary concern on this side. Commerce is all the go, and if Ships can be manned, the day has come to employ them to advantage. An English Vessel made $33,000 from Panama to California by carrying passengers. One of the American Steamers obtained $300,000 from Panama to St Francisco, for freight and passengers. Indeed you can scarcely realize or imagine what is going on in the Commercial world in the Pacific."

McNeill gave up his leave of absence to assist in the moving of Fort Stikine to the new establishment. He performed with energy and success in building the fort and did not take the leave of absence offered to him in Simpson's letter of July, 1848. Why then, did Simpson write to Douglas on 20 February 1850 and say: "…you did quite right in paying no attention to McNeill's application for leave of absence he should have taken his furlough when it came around if he wished a holiday but until it comes around again, & while he is in good health he must attend his duties."

McNeill brought Simpson up to date on the shipping. The *Beaver* was at Fort Victoria having new boilers fitted and he reported that Mr. Thorn, the engineer, was, on the one hand, an excellent person, responsible for making the steamer go faster and on a quarter less wood, but on the other hand he was a troublesome man, John Bull-like, a great grumbler! Mrs. Muir and her family came ashore on 28 September and were served out their rations as per list. George Blenkinsop also wrote to Sir George Simpson on 28 August and reports his pleasure at the friendliness of the Indians as well as the arrival of the miners:

These Indians also have greatly decreased since your Honor's visit to this place in 1841. in fact they are vanishing rapidly from one end of the coast to the other. Ma-ta-hell is well liked by them all, they are, without exception, the most friendly Indians to be met with on the N.W. coast, and are of great assistance to us in carrying on the work. Furs are at present not very abundant, but I trust that the Sea Otter trade will thrive rapidly as they now have a great quantity of property to buy them with. The Indians on the outside of the Island have promised to devote more of their time to hunting them.

The interior of the Island appears to be but little known to the Natives. Wild animals, of almost every kind, are numerous, and hope to be able to give a good account of many of their skins ere long. Bears are particularly so. A party of miners arrived here a few days since, and commence operations immediately. The oversman, a fine intelligent Scotchman, seems in high spirits and fully expects the concern will turn out to be a prosperous one.

This honeymoon lasted but one week before the fort journal records a deterioration of relations between the miners and the establishment!

Charley Beardmore writes to his friend Aaron Chapman on the Board of Governors in London: "The service is a good service, yet every clerk is discontented & most of the commissioned Gents. Why? because of the despotic way that is held over the country, clerks are leaving and those coming are of a letter rank & more enlightened & will not put up with the same treatment as the old hands."

Later in his letter he writes: "...seldom is salt beef or pork furnished. These items are sent to the Russian American Company at Sitka. Cheese and bacon are, unknown save in name. The butter is abominable; we have butter now in the Fort that you would not put to your carriage wheels, for if you did the salt would wear out the axle trees. The good butter is sent to Oahu!"

The Kwakiutl Indians were famous for their marauding warfare with their neighbors and punished any offense against them by setting out to avenge themselves. On one occasion they went to avenge an attempted assassination of one of their chiefs by a northern tribe and returned to the village with fourteen skulls and thirty prisoners. To honor Mrs. Muir, the first white woman to visit their land, they offered her any two of the fine heads of her choosing as a gift and no doubt were willing to show her how to remove the scalp, cure the skin, wrap it with the long hair in blue cloth and place it in a cedar bent box—a special trophy.

Within the first two weeks, Blenkinsop starts to comment in the fort journal on the miners work ethic: "They work at present but little in fact Smith and Macgregor are the only two who keep steadily at their jobs the others merely box attendance." From this time he enters the hours the miners work on a daily basis into the fort journal. The Muirs were dissatisfied with their accommodation. In their contract they agreed to build their own housing on arrival but in spite of that, they demanded the whole of the men's eighty-foot dwelling rather than the half of it. The fort journal records:

> They positively refuse to work at the mine until they can get four fire places. We have done everything to make them comfortable giving them half of the mens house thereby saving them a great deal of trouble as it is specially stated in their agreement they were to build their own houses with nothing towards this. The house commenced today will of course be constructed by both parties as mentioned in this agreement. We have no control over their movements so long as Mr Muir has mining operations in hand or in view, there refusal to work at the shaft to be a troublesome set and so far as my humble opinion is concerned they have fully made up their minds to do just nothing. "Nous verrous".

Blenkinsop had been on the coast for nine years and writes as if flabbergasted: "Mr Muir asked the miners to commence sinking the shaft last Monday they positively refused saying that they had no place to dry their clothing."

By the end of October, 1849, the two sides had fleshed out their positions. Andrew's diary records:

> We are all of us at Pit digging drain to take water away surface water now we are on Vancouver's Island and we are put to the sinking of a Pit to look for coal a thing we never agreed for as we came out here to work coal not to look for it and do all manner of work and I consider the company has broken our agreement as we were only to work as labourers in the event of the coal not succeeding now we never saw a coal at all and on speaking about it we were told we should have to work at anything we were put and knowing we could get no redress we were obliged to work away, thus we have been kept knocked about at every thing away from the Fort with our work and no protection and everything about the pit to do ourselves without any assistance and the Coy. having their Fort here could not get the least assistance and several times the Fort having rows with the Indians has come down and threatened to shoot us, We went to the head Officer of the Fort for assistance and our place made secure from the Indians with Pickets that we might work without molestation but no assistance could we get but was told we must either work away as we are or let it stand altogether as we could get no help from him.

Charley Beardmore goes down to the mine shaft, the rain coming down in sheets and he huddles under the hood of his capote. He passes the miners already leaving the shaft although it is only nine o'clock in the morning! At the shaft, the two Kanakas sent by McNeill to help Mr. Muir are still working.

"You're foolish to work when those lazy buggers have left you!" he exclaims and walks away.

At midday Bottineau hails Charley in the trade shop, tells him the captain is asking for him. As he enters McNeill's office the captain berates him in front of Mr. Muir and Blenkinsop.

"What right, sir, have you to tell the Kanakas to stop work!"

Not a question for Charley, but a severe reprimand that brings an expression of triumph to Muir's face. Charley attempts to defend himself.

"I didn't order them, sir, I expressed a private opinion!"

"Well, sir, in future mind your own business in the trade shop and stop meddling in other peoples affairs," Captain McNeill tells Charley, his face flushed with irritation.

Blenkinsop defends Charley in the fort journal and writes: "Mr. Muir was fully aware as he himself said that an under officer had no business to interfere. Consequently, what happened this morning was only considered to be a misunderstanding between Mr. Muir and Mr. Beardmore and at all events, if two Kanakas still kept at their duty the remainder of the day at 'A' mine, Mr. Muir was put at no inconvenience whatever respecting what took place this morning."

The company's point of view is expressed at great length in the journal by Blenkinsop:

Yesterday a slight disturbance took place outside the fort in consequence of an Indian having stole one of our axes. After a little talk the Axe was returned and things were settled amicably. Some two or three (natives) however went down to the mine and told the miners that the Indians were coming down to cut all their heads off as they had done to some of their enemies and in the evening they came and requested powder and ball to defend themselves with in case of a war. This morning this was given them and after they came back 9 A.M. because it rained a little, demanded to have their mine picketed in. Cap MacNeill refused by telling them our men were required at present to put up buildings for home. But the miners, not e'en ourselves having a dry place to sleep in, this request however was made by the young men of the party and not by Mr Muir. Andrew in particular seems to be the leader in controlling his father. Mr Muir however said he did not want anything of the kind and so that was scotched. How in justice to the company it is necessary to state here that the doings of their men, miners are anything but what is specified in their contract for them to do. From a conversation which passed this afternoon between Captain MacNeill and Mr Muir we have ascertained that these people consider themselves an aggrieved party 'and are going to make out a protest.' God knows for what, this they did not let us know and also 'had something with law when they got back to England or Scotland.'

Before going any further I am quite ready to swear that all I have written concerning them is correct and impartial. There was much valuable time lost by them previous to Octr 25th being very dilatory and idle whilst employed getting ready their houses. Mr Muir and his family viz 4 sons and nephew commenced on the mine on the 25th Octr Smith and McGregor joined them last Monday and as one thought were going to work in earnest. Monday and Tuesday they were away from the fort 8 hours but lo and behold today because it rains they do not work. They 'wet the small of their backs' and knocked off. This after the shameful manner of acting before is too bad. They are well fed, much better than ourselves, housed and have every assistance. They require more than they bargained for, It says in their agreement they were to work 10 hours on the surface.

Now so far it has been all surface work and no one day have they worked more than 8 hours and on average not more than 5 hours. So it is plainly to be seen they have determined to do as little as possible and just what they plan. What can men who act thus have to protect against and go to law about? So for everything away from the fort it is what more or less of our own men have to do every day. So for being exposed who are more so than ourselves and lastly we and our men have to do our duty rain or no rain and why should not they. We expect nothing from them but to act up to their engagement we have fulfilled to the utmost and even more all that was required of us. To make them more comfortable we have employed the very men one wanted to build a house to shelter ourselves from wind and rain in erecting their's. We have deprived our own hard working Kanakas and Canadians of their dwelling place to accomodate these miners. Nay more, we have given them our own pork to eat and actually eating ourselves the very meat they refused. It is certainly as Mr Muir said come to a crisis. We must know their future intentions as well as their reasons for acting as they have done. Mr Muir seems himself to do his best but does not appear to have any control over his men in justice to our employers we must control them for him.

I repeat every justice have been (made) will be done them and at the same time all proceedings will be faced fully noted down in this journal. Those in authority over us will see from its perusal whether or not these persons have fulfilled their several contracts so that it is for them to decide and act accordingly.

◦✺◦

Charley Beardmore has been subdued since reprimanded by Captain McNeill in front of Muir and Blenkinsop. He stays in his trade store, supervises the new building and at dinner each afternoon, listens to the gossip. He learns that the first shaft sunk by the miners has filled with water and cannot be drained. McNeill and Muir have chosen a new site for a second shaft to be sunk closer to the sea and more easily drained. Blenkinsop grumbles that the miners will never get far down if they continue to spell each other off so that only half of them are working at any one time.

Charley sees McGregor and Mr. Muir heading for Captain McNeill's office and hears from Blenkinsop that McNeill supports Muir against complaints by McGregor that Muir's sons did not work more than half the time and did not take their turns at heaving the stuff out of the shaft.

Over dinner Charley nods his head as Captain McNeill and Blenkinsop complain that the miners are shameful and do not promote the interests of the Company even after they had been so generous to the miners in giving up their own housing to them!

Charley hears raised voices from McNeill's office again, violent language from one of the men, countered with cries of mutiny and orders arrive for him to get Bottineau and irons for Smith and McGregor. McNeill, sword in one hand and pistol in the other, guards the two men as he goes over to put them in irons. "You will obey Mr Muir," McNeill shouts at the two men, "cause any more trouble and I will put you on water and salmon with irons on your hands and feet!" The two of them go white and mumble contrition

216

enough to satisfy McNeill who then reads them a lecture on their duty to obey Mr. Muir.

Calm is restored in the room, the irons are taken away by Bottineau. Captain McNeill asks McGregor, "Why have you not worked ten hours a day on the surface as your agreement states?"

McGregor looks surprised and replies, "No one's ask it of me!"

"So that's the truth of it," McNeill observes to them at dinner.

Captain McNeill calls Charley into the office after the steamer arrives to let him know that Blenkinsop is going on a period of sick leave and will be going down to Fort Victoria in the new year.

Charley is to act as second during Blenkinsop's absence and on 27 January 1850, he starts to keep the journal.

The SS *Beaver* brought the governor of Rupert's Land, Mr. A. Colvile and party, on a visit of inspection to Fort Rupert. He was impressed with the progress made and in a letter to Sir John Pelly writes: "We found everything at this establishment to be progressing satisfactorily. The stockades and bastions completed, several substantial buildings erected and others in progress, and a portion of land cleared for planting potatoes. The Indians, about one thousand in number, who live around the fort have been all along well disposed, and industrious and I consider that the state of affairs here reflect great credit on Capt McNeil's management."

Mr. Colvile noted that 1,100 tons of coal, collected by the Indians, were protected and ready for shipment. The shaft half a mile from the fort had been sunk to about forty-one feet and gave the geological formation of the walls and reports to Sir George Simpson: "...the gang of miners appear to be well satisfied with all that has been done for them but will be more contented when we shall be in a condition to supply them with fresh provisions occasionally."

Mr. Colvile also expressed his regret at not being able to report a workable seam of coal, but he adds that: "...the miners are generally of opinion, that they will find a workable seam of coal immediately under the last bed of Grey Freestone." McNeill requested a furlough and in this letter to Simpson, Colvile writes: "I have performed my first administrative act, as will appear from my letter to McNeil herewith enclosed. He had made up his mind to retire unless he got leave of absence & Douglas thinks that Blenkinsop will do very well at Fort Rupert, so I complied with his request 'a tout risque'."

❧

Charley Beardmore sits at his desk writing up the journal and notes that there has been another break into Mr. Muir's tool house. Sixteen chiefs in the fort have a long talk with him about the two axes stolen. He swears that he will have payment or close out the fort and clear off to Koskimos. He tells them they better go in the bush and hide as he does not wish to hurt them. The chiefs are shocked when he tells them that the captain intends to set fire to the houses and burn them down. The chiefs bring in two beaver, two bears and four other skins as payment, very good he tells them, "coupitoilex" which means "we are done being angry." In the journal he writes: "…but this wont do getting into rows each day for Mr Muir. We gained our point however showed we were not afraid yet did not fight which is an Indian Traders policy."

The growling discontent continues, overshadowing some of Charley's anxiety about the late arrival of the *Beaver*. This episode makes Mr. Muir a little repentant about the work done by his men, and Charley writes in the journal: "…Mr Muir now tacitly confessing how wrong he acted in not making his men work 10 hours per day when they first came to the country."

The *Beaver* arrives in snow—heavy southeast wind—and anchors under lee of Shell Island (Deer Island). Charley is relieved to see Blenkinsop and his wife and son safely back home.

Over dinner, Captain Dodd tells Captain McNeill about his troublesome voyage. As the fort journal records: "We were delayed at Fort Victoria by the late arrival of the ship from England. Thirteen days ago we started for this place but in entering Beware Harbour we foundered on a rock that knocked off her nose, two-thirds of the false keel and a third of the keel. Water rushed in and we pitched over our wood, emptied the boilers and got the water mastered. We lay on the rocks ten and a half hours, until the tide rose to let us steam into Beware Harbour. We laid her up on blocks, repaired her in nine days and thank God, did not see an Indian the whole time. She makes about one inch per hour now."

Charley watches Captain McNeill commiserate with Dodd and knows that had this happened to poor old Humphries or some other drunken skipper, he would have been most derogatory! Next day Charley hands over the fort journal to Blenkinsop and returns to the trade store.

⌒◞)

Three days later they greet Governor Blanshard at Fort Rupert. In July, 1849, Richard Blanshard was appointed governor to the new Colony of Vancouver Island. In August, 1849, Sir John Pelly, governor of the Hudson's Bay Company, wrote to James Douglas. In this letter he explains: "It was proposed to appoint you Governor pro tempore of the Island, but you will see by the public press, from the jealousies of some parties, and interested motives of other, how next to impossible it would have been to give you the situation."

The new governor traveled to Panama and on the Pacific side boarded HMS *Driver*, under Captain Johnson, in November, 1849. The *Driver* arrived at Fort Victoria in March, 1850, a little before the Norman Morrison. At Douglas' request, HMS *Driver* transported some livestock to the Puget Sound Agricultural Farm at Nisqually. Dr. Tolmie met Governor Blanshard at Nisqually and describes him in a letter to Simpson: "...a tall, thin person with a pale, intellectual countenance — is a great smoker, a great sportsman — a protectionist in Politics and a latitudinarian in religious matters. His manner is quiet, and rather abstracted, tho' free from hauteur, or pomposity, he does not converse much."

Since there was as yet no residence for the new governor at Fort Victoria, Blanshard stayed on board with Captain Johnson. HMS *Driver* then took Governor Blanshard on a circumnavigation of his colony. Only one other white settlement existed on Vancouver Island and on March 27 he visited it at Fort Rupert. HMS *Driver* was greeted with a seven-gun salute and then refuelled with eighty-seven tons of coal in replacement for the sixty tons used on Hudson's Bay Company's business.

Governor Blanshard spent a considerable time with the miners listening to their complaints. When the miners signed their contract, they had expected to mine a seam of coal, but they had not expected to have to look for coal. As a result they were unable to reap the piecework reward of working a coal face and wanted recompense for this deficiency. Later Douglas writes to Archibald Barclay in London: "They called upon him in a body during his visit to the mines and appeared in a very discontented state. They made no complaint against Captain McNeill who had treated them with greatest kindness but they were disappointed with the country and the mines."

~~~

Charley Beardmore is delighted with the visit by the governor that coincides with the birth of his daughter, Princess. His wife and her chiefly family are particularly impressed that the Great White Chief, King George's envoy, has consented to christen their new kin. They are intrigued by this, their first brush with the belief in a spiritual being over and above all others, but puzzled by the cross he inscribes with water on the baby's forehead. Charley's translation from English to French for Bottineau loses something of the essence even before Bottineau's translation into their Kwakiutl language.

~~~

The Hudson's Bay Company vessel, *Norman Morrison*, under Captain Wishart, left Gravesend on 21 October 1849 and between the 22 and 24 October was anchored at the Downs waiting for a change in weather to take passage west out of the English Channel at the start of her voyage to Fort Victoria. Aboard were eighty immigrants to the new colony of Vancouver Island. Most of them were under contract to the Company and Doctor J. S. Helmcken, ship's surgeon for the passage, had signed a five-year contract. During his initial interview with Mr. Archibald Barclay at Norway House, Dr. Helmcken was informed that he would relieve Mr. Barclay's nephew, Dr. Forbes Barclay, at Fort Vancouver. When Dr. Helmcken returned for his interview to accept the position, Mr. Barclay told him that he would have plenty of spare time and he would also act as private secretary to the newly appointed governor, Richard Blanshard. This suggestion seemed to highlght a sparse knowledge of the geography of the west coast of North America!

Mrs. Letitia Hargrave wrote of Dr. Helmcken in a letter to her father in 1847 that, "he is young but seems rather cute tho' prodigiously little man seems like a gentn." There were many references to his small stature and also his large head in contrast. Of himself, Helmcken said that he was a London sparrow fond of nonsense and cigars! He was friendly with everyone but intimate with no one. A shy man, with dislike of formal occasion from which he would absent himself whenever possible. In his writing he was thoughtful, almost without prejudice and he assessed individuals as he found them, unimpressed by their precedents.

Soon after his arrival at Fort Victoria, Dr. Helmcken went to see Governor Blanshard. He was under orders to proceed to Fort Rupert although it was a month or more before he took passage in the *Beaver*, under Captain Dodd. The posting of the governor's private secretary away from Fort Victoria by Chief Factor Douglas, no doubt caused another burr in the relationship between those two authoritarian gentlemen.

The barque *England*, under Captain Brown, arrived in Victoria after the *Norman Morrison*. She was sent to take a cargo of coal from Fort Rupert to San Francisco, a destination that excited many of the new immigrants under contract to the Hudson's Bay Company. Four men deserted from the *Norman Morrison* and were taken on board by the barque *England* before it sailed for Fort Rupert.

Blenkinsop kept the fort journal as soon as he returned to duty. He recorded Governor Blanshard's visit and most likely picked up gossip of the discontent between Douglas and Blanshard. He had seen the chaos in Fort Victoria first hand and reports it in the journal: "All disorder at Victoria, no order or work done, master worse off than the men." Now he was to take charge of Fort Rupert in Captain McNeill's absence. Blenkinsop's first act is recorded in the journal: "Weather uncommonly fine Wind NW At 3 A.M. the Beaver started for Fort Victoria. Called in all the principal Chiefs and gave each a small present to induce them to work well and bring in a good supply of coals, they appeared well pleased with their present and went out after making many promises of good behaviour & etc."

The stage was now set for the drama to begin. A large cast of actors, Governor Richard Blanshard, Chief Factor James Douglas, Captain Wm. McNeill, John Muir Sr., George Blenkinsop, Charley Beardmore, Dr. J. S. Helmcken, Captain Brown, Mr. Thorn, Andrew Muir and his colleagues with their wives, Chiefs Nancy and Looking-glass with their Nahwitti Indians, the deserters of the *Norman Morrison*, the Canadians, Kanakas and the new English servants in the fort, were ready to make their entrances and exits in what came to be known as the Fort Rupert Affair.

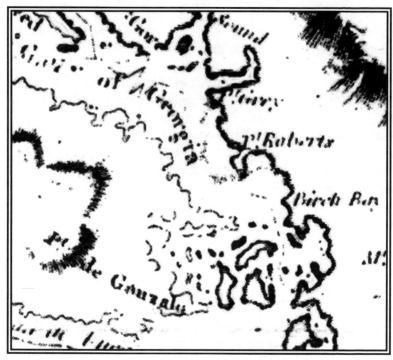

Gulf of Georgia from Captain George Vancouver's map, 1793.

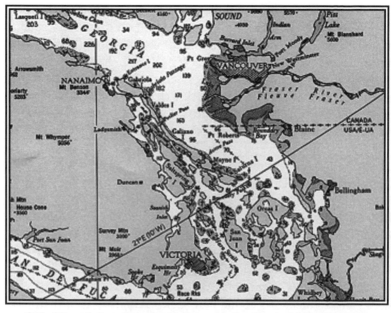

Gulf of Georgia from Canadian Hydrographic Service chart L/C-3000, 1994.

CHAPTER 12

The Fort Rupert Affair

> Have I laid my brain in the sun, and dried it, that it wants matter
> to prevent so gross o'er-reaching as this?
> —Sir John Falstaff, *Merry Wives of Windsor*; Wm. Shakespeare

Andrew Muir summarizes the winter of 1849–50 under a single entry for 29 October 1849, that appears to have been written around April, 1850. He felt that they had a three-point grievance, which he voiced in his diary. He accused the Company of a breach of their agreement:

> We are all of us at Pit digging drain to take water away surface water now we are on Vancouver's Island and we are put to the sinking of a Pit to look for coal a thing we never agreed for as we came out here to work coal not to look for it.
>
> We went to the head Officer of the Fort for assistance and our place made secure from the Indians with Pickets that we might work without molestation but no assistance could we get but was told we must either work away as we are or let it stand altogether as we could get no help from him.
>
> Send my own men with Indians in canoes up and down the beach in the dead of winter in search of clay these are facts thus we wrought away and did everything ourselves.

The last straw came on 16 of April 1850 when Andrew complains: "...we were compelled to work without assistance and protection when our watchman stored with arms and ammunition was obliged to run how could we be thought to stand and work our work without their annoyances by day and their thieving depredations by night we could not stand and men that people sees with their own eyes go out and in 5 minutes return with 2 of their neighbours heads in their hands it certainly teaches this lesson not to be trusted."

At this point, Mr. Muir came up from the mine to see Blenkinsop because of another theft at the miner's hut. According to the fort journal, he told Blenkinsop that he had decided to abandon the shaft and stop work there. However, Blenkinsop writes in the journal: "… the men were ready to do any job I might set them at, it is my intention to employ them at present digging another well in the fort as we are miserably off for want of good water."

The next morning, Chief Warsoaatie invited the miners and officers of the fort to his lodge to give them property to recompense the loss of stolen goods from the miner's hut. Blenkinsop accepted this property for return when the Company's stolen property was returned. On entering to the fort, Blenkinsop told Mr. Muir that this property was all to be deposited in the store and given back to the chiefs on condition of their getting their own things restored. Some short time after his son's articles not being forth coming he again asked Mr. Muir for it. Mr. Muir told him that he considered the property given expressly to himself and his son and that the company had no business with it. Bottineau, the interpreter, asked Warsoaatie, the head chief, for what purpose were these things given? He distinctly answered "for the things stolen from the mine." Warsoaatie, however, told Mr. Muir he might keep the things he gave him.

Andrew's version does not differ except for the indignation that Blenkinsop could suggest otherwise: "I said the goods were given freely to me and I thought I had no right to give them to him. I then went and asked at the Chiefs whither these articles were given to me as a pledge for the things stolen they said no such thing in their own language they patxhittled to me closh keep you when Mr Blenkinsop with his interpreter & Mr Bermore interrogated them they gave the same answer they had given to me and I was to give them to no one unless I choosed myself."

As far as Blenkinsop was concerned, things had reached a head and he needed advice on how to deal with the miners who had stopped work. On 18 April 1850, he dispatched a canoe with Bottineau, Tiger, two women and eight Indians along with Chiefs Warsouatie and Jani to Fort Victoria with letters to the board. He provided the canoe with muskets, ammunition and provisions necessary for the voyage. The work continued at the fort for a week while Blenkinsop waited for an answer from Fort Victoria. On 26 April 1850, Andrew confides to his diary: "At work today at drain after breakfast Mr Blenkinsop came and charged me with neglect of duty and a penalty of £50 which I said was false I was at my duty he said we were not doing half work but sitting idle I said I was doing as well as I was able and that I never was acquainted with such work as taking out roots he also charged me with these words that I was a rebellious person and kept the men of their duty, which I put down as defamation of character, and have witnesses to prove that he said so, so that when we could not please with our work we stop for the present until matters settled."

During the period that Blenkinsop waited for a reply from Fort Victoria, he made an extensive report in the journal. In this report he criticizes the quantity of work done by the miners and asks Mr. Muir if he was satisfied with the output of his men. Mr. Muir was careful not to answer this question directly as the journal entry records: "Mr Muir said he did not consider himself a good judge of labourers work but that he thought what they had done was sufficient for the number of hours they had been at work. Now I am quite ready and willing to take oath that any one man would perform the same amount of labour in six hours at most. I mean any one of the Kanakas or Canadians. Mr Beardmore and all the servants of the Establishment are also ready to come forward and bear witness to the shameful idle way of working of these two miners, Macgregor and Andrew Muir."

Blenkinsop was extremely displeased with the Muirs in general and with Andrew's belligerence in particular, as he records in the journal:

Mr Muir allowed that he was impudent and forward saying it was his failing &c. Andrew, after some further talk on Mr Muirs part saying how the Company had broke their agreement with him and he should see himself righted & etc stepped forward and began in the impudent way as on Wednesday last to abuse the Company and threaten to make them suffer for deceiving him &c. I checked him instantly telling him if he made use of such language again as he did the other day inst, Revolution was approaching the Companys day was gone by and that the men were beginning to hold their heads up & etc and a lot of other rebellious language, I should most certainly treat him in a way anything but pleasant as to allow him to hold forth such mutinous talk, mutiny it was to all intent and purpose, would be to endanger the peace and even safety of the Establishment by sowing the seeds of discontent and perhaps even mutiny amongst the other servants of the establishment.

Blenkinsop was vociferous in condemning Mr. Muir's ability to oversee his men and his failure to insist on a reasonable output of work as the journal states:

When Mr Muir informed me that he was going to abandon the mine and bring his men to the Fort to work I said to him, 'now my orders will be given to you and you will see the men carry on their work properly and tell them what to do. He in reply said 'that was the proper way and according to his agreement.' When the drain was marked out Mr Muir was told to put on two men. Of course he should have pointed out to them the proper mode of working not me and so I told him he being their overseer or oversman. After some little further conversation in much the same purpose I left them but not without telling Mr Muir that his men would certainly be liable to the full amount of penalty if they did not work steadier and a little faster. Mr Muir came a little while after and told me that Macgregor and Andrew Muir had refused to work anymore as labourers as they could not please me and did not like to be talked to as they were this morning. I requested him to give me in writing what they had to say, in the course of a few minutes he returned with a letter addressed to the Board of Management which was as follows: Gentlemen, being obliged to abandon work at the shaft as I have already stated to you I brought my men to the Fort to do anything they could do the consequence was two of them were set to cutting a drain through the Fort but the head officer Mr Blenkinsop quarreled with them saying they were not doing a sufficient quantity of work and threatened them with the penalty so that when they could not please they stop for the present until matters are settled. Signed John Muir Manager Coal Workers.

The next day Andrew and McGregor went in a canoe after breakfast with two Indians found the small islands in the harbor to visit a camp of "Belbbella" Indians. They hunted for some fresh provisions and returned for their dinner. The young Muirs, somewhat agitated with spirits, accosted the officers dining in the big house, as Andrew writes in his diary:

...went to Bredmore before Mr Blenkinsop's house in the court to ask what he meant by impeach them - without knowing their duty, the first word spoken he called out to Mr Blinkinsop who came out immediately and upbraided them saying he would say anything in his house he choosed, concerning any person and swore oaths that whatsoever his officer said he should say and would sware to it. Mr Blinkinsop went on for some time with threatening language, When I charged Mr Bredmore with saying I did not know my duty which I can prove to the contrary, and in the midst of the conversation he said Mr Douglas was the Damdest lier on the coast and he could prove it, Mr Blinkinsop went on talking for some time but got rather calmer with my Father and saw he could find no fault with him but he had never got respect from his sons so the matter finished 4 O.C.P.M..

Immediately after the altercation between Blenkinsop and the Muirs there is a subtle change in Andrew's diary. It is easy to imagine one of the Muirs in full-flighted irony, naming him "a blinking sop!" Never again does Andrew spell the name correctly. And had Charley Beardmore "bred more" half-breed bastards?

McNeill went in the *Beaver* with Captain Dodd to Victoria. His young daughter Fanny, who was to attend the Reverend Staines School traveled with him and he left Mr. Blenkinsop in charge of the fort with Mr. Beardmore as his second. He was going on his furlough and Fanny would join Alfred, Lucy and Matilda who were already boarding at school. For all the children, this was their first experience of a formal education. McNeill was not long in Fort Victoria before Bottineau arrived with the dispatch from Blenkinsop to Douglas. As soon as he heard of it, he offered his services to Douglas and since the *Beaver* was on the point of leaving to tow the *Cowlitz* up to Fort Rupert, he boarded the steamer, as he explains to Simpson in his letter of March, 1851.

The Cowlitz was on the eve of being towed to Rupert by our steamer with supplies for that Establishment and Langley on board. Mr Douglas wished me to return back in the Steamer and endeavour to make up matters with the miners, I consented, although I did not expect that they would go to work again as I was aware of their wishes and plans long before. On our arrival at Rupert I found that Mr Muir had left off work at the shaft saying that it was not safe on account of the hostility of the natives &c.

which was notoriously false, as the miners were in the habit of going several miles from the fort shooting fowl &c. and on two occations slept out all night, this will show you that the Indians are or were not badly inclined to anyone at the place or inmates of the fort. Our men to this very moment are at work miles from the establishment and are on the very best of terms with the natives in fact a few of them are always at work with our own men. Eight of our men have Quacolt wives in the fort, no Indians could be more kind or friendly, and I think you will allow me to be a judge, they are ever ready to work for us, for instance, it was the natives who have worked every pound of coals collected at fort Rupert, and an immense labor it has been to them, with nothing but worn out axes chiefly they make themselves useful in various other ways, And were very indignant when the miners left off work, the Chiefs told Mr Muir that they would do anything to assist him, why, the miners Wives used to be through the Indian camp daily.

Once more McNeill showed his willingness to put the Company's interests before his own and return to Fort Rupert to try to sort out the problem. Dr. Helmcken was also on board, going to the fort as physician. It was on this trip that Helmcken asked Captain Dodd the name of the island between Current and Race Passages. Dodd replied, "it has no name, but I will call it after you Doctor, for it is always in opposition!"

As soon as they arrived at Beaver Harbor, McNeill, Dodd and Helmcken went ashore and were briefed by Blenkinsop and Beardmore who presented them with a written statement which they were prepared to take on oath for its impartial truth:

Note. This morning Mrs Macgregor applied to me through Mr Beardmore for a gallon of molasses on her husbands a/c. I refused her and told her to speak with her husband, he came shortly after when I acquainted him he would get no more supplies as I considered by his refusing to work he has forfeited all money that may be due him and any right or claim to obtain more goods from the store. I however offered to sell him some for cash which he declined.

Before Macgregor left I told him he would most certainly have to pay the penalty of fifty pounds and expressed my surprise at his being led by such a person as Andrew Muir who neither did his duty nor knew how to do it. Mr Beardmore who was present made use of a remark much to the same effect vizt 'you know it to be true Macgregor that Muirs sons are not able to work with you and

Smith. This was all that passed and Macgregor left. Had he not been as I am almost certain he was led by Andrew Muir to refuse doing his duty I should have said nothing to him on the subject, what I did say was merely warning him of the consequences of his refusal to work. Macgregor went and told Muirs sons what Mr Beardmore and myself told him. Whilst sitting at dinner Archibald Muir, Robin Muir, John Muir and Michael Muir, boy, came and accosted Mr Beardmore who had gone into the yard from the dinner table for a few moments and demanded to know what he had said to Macgregor about them. Their manner was so threatening and language so violent and one of theirs being in liquor also (Archibald Muir) that Mr Beardmore came and called me when they began to be so insulting that I immediately ordered them off the premises but if they had any complaint to make to come and lay it before me and I would listen to it provided it was done in a respectful manner. What their object was in coming I know not but this I am certain of they came with the intention of bullying & had I not, backed by Mr Beardmore, shown them they would gain nothing by their mutinous behaviour God knows what would have been the consequences as they were the greater part of them much excited and evidently bent on mischief. I have put up with this rebellious conduct of theirs long enough it is time for the safety of the Establishment that I should put a stop to it. Up to this time I have acted peacably and with a great deal of forebearance not wishing to give them any cause to discontinue working and thereby defeat the object the Company have in view of sinking for coals.

I have passed over many things that Cap MacNeill would have put them in irons for after this any or either of them who make the least objection to do as I bid them they will most certainly be put in confinement and kept there till an opportunity offers of sending them down to Fort Victoria to be tried by the Laws of their country for mutiny. Mr Muir too instead of teaching his sons to obey the authority encourages them by all means in his power to set them at nought. He was as violent as either of them in his language and as much in liquor as Archibald Muir. This latter person, to Mr Beardmore informed me this evening, said whilst I was engaged in talking with Mr Muir that if I wanted him for anything after this I should come to his court for him as he would not come to mine. Had I been aware of this at the time I would have called him to come to my court and had he refused have put him in irons I intend tomorrow to send for him to see if he is game to keep his word. Nous verrous just after supper Balthasard came to me from all the men and said that, at any time, if I sought their assistance necessary to quell any disturbance I might have with the miners they were all willing and ready to come forward and assist, he further said all the men were convinced that the miners were bent on having a row and came expressly for that purpose this afternoon. In return I told him I should be very sorry for anything to occur, to render their assistance necessary I should however call on them if required and was glad to find them so ready to uphold discipline and the Master of the Fort.

Would any reasonable man question for a moment the right of a Master of an Establishment of this kind to say what he thought proper or even what he liked about the working quality of any of his servants no matter to whom it was said or of whom it was said? I know of no man in his right senses who would. Their excuse this afternoon was they did not come to say anything to me but to my officer Mr Beardmore who merely repeated my words to Macgregor. I was so completely taken aback by their audacity that I allowed them to depart without pursuing the proper course vizt placing them all in confinement. The warning I gave them I trust will put a stop to all this sort of work I have been bound with it long enough I said before the safety of the Fort makes it imperative on me to lay aside all mild measures and let them see I am not to be insulted with impunity. They are constantly telling me the Company has broken their agreement with them but what is that to me it is no fault of mine so long as they remain here and under my charge they must and shall do their duty if not, I shall not consider them having to pay a penalty of £50 a sufficient punishment anymore, as in the case of Andrew Muir and Macgregor the other day for refusing to do their work under the plea that the Company had broken their engagement with them, no I shall put them in Irons and feed them on bread and water and keep them till the order of the Board of Management can be received concerning them.

I am quite ready and willing to take oath before any magistrate or Justice of the Peace that all I have written in this Journal is impartial and true witness.

Witnessed by	Signed by
J.S. Helmcken	George Blenkinsop
Chas Dodd	

I am also quite ready and willing to take oath before any Magistrate or Justice of the Peace that all written by me in this Journal from 27th Jan to 23rd Mar 1850 is impartial and true.

Witnessed by	Signed by
J.S. Helmcken	Charley Beardmore
Chas. Dodd	

McNeill trusted Blenkinsop and was probably authorizing the action his son-in-law suggested as he called the Muirs to the hall of the big house to account for themselves. Who better than Andrew Muir to give a description of the events the morning after the *Beaver* reached the fort:

We were all called over to the Hall in which were Capt. McNeil, Blinkinsop and Bredmore, on going over Capt. McNeil commenced like a madman swearing and threatening and ordered us to work. We said not until we were fairly tried by English Laws for what was charged against us. We were ordered put in Irons and fed on bread and water during the time they were putting the Irons on McGregor and I we were treated in the most shocking manner possible called everything we could be called and threatened to be shot like dogs and dared not open our mouth so we remained silent the time they were putting on the Irons the last words he said on us 2 going out we should remain in Irons and on bread and water for 2 years, the others were to finish the well and then take the same fate. I was placed in the upper Bastion McGregor in the lower on bread and water nothing else. I durst not so much as speak to my Mother such proceedings as these carried on in a British Colony Governed by English Laws, is a disgrace talk of slavery being abolished here it reigns in full force.

They will have slaves who will crawl at their feet even when they look at them such are the officers of the Hudson's Bay Coy not content with starving a man they must also trample on him thus we remained in Irons 6 days the 2nd day McGregor was brought over beside me the place in which he was put being without a roof. the first night I caught a cold through which I am partially deaf, with the Irons on at night and no bed I could not keep myself warm. I applied to the Dr 5 days before he gave me anything for my ears in fact he laughed at me I never shall forget the treatment I have received, the Third night we spoke to get the Irons off at night which was granted. They were taken off at 8 P.M. and put on at 6 A.M. we were a little better after this 2 together we could keep ourselves warm at night. some days we got a walk on the gallery and some days not, with only 2 days we were allowed soup to dinner it was bread and water all the time on the seventh day that was Thursday the 9th after breakfast our Irons were taken off and we were ordered down the Hall where was assembled McNeil, Blinkinsop, Bredmore, Capt. Dodd, Dr and My Father with the rest of our men we were ordered to state our mind freely which we did a great change from last day we

231

were when we durst not open our mouths they implored us to go to our work or do anything until the steamer should return when we should be tried we said no we had been imprisoned falsely and should do no more till our case was tried and settled. We were then told to go outside and consult one another we did so and returned with the same determination as before were told still to go away and consult till after dinner. at 5 P.M. we were sent for and asked what now when we said still the same Capt. McNeil said we should have to go to the Bastion, but not in Irons and our rations served out as before and the wives should cook it, and our beds up 3 together us to our old place what a change all right Bredmore brought up a syringe from Dr. for My Ears. this is rather pleasanter but still in prison.

Captain Brown, in the barque *England* arrived at Victoria and four deserters from the crew of the *Norman Morrison* stowed aboard in order to go to San Francisco and the gold fields. This vessel was on its way to Fort Rupert to collect a cargo of coal before heading to that port. Three of the deserters left the England when they got wind that Helmcken was to come on board to look for them. They went to Hope Island with Chief Nancy to wait for the barque to arrive and take them back on board. The deserters ran foul of some of Chief Looking-glass' men for failing to pay for some halibut and all three were killed on Qoin Island, a small island off Kaleden Bay. Meanwhile, Andrew Muir with the miners, also deserted from Fort Rupert and went to Hope Island to wait for the barque. After some days of anxious waiting the miners went on board the *England* and sailed to San Francisco.

When Charley Beardmore returned from his investigation of the murders, he gave Helmcken a false report, saying that they had been murdered by a northern tribe. He then went to Fort Langley in search of James Douglas who, on learning the truth, sent him back to inform Helmcken. Meantime, Helmcken recovered the bodies of two of the deserters and returned with them to the fort for burial. The Nahwitti refused to give up the murderers to Helmcken. This episode led to HMS *Daedalus* bringing Governor Blanshard to Fort Rupert to punish the Nahwitti when they failed to give up the suspected murderers.

When McNeill left Fort Rupert in April in the steamer *Beaver* with Captain Dodd, they went to Fort Langley with the *Cowlitz* in tow and in March, 1851, he writes to Sir George Simpson:

232

After leaving Rupert we proceeded to Langley, discharged the supplies, and took on board the Cowlitz, think twenty two hundred barrels Salmon, on our way out of the river, the Cowlitz, in tow of the steamer, unfortunately took the ground and remained fast, at half ebb, the tide took a direction, drops her stern post and washed away the quick sand. at low water she was dry forward, with about 16 feet water under her stern in which awkward position she strained so much, that she became slightly "hogged". but made no water to speak of. On our arrival at Fort Victoria. Captain Weynton. Captn Scarborough, and Yates the Carpenter, stationed here tried all in their power to condemn the ship. Weynton said he would not go to Sea in the Ship until she had been hove down and had a complete overhawl or repair, which caused his crew to say the same. Seeing this, I told Mr Douglas that if Weynton refused to go in the Ship, that I would take her to the Islands and give her up to Mr Pelly as Lloyd's agent. Weynton seeing this, offered or volunteered to go if Mr Douglas would take the consequences on himself and order him to go. Mr Douglas refered him to Gov Blanshard, as he had consented to act as Lloyd's agent. The Governor immediately ordered him to proceede to Sea with the Ship, as I had addressed a letter to him i.e. Mr Blanshard, saying the Cowlitz was sea worthy and could go to England if required &c. Captain Dodd too signed it, I never saw men act so scandalously as those three men did, when they did all in their power to condemn the ship, they were a regular trio, to give us as much trouble as possible.

McNeill settled back in Fort Victoria to enjoy and plan his furlough. He wanted to go to California to look at prospects for trade for himself after he resigned from the Hudson's Bay Company. However, Douglas received a letter from Mr. McTavish in Oahu as McNeill writes in his letter to Simpson:

Mr McTavish about this time had written to Mr Douglas that he had a leave of absence, and would not remain at his post at Honolulu later than 1st June, and if no one came to relieve him, that he should be off. Mr Douglas thinking that the business would be left to Mr Pelly, who had been ill, and seldom or ever visited the store would suffer desired me to waive my right of furlough & take McTavish's place for one year, I consented and went passenger on board the Cowlitz, taking my eldest Daughter with me, we had a fine passage of 15 days from Cape Flattery, the "Una", in company, the Cowlitz showing no sign of weakening or strain. "I hear that she was hove down after I left the

Islands, and found to be in condition to proceede to England." On my arrival there Mr McTavish informed me that he had wrote you, that he would remain one year longer at Honolulu, he had received the Consignment of three Ships from China, so he informed me, belonging to a Mr Hubartson or some such name. Mr Pelly had not been to the store for above three months, having my daughter with me, I gave up the idea of going to California or the States. I did not like to leave her unprotected, and besides, the expense would have been heavy. I therefore made up my mind to go back to Victoria, and visit the Columbia, on my arrival back at Victoria.

McNeill, with his daughter Lucy, boarded the HBC vessel *Una* at Oahu and returned to Victoria to continue his furlough. News of the murder of the three *Norman Morrison* deserters reached Fort Victoria soon after he arrived. HMS *Daedalus* was anchored in the harbor, commanded by Captain Wellesly, a cousin of the Duke of Wellington. Governor Blanshard and Captain Wellesley asked McNeill to accompany them to Fort Rupert where they intended to punish the Nahwitti tribe for their part in the murders. As McNeill writes to Simpson: "...the Governor demanded the murderers from the Newittie, they refused to give them up, a party of 60 men in Boats with Nine half breeds from the Fort, went to attack the village, on arriving there found it deserted, and came back without doing anything. I hear a Frigate is to be here soon, and will make another attack, the Newitties, however say they will give up the offenders."

The frigate, HMS *Daphne* did arrive in Victoria and George Blenkinsop, in a private letter to Sir George Simpson, tells of the futility of the action:

H.M.S. Daphne paid us a visit this summer for the purpose of punishing the three Newitty Murderers. Governor Blanshard seemed to think that the Company threw obstacles in the way of having the murderers punished: to prove to the contrary, the Boats were placed in a position by people from the Fort from which they could have taken the whole tribe alive, but, instead of doing so, they contented themselves with firing on the village and eventually burning it. Two of the Newitty people were killed and two of the Sailors wounded, but the murderers escaped.

The Daphne sailed and left the affair if anything worse than it was before, as our men were afraid to stir from the Fort. However, after a few days I prevailed on the Newittie people to give up the murderers, they endeavoured to do so alive, but meeting with resistance, they were all 3 shot and brought to the Fort which of course settled the affair. Govr Blanshard was certainly unnecessarily severe in his strictures on the Hon. Co. doings.

McNeill left Fort Rupert to return to Fort Victoria on the *Una* and once more continue his furlough. Governor Blanshard left Fort Rupert by canoe to return to Fort Victoria and became unwell during the journey. Since there was no physician at Fort Victoria at the time, Douglas sent for Dr. Helmcken to come down by canoe to attend the governor.

⸎

Matilda remained at Fort Rupert because of her impending confinement. Early in her pregnancy, Matilda had wondered if she was further along than her missed menses told her.

In November, she felt unnaturally distended by her pregnancy. At each successive delivery, her labor had become progressively shorter so that it was no surprise to her that soon after her pains started she had a compelling urge to strain and she delivered an infant daughter. The senior midwife took the infant to cleanse its mouth with water. The second midwife gave the alarm as a second head crowned in place of the expected afterbirth. She hastily sat a tired Matilda up again to enable her to deliver the infant, a second baby daughter. Both infants lay on Matilda's chest to suckle, while attendants waited patiently for her to expel the afterbirth.

They did not notice Matilda's increasing pallor and were aghast when they saw blood spreading out from beneath her covers. Matilda felt compelled to close her eyes as a strange lethargy overcame her. Her detachment from her body conjured up a vision. She saw her grandmother holding her close after the battle had destroyed her village and everyone had been killed. A man holding a decorated stick in his hand appeared before them and offered to take them away to the safety of his home on condition they both kept their eyes closed. The stick he held had the power to make the world tilt. Taking Grandmother under his left arm and Matilda under his right, he transformed into a giant bird and they rose into the sky. Matilda saw herself keeping her eyelids tight together but then her

235

Grandmother fell away from the bird into the sea below, because she had disobeyed.

Matilda opened her eyes, the small room was misty with steam and she was surprised she was not in the big house at Fort Rupert. Her attendants took on a luminous glassy appearance and glowed as they prepared her bath. As her skin peeled off her to reveal the spiritual glow, she knew she was in the spirit house of the Commander of the Land. Secure now in the knowledge that she was cleansed at the end of her seventh reincarnation following a life lived in accordance with her destiny, she seemed to glide out of the water and float into the next room to enter the bliss of paradise, never again to reincarnate.

McNeill received the news of Matilda's death from Dr. Helmcken, as he writes to Sir George Simpson: "...he brought intelligence of the death of my poor Wife. As the Canoes was to return, I thought it advisable to go back again and see about my children and how they were to be provided for. On arriving there I found the children with no Nurse and got one from the Camp. I remained there untill the Steamer arrived from Sitka, where she had been undergoing repairs, and came down as passenger to this place, The Steamer has been very well overhawled, and the Russians have charged very moderate prices for their work."

McNeill was back in Fort Victoria in a poor state of mind over his wife's death and worried about support for his family. Helen had care of the children who were not at school in Fort Victoria and she had another child on the way as well as the newborn twins to attend to. He was also in financial difficulties and seriously thinking of becoming a settler as he writes to Simpson for help:

> As I intend to become a settler very soon, I would be greatly obliged if I would be allowed to give up my interest in the Puget's Sound Company of five shares, and be allowed to take horses or cattle to the amount of those shares, will you be pleased to let me know if I can be indulged in such a favor as soon as convenient. Now, Sir, I will trouble you with reading an account of a greivence I have to state. The year that Stikine River was to have been established by us I think in "34", I wished to leave the service and go to the Islands on board the Eagle, Capt Darby. Doctor

McLoughlin said to me why do you wish to leave the service? I said because I could do better at home. Why sayes he, how much could you make, I said $100 per month at least. Why sayes he, you have more than that now, you have had £300 per ann' since Sept. I told him I was not aware of it, but if that was the case, I would remain two years longer. Some time after this took place, "it was the year the Doctor went to England," I found that I was allowed but £270. Stg, I told or spoke to Mr Douglas about it, he told me that £270. Stg was 300 Halifax!!! I was confounded, and said that I had been played a trick, for I can call it by no other name. I wrote to the Doctor afterwards he told me that he thought the bargain was $100 per month, at all events he said it was too late to adjust it now. As no one was present but himself and me, my word, I presume will be taken as soon as his own i.e. the Doctors. I will be much gratified Sir, if you will answer me on this subject also, as I am sure you will see how the thing stands. Unfortunately no agreement was signed. It will amount to £150. Stg. as my Commision was signed in 1834.

And now, Sir, as regards myself, I wish to say that the present Emoluments are not sufficient to pay for the services rendered as I have mentioned before, my family is large say ten children, and it is high time that they were collected together under one roof, and that I commenced house keeping for their benefit. I hope Sir that my services have been of sufficient value for you to recommend me to have an increased salary. If that cannot be done with conscience or propriety, I hope you can give me some situation where I can realize something more than I have at present, you know my abilities and can judge best where they will be most required.

I am in good health and time deals kindly with me as regards age. If you can do nothing more for me. I beg to say that I shall give in my resignation next 1st June. I hope Sir you will not think that I am disconted, no such thing, I am willing to do as I have done for the Company, I can say no more except that I have gained nothing by obtaining a C.Ts commission, as I had, as "acknowledged". £270 Stg per ann when it should have been £300 Stg as promised by Dr McLoughlin. Now my emoluents as a C.T. has never given me over £265 Stg per annum, and that but one year, I came in with outfit 1840, and as you are aware the dividends have fallen off since that time, I think Sir you will say that I have gained nothing in a pecuniary point of view, by being honord with a Parchment.

Under these circumstances I hope you will in proper to do something more for me, or I may more truly say for my young family. If you can, or intend, to do anything to assist me, will you be pleased Sir to inform me by way of Panama that I may know how to arrange my affairs. If you cannot with propriety assist me at present when I retire, I shall at all events wish & hope that you will do at least as well for me as you did for Mr Tod, that is allow me three years leave of absence before my retired share commences, this you can do, with propriety as I am now an old Servant, and never been off duty untill now, and even now I shall start in a few days to seek for Gold on Charlotte Isld on board the Steamer, but will have a short time on furlough after I return. As I have said before, I hope you will take all these matters in consideration, and not think that I have asked for more than is my due. I will leave all to your best judgement. Captain Stewart will take command of the Steamer "as Mr Douglas tells me." I shall instruct him as much as possible both as regards the trade and navigation on the coast.

In the eight months of his furlough, McNeill went back to Fort Rupert to sort out the miner's strike, went to Oahu to relieve Mr. McTavish, went with Governor Blanshard on the *Daedalus* to assist in the reparations for the murdered deserters, and then, on arrival back in Victoria, as Douglas writes in his letter to Archibald Barclay: "Chief Trader McNeill, though on furlough has, with praiseworthy zeal, volunteered his services to conduct Capt Stewart on his first trip round the coast, an offer I gratefully accepted as experience is often too dearly bought. This relieves me of all anxiety on the subject of the Steam Vessel."

McNeill had kept Simpson informed of the Company's affairs on the coast in yearly private letters and had every reason to expect that Simpson thought highly of him as a company servant. Therefore, one extract from a private letter of Simpson's to Douglas seems incomprehensible.

I was astonished to learn from Ogden that you have an idea of sending McNeill to the Islands to replace McTavish. I do not think a more unfortunate choice could have been made. From the little I saw of McNeill on board the Steamer, I know that his temper is such that it would be impossible for Mr Pelly to agree with him, while he is wanting in business habits, is ignorant of accounts and is unaccustomed to commercial correspondence to all these disqualifications must be added the fact, which of itself was sufficient to settle the matter, that he is an American citizen, & that he would be the most likely man in the service to job & traffic on private account, seeking to promote his own interests even at the expense of the Company's. Rather than send McNeill, I should prefer a Clerk being placed with Mr Pelly, should McTavish leave immediately (which I do not now think likely for a year or two at any rate) & that Clouston cannot be forwarded, a clerk will be sent to the Islands from the country or from England. On this subject, you will see I write in the most perfect confidence, which I am sure will not in your hands be abused.

There is no evidence that McNeill ever found out Sir George Simpson's true opinion of him and he continued to write to him until 1857 from Fort Simpson. Sir George Simpson left no summary of reasons for his opinion of William McNeill and McNeill does not feature in Simpson's list of his opinions with regard to the character of the Hudson's Bay Company employees.

Epilogue

After instructing Captain Stewart on the intricacies of various harbors and waterways while aboard SS *Beaver*, McNeill asked the board and council in Fort Victoria to accept his resignation for 1 June 1853. Mr. Douglas put him in charge of the first expedition on board the vessel *Una* to the Queen Charlotte Islands to search for gold.

With only eight men, the Indians disrupted their work and after two weeks McNeill took his people away. He sailed the *Una* to Fort Simpson and in November, 1851, James Douglas appointed him to take charge of the fort to allow Doctor Kennedy to go on furlough. The acquisition of 200 acres of land at Gonzales Point was not achieved without difficulty for McNeill. The governor and committee initially gave their approval and then reversed themselves on the basis that an American citizen could not be given title to land on Vancouver Island. McNeill took an oath of allegiance to the British Crown and as a result was granted title to his farmland. James Douglas supported McNeill as he told Barclay in his letter of 16 February 1853: "...the fact that McNeill as a Company employee and an American, had been in command of British ships contrary to British law had been ignored for years."

In 1851, McNeill asked his sister, Sarah McNeill, to come out to the coast to look after his large family. In the meantime, George Blenkinsop and his family moved to Fort Simpson where Helen acted as mother to her half brothers and sisters. Much to his surprise, Sarah was unable to come, as is indicated when he writes to Sir George Simpson: "I had wrote to my sister to come and join me to take charge of my family &c. She however is now married!!! and in one of the first families in Boston. She of course could not come to me."

McNeill stayed in Fort Simpson, rescinded his resignation of 1 June 1853 and continued to serve the Company. He was promoted to Chief Factor in 1856 and asked Sir George Simpson for a leave of absence in 1857 to go to see his family and to go to England to recover some money held in Chancery there. On his return in 1861, he went back to Fort Simpson until he retired from Company service to live at his farm on Gonzales Point outside Victoria.

Why the about-face from determination to leave the Company in 1853 and such long service at Fort Simpson? Some time around 1852, McNeill met and married Martha. His new wife was also a Nishga chief, Neshaki, a fur trader in her own right and every bit as colorful as Matilda. This, however, is another story, beyond the scope of this book.

McNeill was a signatory to an unsuccessful plea sent to President Grant in 1867, that the United States annex British Columbia. This action would have shocked the emerging English society in Victoria. Some years later McNeill offered land he owned for a site to build the new lieutenant governor's residence—perhaps an act of atonement to restore his goodwill.

Bibliography

The Doors of Perception and Heaven and Hell, by Aldous Huxley (Grafton, 1977).

"During My Time" Florence Edenshaw Davidson, "A Haida Woman," by Mararet B. Blackman (University of Washington Press and Douglas & McIntyre, 1982).

Exploring Puget Sound and British Columbia, by Stephen Hillson (Holland, Michigan: Van Winkle Publishing Company, 1975).

Fort Victoria Letters, edited by Hartwell Bowsfield (Winnipeg: Hudson's Bay Records Society, 1979).

A Guide to Indian Myth and Legend, by Ralph Maud (Talonbooks, 1982).

The Hargrave Correspondence 1821–1843, edited by G. P. de Grazebrook (Champlain Society, 1938).

The Journal of John Work. January to October 1835, introduction by Henry Drummond Dee (C. F. Banfield, 1945).

Journal of the voyage of the brigantine Hope *from Boston to the northwest coast of North America 1790–1792,* by Joseph Ingraham (Barre, Mass: Imprint Society, 1971).

The Journal of William Sturgis, edited by S. W. Jackman (Victoria: Sono Nis Press, 1978).

The Maritime History of Massachussetts, by Samuel Eliot Morison (Boston and New York: Houghton Mifflin Company, 1921).

243

McLoughlin's Fort Vancouver Letters, First Series 1825–1839, edited by E. E. Rich (London: Hudson's Bay Records Society, 1941).

McLoughlin's Fort Vancouver Letters, Second Series 1839–1844, edited by E. E. Rich (London: Hudson's Bay Records Society, 1943).

McLoughlin's Fort Vancouver Letters, Third Series 1844–1848, edited by E. E. Rich (London: Hudson's Bay Records Society, 1944).

Narrative of a journey round the world during the years 1841 and 1842, by Sir George Simpson (London, H. Colburn 1847).

Physician and Fur Trader, the Journals of William Fraser Tolmie (Vancouver: Mitchell Press, 1963).*Totem Poles, According to Crests and Topics,* by Marius Barbeau (Canadian Museum of Civilization, 1950).

The Reminiscences of John Sebastian Helmcken, edited by Dorothy Blakey Smith (University of British Columbia Press, 1975).

Rites & Passages: The Experience of American Whaling, 1830–1870, by Margaret Creighton (Cambridge University Press, 1995).

Totem Poles, According to Location, by Marius Barbeau (Canadian Museum of Civilization, 1950).

Two Years Before the Mast, by Richard Henry Dana (Penguin Classics, 1986).

Voyages of the Columbia *to the Northwest Coast 1789–1790 and 1790–1793,* edited by Frederick W. Howay (N. Israel/Amsterdam: Da Capo Press/New York, 1941).

The Voyage of the New Hazard *to the Northwest Coast, Hawaii and China 1810–1813,* by Stephen Reynoulds, edited by F. W. Howay (Salem: Peabody Museum 1938).

Warriors of the Pacific, edited by Charles Harrison (Son Nis Press, *).

White Jacket, or The World in a Man-O-War, by Herman Melville (World Classic, Oxford University Press, 1990).

Index